SOVIET JEWISH ALIYAH
1989–1992

SOVIET JEWISH ALIYAH
1989–1992
IMPACT AND IMPLICATIONS FOR ISRAEL AND THE MIDDLE EAST

CLIVE JONES
*Institute for International Studies,
University of Leeds*

FRANK CASS
LONDON • PORTLAND, OR.

First pubished in 1996 in Great Britain by
FRANK CASS & CO. LTD
Newbury House, 900 Eastern Avenue, Newbury Park
London IG2 7HH, England

and in the United States of America by
FRANK CASS
c/o ISBS
5804 N.E. Hassalo Street, Portland, Oregon 97213-3644

Copyright © 1996 Clive Jones

British Library Cataloguing in Publication Data
Jones, Clive
  Soviet–Jewish Aliyah, 1989–92
  I. Title
  304.85694047089924
  ISBN 0-7146-4625-3

Library of Congress Cataloging-in-Publication Data
Jones, Clive, 1965–
  Soviet Jewish Aliyah, 1989 to 1992: impact and
implications for Israel and the Middle East / Clive Jones.
    p. cm.
  Includes bibliographical references and index.
  ISBN 0-7146-4625-3
  1. Jews, Soviet–Israel. 2. Soviet Union–Emigration and
immigration. 3. Israel–Ethnic relations. 4. Israel. Knesset–
Elections, 1992. I. Title.
DS113.8.R87J66 1996
956.94'04924047–dc20   95-17863
                                                       CIP

All rights reserved. No part of this publication may be
reproduced in any form or by any means, electronic,
mechanical, photocopying, recording or otherwise,
without the prior permission of Frank Cass & Co. Ltd.

Printed in Great Britain by
Bookcraft (Bath) Ltd, Midsomer Norton, Avon

To my mother and father

CONTENTS

Acknowledgements ix

1: Soviet Jewish Aliyah 1989–1992: An Introduction 1

Transnationalism: The Influence of Society and Societal Actors 2
Migration as a Transnational Activity 7
Soviet Jewish Aliyah: A Conceptual Approach 11
Conclusion 13

2: The Migration of Soviet Jewry: 1970–1989 16

Emigration and the Superpowers: 1970–1980 17
The Process of Soviet Jewish Emigration 22
Soviet Jewish Immigration to Israel: 1970–1980 28
Soviet Emigration Policy: 1980–1987 35
Gorbachev and Soviet Jewry 38
Soviet-Israeli Relations: 1985–1989 40
The United States, Israel, and Soviet Jewish Emigration: 1987–1989 48
Conclusion 50

3: The Political and Ideological Context of Soviet Jewish Migration to Israel 57

Soviet Jewish Aliyah: The Ideological Context 59
The Demographic Debate 66
The Occupied Territories: the Strategic Debate 69

4: Absorbing the Soviet Aliyah: Practicality versus Ideology 75

Organizing the Soviet Aliyah: the Role of the Jewish Agency 78
Financing Immigration and Absorption 81

Israel, the United States, and the Loan Guarantees	87
Soviet Aliyah, Construction, and the Double Agenda	96
The Stars Programme and East Jerusalem	104
Conclusion	111

5: Absorption of Soviet Jewry: Integration and Dislocation — 118

The Soviet Olim: A Profile	120
Employment and Housing	124
Soviet Jewish Identity: Acculturation and Alienation	132
The Issue of Yordim and Noshrim	140
Soviet Jewish Aliyah: The Popular Response	143
Conclusion	148

6: Arab Responses to Soviet Jewish Aliyah — 154

The Arab Regional Response to Soviet Jewish Immigration	156
Washington and the Arabs	165
The Palestinians and the Israeli Arabs	168
Conclusion	175

7: The June 1992 Israeli General Election: The Impact and Influence of Soviet Jewish Immigration — 179

Immigration and the Political Right in Israel	181
The Politicization of Soviet Jewish Aliyah	187
Labour, Rabin, and Soviet Jewish Immigration	192
The Israeli Left and the Soviet Jews	198
The Election Results	204
Conclusion	208

8: Conclusion — 213

Appendix	221
Select Bibliography	223
Index	239

ACKNOWLEDGEMENTS

This book, and the thesis on which it was originally based, could not have been completed without the help and support of so many people. I would like to thank in particular those whose names follow to whom I shall always remain indebted for their knowledge, kindness, generosity, and above all friendship. During the course of two research trips to Israel, Tamara and Yigal Amitai were a continuous source of intellectual encouragement, furnishing me with much of the material that has been used throughout this work. Arnon Dunetz of Mapam deserves special mention for arranging many of the interviews, while the hospitality of Dikla Halevy and Alon Hornstein was generous in both its warmth and scope.

In the United Kingdom I owe a considerable debt to many friends and colleagues, without whom, little of value could have been achieved. Guy and Nurit Abrahams, Fiona Butler, Louise Campbell, Jan Goodey, and John Stone all gave freely of their time and support, particularly when it was needed most. Dr Caroline Kennedy-Pipe and Dr Moorehead Wright provided invaluable comments on earlier draft chapters, while Professor Ritchie Ovendale was a constant source of advice and encouragement throughout. Professor Robert O. Freedman of the Baltimore Hebrew University was particularly helpful in providing me with much useful information. Finally, the successful completion of this work could not have been accomplished without the support and guidance of Professor James Piscatori. As a supervisor, he was an intellectual inspiration, encouraging at every opportunity yet providing the whole endeavour with an academic rigour second to none. But more than this, he has been a friend. For this, and his support, I shall be forever in his debt.

1 Soviet Jewish Aliyah 1989–1992: An Introduction

Between October 1989 and June 1992, over 400,000 Jews left the former Soviet Union for the State of Israel. A comparable wave of migration would be the movement of 50 per cent of the population of France to the United States over a four-year period.[1] The very magnitude of this exodus affected superpower relations, American–Middle Eastern relations, Middle Eastern relations themselves, and the internal political equilibrium of Israel as a nation-state. To this end, this book is an examination of the political impact of Soviet Jewish migration as a transnational flow, how it complicated the decision-making of key actors, helped redefine Israel's domestic political agenda, and, by extension, the approach of the Jewish State towards regional peace. This approach demonstrates clear linkages between developments in domestic politics and the implementation of foreign policy by a state élite: in this case, the Likud dominated National Unity government of Yitzhak Shamir. The use of the term transnational to describe the process of migration is deliberate, not least because it widens the remit of what has traditionally been understood to constitute such activity.

Emerging in response to the perceived movement towards greater global interdependence throughout the 1960s and early 1970s, the transnational debate concentrated on the role of non-state actors in eroding the hegemony of states as the dominant actors in world affairs. While the role of economic organizations such as international banks and multinational corporations in this debate elicited the most interest, other examples of transnational activity included cross-border contacts among groups and individuals, and the permeability of borders through the revolution in telecommunications.[2] Writing in the winter 1992 edition of *Millennium*, however, M.J. Peterson argued that the study of transnationalism in international politics had been somewhat constrained, since the 'empirical work seldom went beyond proving the existence of such activity'.³

Transnationalism: The Influence of Society and Societal Actors
Peterson has sought to widen the scope of transnational activity to include the role of 'societal actors' in the study of international politics. Set within a domestic environment these include the activities of individuals, companies, interest and social pressure groups, and their effect upon state behaviour. As Peterson explains:

> These societal actors have significant effects on the flow of material resources, know-how and ideas around the world, and cannot be ignored in any full account of international relations. At the same time, they co-exist and interact with states. A sound understanding of world politics depends on understanding the different types of societal actors operating transnationally, the various relations that can exist between them and states, and the sort of tactics they adopt in their efforts to influence states.⁴

In short, while continuing to place primacy on the state as the main actor in international politics, Peterson is concerned to examine the impact of these societal actors on state behaviour. This is a notably different approach from the original study of transnationalism, which viewed non-state actors as largely autonomous from their domestic setting. By enclosing societal actors within the remit of transnational activity, Peterson sets out to establish clear links between the conduct of domestic and international politics.⁵

Implicit within the concept of societal actors affecting state behaviour in the international system is the assumption that society is autonomous from the state. A state in this context may be defined as the 'institutionalized apparatus of rule' that is expected 'to maintain the physical security of the country as a whole and of the groups and individuals within it'.⁶ From this, the concept of the state élite clearly emerges, encompassing those individuals and associated bureaucracies who formulate policies to be implemented by the state apparatus. In short, such individuals and bureaucracies form the government of the state. This definition clearly places the state at the nexus of domestic and international politics, but, as Michael Barnett explains in his study of Israeli security policy, one that is complex. The state has to construct strategies to meet external challenges and 'for mobilizing societal resources' in order to implement foreign policy decisions.[7] The failure of the state élite to reconcile both challenges can undermine the legitimacy of its standing with its own society.

In the context of Israeli politics, the public reaction to the massacre of Palestinians at the Sabra and Chatilla refugee camps in Beirut in 1982 provides a prime example. In this instance, a societal actor – the pressure group Peace Now – was able to mobilize mass public support against the government. This ultimately led to the resignation of Ariel Sharon as defence minister and to the establishment of the Kahane commission to examine the extent of Israeli culpability.[8] These events anticipated the growing debate concerning the relationship between the state and society that has developed since the end of the Cold War. In particular, there has emerged a growing interest in concepts of 'civil society' and its effect upon the state as an institution. No precise definition concerning the parameters of civil society exists, but a broad consensus as to its intellectual origins and key constituent elements can be traced. This rests in turn on a definition of society that posits clear distinctions between society and the role of the state.

According to the Danish political scientist Ole Waever, the constitution of society is an implicit act, broad enough in scope to encompass an identity that is communal in nature. This can manifest itself in various forms, ranging from small group cohesion associated with tribes, to the mass identity associated with a nation. The semantic link to societal identity is the word 'we' in the sense of we Germans, we French, we British. This rests heavily upon the concept of *Gemeinschaft* first articulated by the German sociologist, Ferdinand Tonnies. This conceptual approach defines the reduction of society to a rational concept since it contains moral and social structures that represent an identity which is more than the 'sum of its parts' and 'which reproduces itself from generation to generation'.[9]

This conceptualization does not preclude the possibility of dissonance within society. Again, the example of Israel provides us with evidence of ethnic dissent that has marked the development of the Jewish State, most notably the divisions between Ashkenazim and Oriental Jews. However, if a nation constitutes a broad definition of society, we can clearly identify the generic term 'Israeli' as falling within the remit of this sociological interpretation. In this sense, as Waever argues, a nation as a broad form of society exists when certain elements are present: affiliation to a territory; a continuity among society that links past, present, and future members; and a belief that as a manifestation of society, a nation is an important constituent unit of global society with a concomitant right to statehood.[10]

Such criteria allow for the term nation to be applied to societies yet to achieve territorial sovereignty, including the Palestinians and the Kurds. But even where a nation resides within clear territorial boundaries, a distinction can be made between the homogeneity of society and the role of the state. A state comprises those actors that perform governmental functions which are subject to change, while society can comprise non-governmental actors, also subject to change. But society itself is 'not only robust enough in construction, and comprehensive enough in its following, but also broad enough in the quality of identity it carries, to enable it to compete with the territorial state as a political organizing principle'.[11]

This organizing principle is most obvious in the activity of political parties, usually associated with strong, democratic regimes that allow constraints to be placed on the activities of the state. Yet this political society, as outlined by the nineteenth-century French historian Alexis de Tocqueville, does not include those organizations, groups, or individuals who also, in the words of Augustus Richard Norton, 'provide a buffer between the state and the citizen'.[12] Within the context of Israeli politics, Peace Now, Women in Black, and even the settlers' movement, *Gush Emunim*, all constitute units of what can be termed civil society. On a global scale, Amnesty International and Greenpeace are perhaps the two best examples of groups that operate transnationally across civil societies in their efforts to influence state behaviour. However, multinational corporations, as well as interest groups that actually support state actors, can also be included within the realm of civil society.

But if actors which constitute civil society operate outside the confines of the state, society nonetheless still requires the state to afford both physical and, in the case of most democratic regimes, social and economic security. Moreover, societies in developed countries require that the state continue to foster the necessary conditions that allow civil society to flourish.[13] Where a state apparatus fails to fulfil its responsibilities towards civil society, or, at a more profound level, attempts to alter the identity of society at large, the result can be violent resistance to the policies of the ruling élite. The tumultuous events surrounding the overthrow of the Peacock throne in Iran provide one obvious example.

Yet far from undermining the role of the state in international politics, interaction between transnational societal actors and the state can serve to reinforce the state as the primary actor in international politics. According to Peterson, the relationship between societal actors and the state may be divided into several main categories, depending on which actor initiates the contact.

First, societal actors in one country may interact with societal actors in another without involving any state, in order to pursue shared goals or to help each other carry out mutually desired activity. Second, a state may seek the assistance of its own societal actors in implementing its foreign policies. Third, a state may appeal to societal actors abroad in efforts to influence the policies of other states or tap resources for a policy that it lacks at home. Fourth, a societal group may seek the assistance of its own state in furthering its activities. Fifth, a societal group may seek the assistance of a foreign state in furthering its goals.[14]

These categories are by no means mutually exclusive, nor, as Peterson points out, premised upon the state as a unitary actor. Competition between bureaucracies can, as Graham Allison points out, result in 'sub-optimal' outcomes in foreign policy implementation.[15] But these categories do make clear linkages between the state and societal actors, thereby moving the transnational debate away from its previous emphasis on economic non-state actors. Furthermore, the framework developed by Michael Barnett, in his analysis of Israel's security policy, demonstrates that society itself can impose severe constraints on the implementation of state policy, both foreign and domestic.

Barnett's work is a challenge to those who assume that state security 'is autonomous and therefore distinct from "low politics", societal pressures, and the domestic political economy'.[16] Such an assumption, he feels, is made without seriously considering the response of society to the mobilization strategies of the state.

While not denying that international pressure can both mould and restrict state behaviour, the framework constructed by Barnett is significant precisely because it shows that state representatives, in this case, successive Israeli administrations, may be subjected to implicit and explicit societal constraints.

With reference to meeting the demands of national security, Barnett remarks that the state not only has to meet the challenge of an external threat, but also to face the prospect that policies designed to meet this challenge can elicit widespread societal antipathy. This forces the government or state élite to embrace solutions that 'mobilize the required resources at a minimal political cost'.[17] These resources can be material, for example, oil, coal, steel, high technology and so forth, but are more likely to involve finances. According to Barnett, these solutions lie within three broadly defined strategies that identify the location of the resource in either a domestic or international milieu and the costs involved in pursuing any one of them.

The first of these strategies is termed accommodational, and requires little reform to the existing relationship with society for resources to be extracted. In short, the external challenge facing the state can be met by the use of domestic resources with little change in societal equilibrium. The second, labelled restructural, requires the state to redefine its relationship with society if its foreign policy commitments are to be met. This strategy can involve the raising of taxes or the nationalization of key industries to meet a threat, or involve the liberalization of the economy in the belief that this will improve the productive capacity of the state. However, the viability of either of these strategies remains dependent upon the economic structure of a society. For example, the decision to embrace the free market or raise taxes often has a deleterious effect on the welfare of certain sections of society. Israel, with its matrix of competing ethnic identities, is not immune from such pressures.

If unable to extract the necessary domestic resources due to societal constraints, the state may have to adopt a third strategy, an international one. This strategy attempts to offset the costs involved in pursuing a given policy, by involving other states, or eliciting the support of societal actors, most often banks, in the international arena.[18] But there are drawbacks in pursuing an international strategy: an alliance with other actors over a given issue may not be possible; and the price attached to foreign assistance may impede the attainment of other policy objectives. While Barnett constructed this framework as a means to examine domestic constraints on Israeli defence policy, it also provides a ready framework in which the impact and influence of Soviet Jewish migration, as a transnational flow, can be assessed on Israeli society in general, on particular societal actors, and on the foreign and domestic policies of the Likud coalition government of Yitzhak Shamir.

Migration as a Transnational Activity

As with much of the early work on transnationalism, the very act of migration was dominated by economic factors in explaining the movement of people across international borders.[19] Two main schools of thought existed: microanalytic and macroanalytic. The former took individuals as the main unit of analysis and traced population movement against opportunities that were unevenly distributed worldwide. The latter placed emphasis upon the uneven development of world capitalism in explaining the mass migration of people from one area to another. However, the problem remained that both approaches reduced migrations to a one-dimensional process of 'uneven economic exchange between states of origin and destination'.[20]

Reducing migration to the realm of economic theory negated the importance of ethnic, ideological, and political reasons behind population flows. In this respect, the works of Aristide R. Zolberg and Myron Weiner have challenged the hegemony exercised by economic factors in explaining population movement. Indeed, as Weiner explains, the very act of migration is necessarily a political one since it impacts upon concepts of state sovereignty, citizenship, and the rights of the individual.[21] From this, the state emerges as an important actor in determining migration flows, but, equally, the very act of migration demonstrates that states cannot be immune from an activity that is, by its very nature, transnational. While economic factors obviously play a large part in determining migratory movements, it is still the state that mainly determines if its citizens may be allowed to leave or immigrants to enter.

Weiner posits several categories in which the transnational flow of people can impact upon international politics: migrants can produce tension between sending and receiving countries simply because the migrants are unwanted; diasporas can create security problems for both the sending and receiving state; migration can affect the homogeneity of the host society, raising questions of citizenship and loyalty among states; and migration can impact upon the transfer of capital, technology, and the spread of ideology or religion.[22]

The first two categories of transnational flow have had an obvious impact on interstate relations. The movement of one national grouping into the territory of another has been a common occurrence in world history that has often led to conflict. The insurgency in Northern Ireland has it roots in the Protestant colonization of that country in the seventeenth century. More recent examples include Rabat's movement of 350,000 Moroccan citizens into the Western Sahara, the resettlement of Russians in the Baltic Republics under Soviet rule, and, indeed, the expansion of Israeli settlements on to occupied Arab land following the June 1967 war. All these migratory flows have plagued, or continue to bedevil, regional interstate relations.

Implicit within Weiner's work is the realization that migration as a transnational flow has the ability to shape the internal structure and borders of a state. The regional focus of this thesis provides many empirical examples of this effect. The very existence of Israel is testimony to the impact that Jewish immigration had on the establishment of the new state and its impact on the Arab world. The subsequent flight of Palestinian refugees from their erstwhile homes in 1948 and 1967 had direct and violent consequences for political stability in Jordan, and destroyed the confessional order that had dominated modern Lebanese politics since at least the National Pact of 1943. In short, migration as a transnational activity has had a profound impact on the politics of the Middle East since 1945, helping to redefine the idea surrounding the permeability of international borders. Thus, borders not only are traversed by migration flows, but, in the case of the Arab–Israeli dispute, have actually been shaped by them.

Such examples demonstrate the use of migration as an instrument of state policy. Trade relations between Washington and Moscow throughout the 1970s and 1980s remained dependent on Soviet concessions on Jewish emigration and continued to be so until December 1990. More recently, the Israeli bombardment of southern Lebanon in July 1993, induced a deliberate exodus of refugees designed to pressure the governments of Elias Harawi and Hafez al-Asad into curtailing the activities of Hezbollah.²³ Thus, in the Middle East migration has come to be associated with the destabilization of the existing order. In this context, the mass influx of Soviet Jewry into Israel was met with some despair throughout the wider region. For Arabs in general, and Palestinians in particular, such large-scale immigration represented the continued Zionist subversion of what little remained of Palestine.²⁴

Yet at the same time Israel provides an obvious example where migration, as a transnational flow, remains central to the wellbeing of the nation-state. Indeed, *aliyah*, the ingathering of Jews to Israel from the diaspora, is the *raison d'être* of the Jewish State. In a very real sense, therefore, Israel has consistently laid claim to a nation beyond its present state borders, a position enshrined in the 'Law of Return'. This confers Israeli citizenship on any diaspora Jew, or any person who can prove one female Jewish grandparent, thereby allowing them to make *aliyah* to Israel. For the state, immigration is an ideological process, divorced from the more prosaic motives that propelled many Soviet Jews to leave for Israel.²⁵

This process, however, can have a dual effect. While reinforcing the demographic base of the state, mass migration can provoke dissonance between immigrants and the receiving society, and, more broadly, between the state and society. Immigrants present an economic and cultural threat to the host society, and therefore to prevailing conceptions of societal security ... as a transnational flow actively sought by the state, migration in a very real sense threatens the 'we' identity of society. *Pieds noirs* arriving in France following Algerian independence in 1962 were met with considerable societal hostility, while ethnic Germans experienced similar treatment as the government of Chancellor Helmut Kohl struggled with the momentous challenge of German unification in 1990.²⁶ As Barry Buzan writes, 'Even if some immigration is allowed or welcomed, there may come a point when simple numbers begin to change the identity, and therefore the social and political life, of the population within a given locality.'²⁷

The most overt threat to societal security is economic. Large-scale migration represents a threat to established wage and employment structures. Moreover, by qualifying for citizenship, immigrants are usually entitled to benefits that generally can only be paid for by raising tax thresholds or borrowing money from other states or transnational actors. In turn, problems of economic adjustment are often compounded by cultural estrangement. Therefore, despite a racial affinity, the desire to maintain a specific communal identity complicates the relationship with the host society. While often the product of linguistic barriers, the certainty of communal continuity can both protect and isolate the immigrant from an alien milieu. The absorption of Oriental Jews into the new Jewish State between 1949 and 1960 featured many of these difficulties. Arabic remained the preferred language particularly among the elderly, while the secular, socialist, and distinctly European environment of the Jewish State remained at odds with the Judaic piety and individual work ethic previously so widespread among Jewish communities throughout the Middle East. The latent, but none the less collective, reaction to this absorption experience proved crucial to the ascendancy of the right wing in Israeli politics.[28]

Israel remains one of the few countries to encourage immigration actively on ideological grounds alone, irrespective of societal constraints. Because of the emotive appeal in fulfilling the highest ideal of Zionism, the state continues to engage actively in promoting the value of *aliyah* throughout the Jewish diaspora and among governments able to facilitate Jewish immigration to Israel. Accordingly, such activity has become a foreign policy value rather than just another foreign policy objective. In his study, *The Foreign Policy System of Israel*, Michael Brecher describes the dominant Jewish character of the state as the prism through which all policy decisions are made. As he wrote, 'For Israel's High Policy Elite, as for the entire society, there is a primordial and pre-eminent aspect of the political culture – its *Jewishness*: this pervades thought, feeling, belief, and behaviour in the political realm.'[29] This approach is self-evident in Israel's relationship with the Jewish diaspora. Brecher notes that David Ben Gurion regarded the two as indivisible. Israel's first prime minister is cited as declaring that 'The two groups are interdependent. The future of Israel – its security, its welfare, and its capacity to fulfil its historic mission – depends on world Jewry. And the future of world Jewry depends on the survival of Israel.'[30]

Brecher's work is an attempt to construct what he terms a 'Research Design' in which the 'interplay of different pressures' on Israeli foreign policy making and implementation 'can be observed and measured'.[31] The design traces the impact and influence of various actors in the process of foreign policy making and implementation, including the interaction beween state and non-state actors in the formulation of Israel's foreign policy. In the domestic context, Brecher highlights the role of military and economic capability as well as what he labels interest groups. These he divides among 'institutional', 'associational', and 'non-associational' groups. Institutional include bureaucratic institutions, the military establishment, and religious organizations which affect foreign policy decision-making. Associational groups include trade unions, business and civic groups, while non-associational include the role of individual citizens or broad groupings in the foreign policy process. These may range from class groupings within society to individual journalists or even academics.[32]

Clearly, Brecher's definition of interest groups falls within the broad remit of civil society. Yet he is primarily concerned with the *direct* influence of these interest groups on state foreign policy implementation, rather than how transnational activity can impact upon societal security, complicate the relationships between society and a state élite, and, consequently, change the agenda in interstate relations. Thus while Brecher is clearly of some use in understanding the role of the state in encouraging Jewish migration to Israel, his focus is of limited utility in understanding the impact of a transnational flow on domestic and international politics. Therefore, this study offers an alternative framework. By using the ideas of several of the authors discussed, the thesis sets out to offer a more complex examination of the impact and implications of Soviet Jewish migration upon Israel and the Middle East.

Soviet Jewish Aliyah: A Conceptual Approach
What follows is an attempt to place the significance of migration as a transnational flow within the context of both the Israeli political milieu and the wider realm of international politics. While migration clearly affects interstate relations, several categories in particular are identified with regard to the process of *aliyah*: the relationship between the superpowers, between the United States and Israel, between the Soviet Union and Israel, between the Arabs and the United States, and between the Arabs and Israel. Furthermore, the very nature of migration provides the continuity between the international and national political environments. In short, migrants have to settle somewhere regardless of their final status. The state, such as Israel, exists at

the nexus of this process, facilitating migration to it as best it can, while providing the resources required to absorb immigrants into the host society.

The relationship between the state élite and society can be fully appraised if we adopt the framework developed by Michael Barnett in his analysis of Israel's security policy. In this regard, the ability to absorb a mass influx of immigrants depends on several categories of resource mobilization, whose utility depends in turn upon both existing policy goals of the state élite and societal constraints upon the decision-making of this élite. In the case of 'accommodational' and 'restructural' resource mobilization, the state élite can gain access to the necessary resources domestically, without upsetting the societal equilibrium or provoking tension between society and state. However, with 'international' resource mobilization, the state élite can only obtain the required resources in an international environment. This need to obtain international resources demonstrates that migration, as a transnational flow, is beyond the resource capabilites of society to absorb.

Commensurate with this is the pursuit of an ideological goal by a state élite. It may lie outside the capacity of societal resources to cope with both this ideological goal and immigrant absorption, but ideology remains none the less intrinsic to the agenda of a particular government. Since 1977 in Israel, this ideological goal has been the consolidation of *Eretz Y'Israel*, the belief by the right wing that territories captured and occupied by Israel since the June 1967 war form an integral part of the Jewish State. As the state élite struggles to reconcile competing demands, the élite is forced to interact once more with the international environment. This necessary linkage with the international environment has ramifications, however, on the nature of societal security within Israel and the relationship between society and the state élite. Failure by the élite to foster the necessary conditions in which the physical, economic, and social security of society are allowed to flourish can provoke a challenge to the political legitimacy of the state élite. With this broad conceptual approach in mind, the book aims to highlight the following themes:

1. As a transnational flow, Soviet Jewish migration *simultaneously* affects several types of international relationships – those between the superpowers, between the superpowers and a local state, and between local states themselves. This theme suggests an examination of the manner in which the migration

process renders the foreign policy decision-making of the key actors more complex.

2. The migration process has a dual effect on Israeli conceptions of security: on the one hand, it bolsters the central tenet of Zionism and hence the concept of a Jewish State; but, on the other hand, it affects the position of the state élite by exacerbating ideological cleavages inherent within the concept of Zionism among the Israeli populace. These differences are a manifestation of the ongoing debate concerning the exact borders of the Jewish State.

3. The scale of migration presents a challenge to the conceptions of societal security affecting the economic, cultural, and social cohesion of both Israeli society and the immigrant community. In turn, this raises questions concerning the homogeneity of Israeli society and its relationship with the state élite. These include the relationship among Oriental, Ashkenazim, and Soviet Jews, as well as the impact of a secular migratory wave on the religious structures of the Jewish State.

4. Because Soviet Jewish migration inevitably affects the domestic Israeli equilibrium, and because the Arab–Israeli conflict is central to Middle East politics, the process of migration impacts upon regional order, and, in particular, Israel's relationship with the Palestinians.

Conclusion
It should be noted from the outset that the themes outlined above are not mutually exclusive. Rather, they demonstrate that migration as a transnational flow highlights clear linkages between domestic and international politics. This study of Soviet Jewish *Aliyah* between 1989 and 1992 is, none the less, historical in its methodological approach, beginning in Chapter 2 with a brief examination of Jewish emigration from the Soviet Union between 1970 and 1989. This is important for two main reasons: first, it allows us to examine the impact of Soviet Jewish migration on the relationships between the superpowers, between Israel and the Soviet Union, and between Israel and the United States; second, it allows an examination of the changing motives for migration among Soviet Jews. The question of allegiance to Zionism was to play an increasingly central role as Israel struggled to cope with mass *aliyah*.

Chapter 3 examines the domestic political milieu of the Jewish

State, focusing on the diffuse nature of Zionism as an ideology, the ethnic and cultural divisions in Israeli society, and an explanation of the ascendancy of the right wing in Israel. The intention is to highlight the continuing political, ideological, and security debates that greeted the mass influx of Soviet Jewry to Israel. It is on these debates that Soviet Jewish immigration had such a profound effect; consequently they provide the focus of discussion in the following chapters.

Chapter 4 examines the ideological and economic constraints facing the Likud government as it sought to correlate successful immigrant absorption with its own ideological agenda. It also addresses the issue of competing bureaucracies within the state élite and the ways in which these shaped the absorption process. Chapter 5 looks at the process of absorption itself, exploring how this affected the cultural, economic and social well-being of immigrants and Israelis alike. Chapter 6 discusses the Arab responses to Soviet Jewish *aliyah*, their effect upon interstate relations, and the ways in which this duly affected the Israeli political scene. Finally, Chapter 7 examines the total effect that Soviet Jewish *aliyah* had on the relationship between the state élite and Israeli society, the consequences of which have proved influential in redefining state conceptions of regional and societal security.

NOTES

1. See Annex 1. Breakdown of Immigration to Israel from the former Soviet Union. The comparison with France is made in' 'At Ease in Zion', *The Economist*, 22 Jan. 1994.
2. See for example Robert O. Keohane and Joseph S. Nye (eds), *Transnational Relations and World Politics* (Cambridge, MA: Harvard University Press, 1972).
3. M. J. Peterson, 'Transnational Activity, International Society and World Politics', *Millennium*, Vol. 21, No. 3 (1992), p.372.
4. Ibid., p.371.
5. Ibid., p.372.
6. Ibid., p.374.
7. Michael Barnett, 'High Politics is Low Politics: The Domestic and Systemic Sources of Israeli Security Policy, 1967-1977', *World Politics*, Vol.42, No.4 (1990), p.530.
8. Zeev Schiff and Ehud Ya'ari, *Israel's Lebanon War* (London: Unwin, 1984), p.281.
9. Ole Waever, 'Societal security: the concept', in Ole Waever, Barry Buzan, Morten Kelstrup and Pierre Lemaitre, *Identity, Migration, and the New Security Agenda in Europe* (London: Pinter Publishers, 1993), p.18.
10. Ibid., p.21.
11. Ibid., p.23.
12. Augustus Richard Norton, 'The Future of Civil Society in the Middle East', *Middle East Journal*, Vol. 47, No. 2 (1993), p.211.
13. Peterson, op. cit., p.376.

14. Ibid., p.380.
15. The bureaucratic politics model was first applied in an analysis of the Cuban missile crisis. See Graham T. Allison, *Essence of Decision: Explaining the Cuban Missile Crisis* (Boston: Little and Brown, 1971).
16. Barnett, op.cit., p.531.
17. Ibid., p.542.
18. Ibid., pp.542–4.
19. Aristide R. Zolberg, 'International Migrations in Political Perspective', in Mary M. Kritz, Charles B. Keely, and Silvano M. Tomasi (eds), *Global Trends in Migration: Theory and Research on International Population Movements* (New York: Center for Migration Studies, 1983), pp.3-4.
20. Ibid.
21. Myron Weiner, *The Political Aspects of International Migration*, paper presented to the International Studies Association, London, 30 March 1989, p.1.
22. Ibid., pp.1-2.
23. Hirsh Goodman, 'Why Israel went into battle', *The Jerusalem Report*, Vol. IV, No. 7 (12 Aug. 1993), pp.10–11.
24. Gil Loescher, *Refugee Movements and International Security*, Adelphi Paper No. 268 (London: IISS,1992), p.32.
25. Ibid., p.35.
26. Ibid., p.48.
27. Barry Buzan, 'Societal security, state security, and internationalization', in Waever *et al.* op. cit., p.43.
28. With reference to the origins of the divisions between Ashkenazim and Oriental Jews in Israel, see Tom Segev, *The First Israelis* (New York: Free Press, 1986).
29. Michael Brecher, *The Foreign Policy System of Israel* (London: Oxford University Press, 1972), p.229.
30. Ibid., p.232.
31. Ibid., pp.1–2.
32. Ibid., pp.1–20.

2 The Migration of Soviet Jewry 1970–1989

On 7 December 1988, Mikhail Gorbachev stood before the United Nations in New York to announce radical arms cuts in Soviet conventional forces and weapons. The scale of these proposals, which totalled a unilateral reduction of some 500,000 men, overshadowed the remainder of the Soviet leader's speech which encompassed his vision of a new world order. He went on to declare:

> The problem of exit from and entry to our country, including the question of leaving it for family re-unification, is being dealt with in a humane spirit. As you know, one of the reasons for refusal to leave is a person's knowledge of secrets. Strictly warranted time limitations on the secrecy rule will now be applied. Every person seeking employment at certain agencies or enterprises will be informed of this rule. This removes from the agenda the problem of the so-called 'refuseniks'.[1]

This statement of intent paved the way for the mass exodus of those Jews who wished to leave the Soviet Union. The emphasis on arms control was designed to facilitate the establishment of a benign international environment, conducive to the restructuring of the Soviet economy. However, Moscow had come to the realization that concessions over the issue of Soviet Jewish emigration would help remove domestic political constraints in the West, and in particular the United States, to closer economic ties with the Soviet Union.

This strategy was not new. Between 1968 and 1980 Moscow had allowed nearly 250,000 of its Jewish citizens, from a total population of two and a quarter million, to leave the USSR for new lives in Israel and the West.[2] The decision to allow large-scale, but none the less restricted, Soviet Jewish emigration resulted from sustained United States pressure over the issue. It was seen as a price worth paying if concomitant political, economic, and technological benefits in the era of *détente* were subsequently forthcoming.[3] Therefore, while Jewish dissidents, especially in the early 1970s, were important in highlighting the plight of Soviet Jewry, the issue of Jewish emigration became an issue dominated by superpower politics and thus a function of interstate relations.

An understanding of the dynamics and development of Soviet Jewish emigration throughout this period becomes a prerequisite in analysing the more recent and considerably larger exodus of Soviet Jews to Israel. As well as pointing to the role of Soviet Jewish migration as a transnational flow in the development of superpower relations between 1970 and 1989, this chapter offers a brief analysis of the following: internal Soviet constraints on Jewish emigration; the changing ethnic and ideological composition of the emigrants themselves; Israel's absorption strategy of the 1970s; the issue of the *noshrim*, those Jews originally destined for Israel, who in growing numbers, looked to the West and particularly the United States and Canada to provide them with a new home; the development of Soviet Jewish emigration under Mikhail Gorbachev; the evolution of Soviet-Israeli relations; and finally, Washington's response to the growing tide of Soviet Jewish emigration in the wake of Gorbachev's reforms.

Emigration and the Superpowers: 1970–1980
Initially, Soviet Jews had to rely on their own efforts in demanding the right to emigrate from the Soviet authorities. While the overwhelming military victory achieved by Israel in the June 1967 war had led to a groundswell of Zionist sentiment among many Soviet Jews, Moscow's swift abrogation of diplomatic relations precluded any effective role for Tel-Aviv in supporting Soviet Jewish emigration.[4] At first, Jewish activists, drawn mainly from the intelligentsia in urban areas and highly motivated by Zionist ideals, confined their protests to petitions that demanded the right of exit, usually addressed to the United Nations. *Aliyah* activists also used underground *samizdat* publications to highlight their struggle. Much of this work subsequently went on to be reprinted in the Western press. The most notable of these was the 'Letter of the 39', a petition by *aliyah* activists that demanded the right to emigrate to Israel.[5]

However, despite messages of world support for the Soviet Jewish dissidents, the increased harassment by the Soviet authorities, resulting in mass arrests in 1970, led some Jewish activists to adopt more militant tactics in order to highlight their plight. These usually centred around the peaceful occupation of a government building but, occasionally, more dramatic episodes were plannned. In 1970, nine Soviet dissidents, including seven Jews, were found guilty by a Leningrad court of plotting the hijack of a Soviet airliner to Sweden. While the conviction of the accused was seen to be a foregone conclusion, the death sentence pronounced on two of the Jewish dissidents resulted in a huge international outcry, forcing Moscow to climb down. More than any other incident, the Leningrad trial highlighted the plight of Soviet Jewish activists in their struggle to emigrate from the USSR.[6] Within the context of Soviet politics, this was a rare example of individuals placing demands before an all-powerful state apparatus.

By March 1971 though, it appears that the Soviet leadership had carried out a review of its policy towards Jewish dissidents. On 10 March, just before the start of the 24th Congress of the Communist Party of the Soviet Union (CPSU), 156 Jews staged a demonstration in the Supreme Soviet itself. This act, in conjunction with a demonstration through the streets of the Soviet capital the following day, were dealt with in a conciliatory manner by the Soviet Interior Ministry. This was in sharp contrast to the intimidation and recourse to violence that had marked previous acts of protest by Soviet Jewish dissidents.[7]

Soon after the Leningrad trial, a decision to increase the number of exit visas appears to have been taken by the party leadership. By the end of 1971, over 12,000 Jews had left the Soviet Union, a figure that surpassed the total number allowed to leave throughout the whole of the 1960s. This marked the beginning of the mass Jewish exodus of the 1970s. The rationale behind Moscow's decision was not hard to find. As one commentator wrote:

> The courting of favourable opinion in the West – or at least an unhostile opinion – had assumed special importance in the context of new foreign policy undertakings of the USSR in early 1971. These undertakings, which came to be summmed up in the word *détente* flowed from defence considerations and economic needs, and events in early 1971 gave these a pressing and urgent character.[8]

Throughout the period known as *détente*, a clear correlation was discernible between the state of superpower relations and the number of Jews allowed to leave the USSR. The years 1971 to 1973 saw a rapid increase in emigration, coinciding with the Strategic Arms Limitation Talks (SALT) and their successful conclusion in a series of bilateral agreements, signed between Presidents Brezhnev and Nixon in May 1972. From Moscow's perspective, the SALT 1 accords codified the status of the Soviet Union as a superpower, while the signing of the US–Soviet trade agreement promised an influx of American technology and capital, badly needed in an already stagnating economy.[9]

Unwittingly, however, Moscow's initial gestures of goodwill concerning Soviet Jewry set a precedent in which the issue of trade became subject to increased Soviet concessions on the very issue of Jewish emigration. In Washington, critics of *détente* viewed the issue of Soviet Jewry as a means by which the United States – its foreign policy in apparent crisis following the debacle of Vietnam – could exercise some control over the Soviet Union. Consequently, the Jackson–Vanik Amendment to the trade agreement of October 1972, linked the level of Soviet Jewish emigration with the granting of Most Favoured Nation status (MFN) to the Soviet Union. MFN meant the abolition of import taxes on Soviet goods entering the United States, which was crucial if the envisaged expansion in trade, and the consequent benefits for the Soviet economy, were to be realized.[10]

The Brezhnev leadership was willing to make further concessions on the issue of Soviet Jewry. The emigration tax imposed on would-be emigrés was waived in March 1973, with total emigration numbering some 34,733 for that year.[11] In September 1973, the Soviets became signatories to the UN Covenant on Civil and Political Rights, which, among its articles, enshrined the right of emigration. However, Moscow's perceived failure to warn the United States over the Egyptian–Syrian assault against Israel in October 1973, and its consequent threat to intervene on behalf of Presidents Asad and Sadat, eroded support for the *détente* process in the US Congress. Already, serious doubts existed as to the wisdom of SALT 1 in which the freezing of missile delivery systems at present levels had given an asymmetric advantage to the Soviet Union. Critics of *détente* argued that while feasting upon the 'carrot' of economic co-operation, Moscow had failed to take heed of the American 'stick'. Consequently, increasing efforts were made in Congress to limit the scope of the US–Soviet trade agreement. These culminated in the Stevenson Amendment, a bill designed to limit US credit to the Soviet Union to $3,000 million over a period of four years. By international finance standards, this was a paltry figure, insufficient to sustain the import-led growth badly needed by the Soviet economy.[12]

The passing of both the Stevenson Amendment and the Jackson–Vanik Accord by the US Senate was a major setback for the Soviets. In particular, Brezhnev felt humiliated, regarding the Jackson–Vanik Accord as an unwarranted intrusion into the internal affairs of the Soviet Union. Unable to accept continued Soviet adherence to the trade agreement under these conditions, Moscow announced its abrogation on 10 January 1975.[13]

The period between 1975 and 1977 proved to be lean in terms of the number of Soviet Jews allowed to leave. From the highest level of emigration in 1973, the numbers were severely reduced. In 1975, only 13,221 Jews were recorded as leaving the Soviet Union.[14] This reflected the increasingly fractious relationship between the two superpowers. Caught in a foreign policy strait-jacket in the aftermath of Vietnam, Soviet involvement in the Third World seemed only to underline American impotence. Powerful lobby groups, such as the Committee for the Present Danger, whose members included Paul Nitze and Richard Perle, future members of President Reagan's cabinet, argued that asymmetries conceded by the United States in nuclear arms control had allowed Moscow to implement an aggressive foreign policy. Events during the October War of 1973, the collapse of South Vietnam, and the establishment of Communist regimes in Angola and Ethiopia, only served to vindicate such an analysis.[15]

The election of Jimmy Carter to the White House in November 1976 appeared to herald a new chapter in Soviet policy towards emigration. As apparent progress was being made on the SALT 2 accords, 28,864 Jews were allowed to leave the USSR during the course of 1978. The following year, the number almost doubled: 51,320 Soviet Jews, the largest number ever recorded in one year, were allowed to exit the Soviet Union. This corresponded with record trade figures between the two superpowers.[16]

Given the abrogation of the 1972 trade agreement by the Soviet Union, Moscow's decision to allow a vast increase in Jewish emigration can be attributed to a greater understanding of internal American politics. Although traditionally a bedrock of Democratic

Party support, American Jewry had, following the October 1973 war, become more militant towards the Soviet Union. Consequently, opponents of *détente* discovered a reservoir of growing support amongst America's own Jewish community. Concerns over the security of the State of Israel dovetailed neatly with the expansionist interpretations placed upon the conduct of Soviet foreign policy. Moreover, continued restrictions on the right of Soviet Jews to emigrate had only served to harden opposition to *détente* in the United States. In short, interest group pressure over the issue of Soviet Jewish emigration, amplified by opponents of *détente* in Washington, proved influential in determining the United States relationship with Moscow.

This influence was highlighted once more by President Carter in a speech before the UN General Assembly on 17 March 1979. While addressing the general theme of human rights, it became apparent that Carter planned to raise the issue of Jewish emigration with the Soviet leadership in any negotiations towards the conclusion of the SALT 2 talks. Thus, while the conclusion of an arms control agreement remained the centre of attention during the course of the Vienna summit in May 1979, Soviet Jewish emigration and related trade issues were discussed in private and in some detail by Carter and Brezhnev. Although the Soviet leader remained keen to deny any links between the two issues, it was noticeable that increasing numbers of Jews were being allowed to leave the USSR.[17]

By permitting record levels of Jewish emigration, Moscow hoped to demonstrate that tangible benefits were to be had from *détente*, thereby undermining American domestic opposition to the arms control process and allowing SALT 2 to be concluded. Most vocal in his opposition to the SALT process remained Senator Henry Jackson, architect of the Jackson–Vanik Accord, who accused the Carter administration of following a policy of 'appeasement' in its negotiations with the Soviet Union.[18] Yet any benefits Moscow expected to accrue by increasing Jewish emigration were quickly dashed. The Soviet invasion of Afghanistan in December 1979 removed any hope that President Carter had of obtaining ratification of the accord from the US Senate. The failure to ratify SALT 2, and the overall deterioration in bilateral relations between Washington and Moscow, were swiftly reflected in the number of Jews allowed to leave the USSR. In 1980, 21,471 Jews, a decrease of some 44 per cent on 1979, left the USSR. An accelerated decline in the numbers allowed to leave was to mark the next eight years. Not until Mikhail Sergeyevich Gorbachev became General Secretary of the CPSU in 1985 were Soviet Jews allowed to leave the USSR in increasing, and eventually, overwhelming numbers.[19]

The Process of Soviet Jewish Emigration

Prior to the disintegration of the USSR, there was nothing in Soviet legal or criminal law to prevent or prohibit the right of emigration.[20] In practice, however, a number of bureaucratic obstacles, coupled with latent anti-Semitic sentiment widespread among some sections of Soviet society, prevented large-scale Jewish emigration until 1971. Yet the basis upon which Jews could apply to leave the Soviet Union had been established some five years earlier. Addressing a press conference in Paris in 1966, the then Soviet Premier Alexei Kosygin announced that, 'As regards family reunions, if there are, in fact, some families which would like to meet, or to leave the Soviet Union the way is open before them, and this constitutes no problem.'[21]

Until Gorbachev assumed power, family reunion was the only justification upon which Soviet Jews could apply to leave the USSR, despite the fact that Kosygin's statement was never grounded in Soviet law. According to Thomas Sawyer, the decision to ease restrictions on specifically Jewish emigration was the product of a bureaucratic struggle within the Kremlin itself. Throughout the Soviet Union, Jews, both Zionist and non-Zionist, had faced increasing discrimination, particularly in areas such as employment and education. These practices had been condoned by individuals such as Ukrainian party chief Petr Shelest and chief ideologist of the CPSU in 1970, Mikhail Suslov. With the growing appeal of Zionism among Soviet Jewry in the aftermath of the June 1967 war, it was hoped that the Leningrad trial could be used as a pretext to impose increased restrictions upon Soviet Jews. Yet the world outcry following the trial, coupled with the need to court Washington, allowed the reformers within the Kremlin – Kosygin and KGB Chief Yuri Andropov amongst them – to implement measures leading to large-scale emigration.[22]

A set process was established with which Jews wishing to emigrate had to comply. First, the aspiring émigré had to be in receipt of an invitation or *vyzov* from a relative already living overseas, usually in Israel. Having received this, the would-be emigrant had to obtain references from his or her employer. The disclosure of emigration plans to colleagues at work often prejudiced the applicant's position within an organization. Some were immediately dismissed:

> A prospective Jewish emigrant ran the risk of being caught in a state of limbo:unemployed and unemployable because of the desire to leave, and unable to leave due to lack of employment and the necessary references.[23]

Even if references were obtained, the bureaucratic obstacle of the OVIR – *Otdel Vizy i Registratsii*, the Visa and Registration Department of the Soviet Ministry of Interior – still remained. This had offices that were situated in most cities and large towns throughout the USSR. Charged by Moscow to select the successful applicants for emigration, the OVIR was also a useful means to curtail the flow of Jews, depending upon the internal and international situation at any particular time. The number of Jews allowed to leave the Soviet Union varied from republic to republic, and year to year. For example, in 1973, of the 33,500 Jews allowed to leave, fully 90 per cent came from the southern Soviet Republics, most notably Georgia. The rest comprised Jews from the former Russian Soviet Federative Socialist Republic (RSFSR).[24]

Given that the Russian Jews comprised some 38 per cent of the total Soviet Jewish population, the disparity in numbers was profound. Several conflicting accounts have been put forward to explain this. Jerome Gilison argued that while Moscow may have decided on a rough quota of Jews allowed to leave, the constitution of these numbers was very much left to the discretion of the OVIRs in individual republics.[25] Georgia was seen as having a more liberal emigration policy in comparison with the larger Soviet republics. While the attitude of the Georgian OVIRs may, indeed, have been more benevolent towards its Jewish citizens, other considerations reveal that the ethnic composition of Jewish migration was still very much influenced by Moscow.[26]

Taken against the general profile of Soviet Jewry, Jews from Tajikistan, Uzbekistan, Azerbaijan, and Georgia were less well-educated than their Russian and Ukrainian counterparts. Although their affiliation to Judaism, both as a cultural and religious force, remained strong, they were not indispensable to the welfare of the

Soviet economy. Moscow could therefore allow these Jews to emigrate, thereby appeasing Western demands, while maintaining a tight grip on the exodus of Jews from the Ukraine and Russia.[27] These two republics had by far the largest percentage of trained and highly educated white collar workers, scientists, and engineers whose skills were deemed vital to the security of the Soviet Union.[28]

This selective emigration policy went some way to assuaging the concerns of the Soviet military. They had noted, with some alarm, that former Russian Jewish scientists, now gainfully employed by Israel's military industries, were utilising skills acquired at the expense of the Soviet government. It could not have been lost on the military that Soviet technology, developed further by Israel, could be passed on to the United States or used against Moscow's Arab allies.[29]

Soviet emigration policy in the early 1970s developed out of the need to reconcile these competing interests. In placing emphasis upon the emigration of Jews from the peripheries of the USSR, Moscow hoped to engage Western economic co-operation, without endangering the security of the Soviet state. The effect of this policy was apparent in the wave of emigration between 1971 and 1972. Of the 31,500 Jewish émigrés, only 17 per cent had received some form of higher education. Furthermore, Russian Jews comprised just seven per cent of the total allowed to emigrate.[30]

Increased demand for exit visas, particularly amongst Russian and Ukrainian Jews led to the establishment of further restrictive practices designed to forestall any 'brain drain'. On 3 August 1972, the Presidium of the Supreme Soviet passed decree number 572. This stated that:

> Citizens of the USSR leaving for permanent residence abroad in other than socialist countries [must] compensate the State for their education received from institutions of higher education.[31]

Aware that such legislation could adversely effect its position with Washington, Moscow refrained from publicizing the decree's enactment. All Jews who had received a higher education were now expected to pay the new diploma tax as it became known. This applied to all those who were already in receipt of exit visas, and those who were still waiting to be processed by their regional

OVIRs. The tax levied upon individuals was dependent upon their occupation, but ranged from 4,000 to 25,000 roubles, an extortionate rate by Soviet standards. One Soviet Jewish émigré calculated that, on 1973 pay levels, it would take a qualified Soviet Jewish engineer from five to seven years to raise the required sum.[32] In practice, only 1,435 Soviet Jews actually paid the tax before its suspension in March 1973. Following high-level representations from the Israeli government under Golda Meir, Washington invoked the threat of further trade sanctions, forcing Moscow to back down.[33]

However, the numbers of Soviet Jews wishing to emigrate at the beginning of the 1970s should be kept in perspective. Two-thirds of the total Soviet Jewish population lived in either the Ukraine or the Russian Republic. In contrast to the Jews of the southern Soviet Republics, these Jews were largely Ashkenazi, secular, acculturated and, for the most part, urban dwellers. Despite providing the vanguard of the Jewish dissident movement, the majority were loyal citizens of the Soviet state.[34]

But alarmed by the actual number of Jews seeking to emigrate – still a small proportion from a total Jewish population of some 2,150,707 according to a 1970 Soviet census – Moscow initiated policies that affected all Jews, regardless of their affiliation to Zionism. The period between the academic years 1971–72 and 1977–78 saw a 40 per cent decrease in the number of Jewish university students. According to one commentator, this national figure was consistent with a drop in Jewish students entering Moscow's institutes of higher education, regarded as the most prestigious in the Soviet state. The rationale behind the decline in Jewish students was not hard to find:

> If Jews are going to emigrate, surely there is no argument to educate them. Why should the socialist fatherland prepare cadres for the Zionist state or any other capitalist country? Any Jew, whatever his geographic origins, cultural background, or political beliefs, becomes a potential emigre and must be treated as such.[35]

The increased discrimination imposed upon those Jews wishing to enter higher education proved to be a major factor – particularly amongst Russian and Ukrainian Jewry – in sustaining and expanding the wave of emigration throughout the 1970s. In turn, the exodus of large numbers made life increasingly problematic for the majority who remained. Reactions among Soviet citizens, though hard to gauge accurately, ran from jealousy and hatred, to genuine confusion as to why anybody would want to leave the USSR.

Opinions concerning their Jewish compatriots were often shaped by anti-Zionist propaganda in the media. Indeed, attacks on Israel and Zionism provided cover for the latent expression of anti-Semitism which distinguished many newspaper articles. Many themes were used to undermine the position of Jews within Soviet society: Jewish plans for world domination; infiltration of state institutions, surrogates of the Central Intelligence Agency; the equating of Zionism with Nazism. Cartoons, reminiscent of those that featured prominently in Nazi publications, 'depicting Jews as lecherous money lenders complete with hooked nose and beady eyes,' regularly appeared at this time in the Soviet press.[36] As Gilison comments:

> In this way, Government attacks on Zionism, which can be found in Soviet literature..., have taken on new meaning due to the extremity to which the themes are pushed. It is no longer a set of ideas that are attacked, but a set of people who hold them, and by implication that set of people includes all Jews.[37]

Restrictions imposed upon Soviet Jewry only served to increase the number wishing to leave. From 1974 onwards, figures show that rising numbers of assimilated urban Jews, most notably from the Ukraine and the RSFSR, actively sought permission to emigrate. In one survey of such emigres, anti-Semitism was most commonly cited as the main reason for leaving the USSR.[38] By the time emigration was reduced to a trickle following the Soviet invasion of Afghanistan, over 250,000 Jews had left for a new life in Israel and the West.

Moscow's official rationale for allowing large-scale Jewish emigration had been to facilitate the reunification of families dispersed during, and immediately after, the Second World War.[39] In order to stand any chance of being issued with an exit visa, OVIRs required that Tel-Aviv be listed as the intended destination of the would-be emigrant. Despite repeating the official view that the Jews did not constitute a nation, Moscow's insistence upon national migration to Israel was deliberate. It was felt that an open door policy, allowing Jews to settle in the United States outright, would have initiated unrest amongst citizens of the Baltic and Ukrainian Republics. Many would have been able to make a case, with equal validity, for family reunification with members of large expatriate communities in the United States as justification for wanting to leave.[40]

Yet the shift in the ethnic composition of Soviet Jewish emigration in the mid to late 1970s changed the existing pattern of migration. Jews possessing strong religious, or Zionist, convictions had formed the basis of the Jewish migrants between 1971 and 1973. The majority were from rural or semi-rural communities in Georgia or other southern Soviet Republics. In contrast, urbanized Jews from the industrial heartlands of the USSR began to dominate emigration after 1974. Anti-Semitism, rather than adherence to Zionist or religious orthodoxy, provided an understandable incentive for wishing to leave the Soviet Union, but not necessarily to emigrate to Israel.[41]

Rather than allow direct transit to Israel, Moscow had insisted that all emigrants travel via Vienna. It was at this juncture, beginning in 1974, that the dropout syndrome surfaced: those Jews, wishing to emigrate to countries other than Israel, chose to go to the West, most notably to the United States and Canada. The dropout syndrome continued to mark Soviet Jewish emigration until October 1989 when Washington applied strict new immigration quotas. When emigration during this period reached its peak level of 51,320 migrants in 1979, only 34 per cent of migrants chose to settle in Israel.[42]

From Moscow's perspective, the dropout syndrome was curiously beneficial and may have reinforced the decision to allow a sharp increase in exit visas in the late 1970s. The decision to cite Israel as the sole destination on visa applications had been for reasons of internal ethnic stability. However, this had also elicited protests from Arab states concerned at the demographic consequences of large-scale Jewish migration. Although pointing out that 800,000 Jews from Arab countries had settled in the Jewish State, the Soviets, aware of Arab sensibilities and their already weak position throughout the Middle East, refrained from establishing direct flights to Tel-Aviv.[43] The dropout factor served to alleviate the contradiction between internal political expediency and the further erosion of credibility within the Arab world.

That credibility was further endangered by Egyptian President Anwar Sadat's historic visit to Israel in September 1977. This paved the way for the Camp David Accords two years later, an agreement that denied any constructive role for Moscow in the Middle East peace process. With Egypt, the most influential Arab state, firmly within the American sphere of influence, it became imperative for Moscow to shore up its Middle Eastern assets. Large-scale Jewish emigration, therefore, without the dropout factor, could not have been contemplated since Israel would have remained the only destination.

The dropout syndrome was important to Moscow in one more dimension. By allowing record emigration levels, the Soviets could be publicly seen to abide by provisions set forth in the Universal Declaration on Human Rights and the Helsinki Final Act of 1975.[44] This was crucial since Moscow wished to conclude the negotiations towards SALT 2 at a time when increased opposition to the SALT process was gaining momentum in Washington itself.[45] In short, the dropout syndrome provided a vital link, reconciling several competing elements in Soviet internal and foreign policies.

Soviet Jewish Immigration to Israel: 1970–1980
Initially at least, Israel appeared set to be the main beneficiary of Soviet Jewish emigration. By the late 1970s, however, the preference of growing numbers of Soviet Jews for the United States was causing much disquiet in Tel-Aviv. Ethnic composition, low levels of Jewish cultural awareness and an antipathy towards Zionism all provided partial explanations for the issue of dropouts, or in Hebrew, *noshrim*. Israel, however, had to consider the shortcomings of its own absorption process. Tales of disillusion and hardship amongst earlier émigrés, coupled with the ever-present threat of war, did little to endear Israel to those Soviet Jews seeking a new life elsewhere. This immigrant wave provided an early example of the discord that migration as a transnational flow could have on the security of the recipient society, and the ways in which this consequently affected the relationship between society and the state élite.

Between 1948 and 1970, 24,000 Jews left the USSR for Israel.[46] Given the comparatively small number of new immigrants or *olim*, absorption proved to be relatively painless for all concerned. However, from 1971 to 1974, 94,764 Soviet *olim* were received by the State of Israel. The ensuing social and political problems created by the arrival of this exodus gave birth to the phrase,

'Israelis love immigration, but can't stand immigrants'.[47] Moreover, a clear divide was discernible in attitudes. Many *sabras* – native born or totally assimilated Israelis – expected gratitude from the *olim* and perceived themselves as the saviours of a powerless, downtrodden community. Conversely, the early wave of *olim* saw themselves as pioneers, confronting and defeating the obstinacy of Soviet bureaucracy, and now 'marching as a militant reinforcement to a small, far-off, and beleaguered Jewish homeland'.[48] The friction inherent within such contrasting viewpoints was to be compounded by the process of absorption itself.

The Labour government of Golda Meir was unprepared for the size and scale of the Soviet Jewish exodus. The Ministry of Immigrant Absorption faced a severe shortage of trained language teachers, social workers and absorption centres, all crucial if political dissonance and social dislocation were to be avoided. In short, Israel faced a crisis in societal resource mobilization rather than any shortcoming in raising the required sums from other states or international financial institutions. Indeed, despite financial support from the United States and world Jewry, the development of a comprehensive strategy for immigrant absorption proved impossible. This was largely due to the fluctuations in the volume of those arriving, undermining attempts to match numbers to resources.[49]

Housing proved to be a contentious issue. While sanctioning the construction of new homes, great pressure was placed upon privately leased accommodation, particularly in Tel-Aviv and Haifa, to provide temporary housing for the new *olim*. Because of the sudden demand for private accommodation, Israelis faced steep rent rises in all major towns and cities as demand outstripped supply. Particularly hard hit were young *sabras*, many of whom, having just completed their military service, were looking to establish their first home. Too often, Israelis were faced with having to compete with new immigrants whose initial state benefits, however short term, proved decisive in obtaining accommodation.[50]

Israel's Oriental Jews generally comprised the lower socio-economic strata of Israeli society, a position partly attributable to deliberate policy decisions by a succession of Ashkenazim-dominated Labour governments.[51] Accordingly, benefits to which all new immigrants were entitled, for example, exemption from tax on the purchase of consumer durables for three years, were seen as indicative of continued discrimination. Clearly, as a transnational flow, this wave of *aliyah* produced societal discord among established Jewish communities throughout Israel.[52]

The preference accorded to the new Soviet *olim* in the allocation of housing proved crucial in the formation of a group of politicized, young, Oriental radicals: *Panterim Shehorim*, the Black Panthers. Drawn predominantly from the metropolitan slum belts inhabited largely by Oriental Jews, the Panthers demanded 'slum clearance, more jobs, better educational opportunities, an end to all discrimination against Orientals'.[53] As one observer stated:

> It is not by chance that the Panther movement started in the slums of Western Jerusalem opposite the comfortable new Jewish quarters of the 'Eastern city' being rapidly built by the authorities and where many of the new immigrants were housed.[54]

In March 1971, confronted by official indifference to their demands, the Black Panthers organised a major demonstration in Jerusalem. With the government seemingly ignorant of the feelings of anger and frustration, the event soon turned into a major riot. Golda Meir had publicly stated that if ever the choice came down to social equality or *aliyah* – the ingathering of Jews to Israel – the latter had priority.[55] However, although representative of only a small minority of the Oriental community, the aims of the Panther movement enjoyed widespread sympathy amongst the wider population. This support was partly a response to a generation of political neglect by the Labour establishment, but also a protest at the violent action taken by the civil police in breaking up Panther demonstrations.

Belatedly, Meir's government sanctioned projects designed to meet some of the Panther's demands, demonstrating at least that a societal actor could place pressure and constraints directly on the Israeli government. Large-scale programmes to deal with urban problems, education and social rehabilitation were soon instigated. Following these concessions, the Panther organization, never a cohesive political party, quickly splintered into several smaller factions, each eventually merging with other parties mainly on the right of the Israeli political spectrum.[56] However, by focusing on the perceived bias in favour of the new *olim*, the

Panthers proved extremely effective in raising the collective political consciousness of Israel's Oriental community. This consciousness found its self-expression with the election to power in 1977 of Menachem Begin.

Despite the benefits accorded to them by the state, visible discontent soon surfaced amongst the new *olim*. The Ministry of Absorption, struggling to cope with the size of immigration in the early 1970s, had to reconcile employment opportunities and housing needs for Israel's new citizens. Soviet immigrants complained of being sent to the development towns where housing was available, but appropriate employment, in which the new migrant could utilize his or her skills, was not.[57] This in turn created problems in placing succeeding waves of Soviet Jewish migrants:

> Immigrants would arrive armed with letters from friends or relatives, saying 'Don't go to Beersheva. Accept only Holon', [a suburb of Tel-Aviv], and put their trust in these. The result was antagonism that quickly became a public issue.[58]

Tactics that had been used to force concessions from Moscow were now employed against the Ministry of Absorption and the Jewish Agency, all deemed to be inefficient or unresponsive to the needs of the *olim*. Dentists, originally trained in the Soviet Union, regarded the imposition of retraining schemes as an indictment of their professional competence. Consequently, many decided to strike. Such action became commonplace: strikes at absorption centres and letters of protest by the new immigrants concerning resettlement policy were reported widely by the Israeli media.[59]

Of particular interest was the fate of the Georgian Jewish community. Among the least assimilated and educated of the Soviet Jews, they were, however, the most religious with a high proportion adhering to Zionist ideals. Moreover, the Georgian Jews constituted a tightly knit community who 'fiercely resisted attempts to scatter them through different parts of Israel'.[60]

Absorption policy had, since the establishment of the State of Israel in 1948, been dominated by the policy of *mizug galuyot*: the mixing of exiles. This posited that the new *olim* be assimilated as soon as was practically possible into the fabric of Israeli society. While the intention may have been good, the implementation of *mizug galuyot* often resulted in attempts to strip new *olim* of their original cultural identity. This had occurred in the absorption of the Oriental Jews, and was the main cause of the simmering contempt against the Ashkenazim dominated Labour establishment. Because the Ashkenazim were the founders of the modern Jewish state, Orientals charged that to be an Israeli was synonymous with adhering to the norms and values of the Ashkenazim. Little account, it was argued, had been taken of the cultural heritage developed by Jewish communities in the diaspora.[61]

Consequently, the structure of the Georgian community did not easily lend itself to the process of assimilation. This was compounded by a profound sense of disillusion throughout Georgian Jewry at the nature of Israeli society. Israel appeared permissive, irreligious and egalitarian, a reality far removed from the religious and Zionist ideals thought to constitute the Jewish State. The 'promised land' became the antithesis of the ideals and family culture held dear by the Georgian *olim*. Hierarchical family values, including the inferior social status of women, all seemed threatened by a Jewish society that had adopted gentile norms.[62]

In 1975, the Israeli government, now led by Yitzhak Rabin, commissioned a series of studies, designed to target absorption practices to the actual needs of the Soviet *olim*. Such research helped the Ministries of Employment and Absorption to achieve greater efficiency in placing professional skills at the disposal of the wider Israeli economy. Of a sample of migrant engineers, 90 per cent gained employment within two years. The studies also gave Tel-Aviv a greater awareness of the level of professional training an individual had received in the Soviet Union and, therefore, the type of retraining or instruction that they then required to meet an Israeli standard.[63]

The government also expanded training schemes designed to meet the needs of middle-aged, unskilled *olim*. Rabin deliberately expanded the size of Israel's civil service, thereby offering immediate employment to large numbers of immigrants who had been trained as bookkeepers, skilled secretaries and archivists. In addition, language courses, a priority for all *olim*, began to be structured to the needs of occupational groups such as lawyers, teachers and doctors. This enhanced the chances of being able to compete effectively in the Israeli marketplace.[64]

By 1975, Israel's absorption process had been adjusted to meet the needs of its new citizens. Problems did still exist: the nature of Israeli society; the psychological stress involved in emigration; the continuing housing shortage. These problems ensured that Soviet

Jewish migration continued to produce friction both between and among *sabras* and *olim*. Indeed, the Soviet press had been quick to report the problems of integration into Israeli society by their erstwhile compatriots.[65] However:

> While the first immigrants were like pioneers in a wilderness, those arriving later had relatives, former neighbours, friends, or colleagues already in Israel to whom they could turn for reliable advice and information. The absorbed played a crucial role in easing absorption for the newcomers by shortening the learning process, informing the newcomers of their rights, and guiding them in the field of employment.[66]

By 1975, despite progress in overhauling the absorption process, a combination of international and domestic factors severely curtailed the continuing flow of new migrants to Israel. The October War of 1973 served to highlight the security dilemma facing the Jewish State, and did much to undermine its image as a haven from anti-Semitism. This coincided with changes in the ethnic composition of Soviet Jewish emigration and the ensuing phenomenon of the *noshrim*. From 1977–80 – the last period of sizeable migration prior to the Gorbachev era – a majority of Soviet Jews chose to start a new life in the West.[67]

Tales of hardship and disillusion amongst the initial waves of Soviet *olim* helped shape the emigration decisions of subsequent Jewish migrants. The impact of Rabin's reforms came too late to counter such tales and maintain the momentum of Zionist motivated emigration, created in the aftermath of the June 1967 war. Many of the *noshrim* made it clear that their decision to forego a new life in Israel had been taken before they had actually left the USSR.[68] The *noshrim* comprised mainly assimilated Jews, from the Ukraine and Russian republics, whose Jewish national and cultural identity had been diluted by six decades of Soviet rule. Moreover, with many mixed marriages amongst the Soviet migrants, the concomitant problems of integration into Israeli society undermined the appeal of the Jewish State. Figures released for Soviet Jewish emigration between 1974 and June 1979 clearly demonstrated the role of ethnicity in determining the choice of destination. According to Zvi Gitelman, 72 per cent of all emigrants from Russia and the Ukraine went to the United States, even though their exit papers were valid for Israel only. Conversely, migration to the United States among Jews from

Georgia and Central Asia remained low. Only six per cent of Georgian Jews, and 13 per cent of those from Central Asia, chose to make a new life in America over *aliyah* to the Jewish State.[69]

The Jewish Agency, Israel's extra-governmental organization responsible for *aliyah*, found itself having to compete for new immigrants with the North American-based Hebrew Immigrant Aid Society (HIAS). Washington held the view that the mass exodus of Soviet Jews was political, ensuring that refugee status was accorded those who requested it upon arrival in Vienna. Given its vocal support for Jewish emigration, primarily as a means to influence Soviet behaviour in the aftermath of the Vietnam débâcle, the United States had very little choice but to accept Soviet Jews as refugees.

Israeli officials had blamed the drop in Jewish emigration between 1975 and 1977 on adverse Soviet reaction to HIAS activities that resulted in an increasing volume of Jews going to the United States. However, in 1979, Jewish emigration from the USSR reached record levels. Of the 51,000 migrants, just over 34,000 went to North America. Thus, contrary to the assertions of the Jewish Agency, no correlation between levels of *noshrim* and Soviet emigration policy actually existed. Not until 1981 was an agreement reached between the Jewish Agency and HIAS in which the latter agreed to 'refrain, for a three month trial period, from aiding emigrating Soviet Jews who choose not to go to Israel unless they had a first degree relative in the West'.[70]

The crisis in superpower relations negated any benefits that Israel may have hoped to accrue from the agreement. In response to the tough, public posturing of the Reagan administration, Moscow cut Soviet Jewish emigration from 21,471 in 1980, to 9,447 the following year. In 1982, this number sank further to 2,688, reaching a new low in 1984 of 896. Rather than admit the real cause for the sharp reduction in its emigration quota, Moscow cited the family reunification programme – the original basis on which emigration was sanctioned – as having been completed.[71]

This was a particular blow for Israel. It had struggled to reform its absorption strategy, only to see its efforts undermined by a radical change in the ethnic makeup of migration. This, coupled with the shifting sands of superpower politics, left Tel-Aviv struggling to attract, rather than struggling to absorb, Soviet Jewish emigrants. The mass *aliyah* of Soviet Jewry, beginning in

October 1989, was to demonstrate what lessons, if any, Israel had drawn.

Soviet Emigration Policy: 1980–1987
In 1980 Jewish emigration from the USSR stood at 21,471. By 1986 this figure had fallen to just 914.[72] While undoubtedly a response to the prevailing international climate, Moscow used family reunification, until now the official basis upon which emigration policy had been allowed to proceed, to justify its cessation. It was now argued that far from uniting families, emigration only served to produce further divisions, creating a never ending action–reaction cycle.[73]

The decline in emigration in the early 1980s was matched by a renewed anti-Zionist campaign, openly sponsored by Moscow. The distinction between anti-Zionism and anti-Semitism often became blurred, as possession of Hebrew language materials and the practising of Judaism frequently incurred severe penalties.[74] The campaign, a continuation of Soviet policy from the 1970s, served a number of goals. It allowed the Soviets to placate the Arab states, angered by Moscow's apparent impotence to influence events in the region following Israel's invasion of Lebanon in June 1982.[75] Moreover, it was used to vilify those Soviet Jews who had opted for a new life in the Jewish state, depicting them as renegades unworthy of Soviet citizenship.

> Portraying some Jews as traitors reinforced the notion that only the most unworthy Soviet citizens would emigrate. Depicting other Jews as unwitting victims also served to create the sense that Jews were responding to forces outside the USSR rather than electing to emigrate because of circumstances in the Soviet Union.[76]

To this extent, anti-Zionism served an internal purpose by conveniently citing the machinations of Zionism, rather than any structural failing within Soviet society, as responsible for Soviet Jewish emigration. The formation of the Anti-Zionist Committee (AKSO) in Moscow on 21 April 1983 only served to reinforce this theme, albeit in a more concise and cohesive form. Under the patronage of the USSR Ministry of Foreign Affairs, AKSO held their first press conference in Moscow on 6 June 1983. The legitimacy of the committee was enhanced by the fact that several of its members were themselves Jews, including the chairman

David I. Dragunskii, and first deputy chairman, Samuil L. Zivs. Letters were produced from former Soviet Jews, detailing the misery they were now experiencing in their adopted countries. Zivs then went on to state that 'The Anti-Zionist Committee will defend Soviet Jews from the intrigues of Zionism and imperialism in general, and work in all fairness not to let people go, condemning them to misery'.[77]

The embodiment of such statements was most visibly illustrated by the continuing impasse in Soviet–Israeli relations. While in principle accepting Israel's right to exist, emphasis was placed upon Zionism as an aggressive, expansionist ideology that dovetailed all too easily with the designs of American foreign policy. The signing of an agreement on strategic co-operation between Washington and Tel-Aviv in 1983, allowing the pre-positioning of US military equipment in Israel, served only to reinforce Soviet fears that a 'Pax Americana' would be established from Egypt to Lebanon.[78] The modernization of the Syrian Armed Forces, and the stationing of Soviet manned missile batteries in and around Damascus, clearly signalled Moscow's intent to prevent further erosion of its position throughout the region. This support was crucial in according Syrian President Hafiz al-Asad the necessary means to undermine the Israel–Lebanon treaty of May 1983, concluded under the aegis of United States Secretary of State, George Shultz.[79]

With bilateral relations between Washington and Moscow now marked by a renewal of ideological hostility, Soviet Jewry was subjected to an array of draconian internal legislation, including a circumscribed interpretation of international law, to negate any justification for continued large-scale emigration. By 1980, the number of known refuseniks, those Jews in open opposition to Moscow's denial of emigration rights, totalled at least 3,000.[80] Selective use of the 1966 International Covenant on Civil and Political Rights (ICPR) was one example where Moscow applied a narrow interpretation of an international agreement to impede large-scale emigration. The ICPR codified the rights of migration across international borders, and had often been cited by Jews in support of their struggle to leave the USSR. However, the ICPR did sanction the imposition of restrictions deemed 'necessary to protect national security, public order, public health or morals or the rights and freedoms of others'.[81]

This provision, coupled with a Soviet decree passed in 1956 on the dissemination of classified information, allowed the authorities to apply a broad interpretation of what exactly constituted a threat to Soviet national security. Yet while the desire to prevent a 'brain drain' was often cited as the rationale behind the secrecy statutes, such skills were usually lost to the Soviet Union because applying to leave the USSR often entailed either job demotion or unemployment. Given the climate of mutual hostility and suspicion between the superpowers, the loss of highly skilled labour was more than offset by the denial of such expertise to the United States and Israel.[82]

Refusal to emigrate on the grounds of national security largely applied to refuseniks such as Anatoly Sharansky, Vladimir and Maria Slepak, and Ida Nudel. Sharansky, a leading Soviet cyberneticist, had been sentenced in July 1978 to 13 years in prison with hard labour. Despite repeated denials, TASS, the Soviet news agency, claimed that 'commissioned by his masters he [Sharansky] supplied the West with facts about Soviet enterprises and institutions'.[83]

The issue of the refuseniks may have helped to highlight the continuing plight of Soviet Jewry, but Moscow denied the continuing validity of family reunification as the basis for mass emigration. Indeed, by 1983 Samuil Zivs stated that migration on such grounds had now been satisfied.[84] Given that reunification had provided the umbrella under which the majority of Jews had been allowed to leave the USSR, its withdrawal resulted in the steep decline in the number of exit permits issued by the OVIRs between 1980 and 1986.

Moscow's curtailment of mass emigration was cited by the West as a violation of the spirit, if not the word, of 'Basket Three' of the Helsinki Final Act of the Conference on Security and Co-operation in Europe (CSCE), signed by the USSR in 1975. In order to gain acceptance of the inviolability of post-war borders in Europe, the Brezhnev leadership had acceded to the Western demand that provisions covering human rights be included in the Final Act. While rights of free movement were not enshrined within the declaration, reunification of families was. Despite further conferences on human rights under the auspices of the CSCE, Moscow's adherence to these provisions remained poor until 1987.[85]

The denial of emigration rights, coupled with increased attacks on Judaism and Zionism, failed however to influence those Soviet

Jews who still wished to leave the USSR. In 1986, the number of Refuseniks had risen to 11,000. These had been informed by OVIRs throughout the Soviet Union that their cases for emigration were now closed. Thus the policy of the 1970s, which allowed the identified leaders of the emigration movement to leave, was rescinded.[86] Yet increased repression of the Jewish community only led to a renewal of national consciousness, particularly amongst the young. The establishment of covert groups, designed to facilitate the study of Jewish culture and Hebrew, was reported in at least 30 cities across the USSR.[87] The risks taken were apparent enough: by 1985, 26 Jews had been imprisoned or committed to psychiatric wards for the practice of Judaism.

Gorbachev and Soviet Jewry
Immediate improvement in emigration policy was not forthcoming following Gorbachev's appointment as General Secretary of the CPSU in March 1985. Indeed, despite the release of Anatoly Sharansky in March 1986 after continued Western pressure, the instant arrest and imprisonment of nine other Jewish activists soon followed.[88]

However, by 1987, a clear shift was discernible in Soviet policy towards Soviet Jewish emigration, though this did not amount to an endorsement by Moscow of mass migration. The gradual change resulted from a confluence of external considerations and internal assessments associated with the implementation of *glasnost* and *perestroika*. It was felt by the Soviet leadership that allowing refuseniks to leave the USSR would produce benefits: Moscow could rid itself of a troublesome group that had become an international liability, while fulfilment of international statutes governing freedom of movement would establish the credibility of Soviet adherence to the rule of law. The latter was crucial in persuading the West that fundamental, rather than cosmetic, reforms were now shaping the USSR.[89] In September 1987, large numbers of Jewish political prisoners held in Soviet jails had been released. The total number of emigrants for the year reached 8,155, a massive increase on the 1986 total of just 914. Approximately two-thirds of the emigrants were refuseniks, clearly reflecting Gorbachev's desire to solve the problem once and for all. Still, as late as January 1990, 1,500 refusenik cases remained outstanding.[90]

None the less, it had not been the intention of Gorbachev to sanction mass migration on a scale last seen in the late 1970s. While moving to disentangle the issue of the refuseniks, a revised decree, limiting emigration to only those with invitations from first degree relatives abroad, was passed on 1 January 1987.[91] Although representing an improvement over the blanket denial of family ties as the basis for migration, the new law appeared to penalize the growing constituency of Jews, who, under *glasnost*, expressed a clear desire to leave the USSR.

Theoretically, at least, Gorbachev's agenda for internal reform offered Jews the opportunity to participate in Soviet society on an equitable basis, free from social and political prejudice. But social pressures and a concomitant rise in ethnic nationalism unleashed by *glasnost*, compounded by the continuing crisis in the Soviet economy, led to a sharp increase in Jews wishing to leave.[92] Allowing predominantly refuseniks to migrate had done little to dilute the demand for exit visas among Soviet Jewry. With fear of repression lifted, increasing numbers began to apply. Of the 18,965 Jews who left the USSR during the course of 1988, just over half were refuseniks.

The decision to ease substantially emigration restrictions, irrespective of previous individual commitment to leave the Soviet Union, was inextricably entwined with the dynamics of Gorbachev's domestic reforms. One analyst commented that: 'Continuing a restrictive emigration policy would undermine *glasnost*, the new image of the party (CPSU) and government responsiveness and the fresh commitment to the integrity of international documents such as the Helsinki Final Act.'[93]

The onset of *glasnost* had brought about a revival in open Jewish expression throughout the USSR. Cultural, religious, political, and sports associations appeared, while Jewish newspapers, museums, restaurants, and theatres were allowed to open and flourish unhindered.[94] Nevertheless, increasing numbers of Jews began to seek exit visas, spurred on by economic uncertainty and a tangible rise in levels of openly anti-Semitic sentiment expressed throughout the USSR.[95] Indeed, the Soviet leadership miscalculated the effect that *glasnost* would have on the whole question of national relations throughout the Soviet Union. While an attempt to expose past mistakes in order to justify Gorbachev's economic reform programme, *glasnost* in fact allowed the rise of nationalist sentiment among the constituent republics of the USSR. This, coupled with the rise in inter-ethnic tension, particularly in the Baltic republics and Transcaucasia, persuaded many Soviet Jews at least to consider a new life elsewhere. However, unlike the refuseniks, empathy with Zionism played little part in the decision to migrate. Of the 18,865 Jews who left the Soviet Union on Israeli visas during 1988, some 88.6 per cent became *noshrim*, opting for a final destination other than the Jewish State.[96]

Gorbachev's announcement at the United Nations in December 1988 lifted one of the few remaining obstacles to unrestricted Jewish emigration. Yet fearful that the *noshrim* factor would, once again, distinguish a new wave of Jewish emigration, Israel embarked upon a diplomatic campaign designed to offset this phenomenon. By exerting its political influence in Washington, and utilising a burgeoning relationship with Moscow, Tel-Aviv hoped to exert some influence on the scope and direction of Soviet Jewish emigration. Once more, Soviet Jewish migration as a transnational flow became a factor in the development of interstate relations.

Soviet-Israeli Relations: 1985–1989
The necessity to restructure the Soviet economy was linked by Gorbachev to the establishment of a benign international environment. *Novoe Politicheskoe Myshlenie*, New Political Thinking (NPT), aimed to accomplish that goal. By redefining the role of ideology in the formulation of Soviet foreign policy, NPT hoped to erode Western threat perceptions, allowing, in theory, the diversion of scarce resources from the military to civilian sectors of the Soviet economy. NPT contained four main principles: the threat of nuclear war requires the superpowers to realize human interests over national or ideological goals; the zero-sum game approach to dealing with events in the Third World must be abandoned; a balance of interests involving relations between Washington and Moscow and the regional states should exist; and reliance on political means to resolve regional disputes, with the active involvement of the United Nations, should become the international norm.[97]

Although significant progress in arms control negotiations marked the most tangible outcome of NPT, Moscow also embarked upon a more sober reappraisal of the role that regional conflict played in superpower relations. Moscow had denied any overt linkage between bilateral ties with Washington, and unilateral action in Third World conflict throughout the 1970s. This position underwent a radical revision with Gorbachev now urging co-operation rather than coercion if regional conflicts were not to engulf the superpowers in a much wider conflagration.[98] Concurrently, the new Soviet approach to the Third World offered the prospect of economic development with emerging capitalist economies, emphasizing Moscow's preference for state to state relations, rather than class-based relations, for the future conduct of international affairs with less developed nations.[99]

New Political Thinking had a gradual, but none the less highly significant, role in redefining Soviet policy towards Israel, and, by extension, the moribund Middle East peace process. Following Israel's emphatic victory in the June 1967 war, Moscow had severed official ties with Tel-Aviv. Although it was an attempt to curry favour with the Arab world, it meant that little leverage could be directly exercised over Israel without recourse to Washington. Such impotence had allowed Egypt and Israel to conclude the Camp David Agreement of February 1979 under the auspices of the United States. Indeed, what influence the Soviet Union did exercise throughout the region was further undermined by Moscow's intervention in Afghanistan in December 1979.[100]

Therefore, improved ties with Tel-Aviv became a prerequisite if the Soviet leadership were to exercise some authority over the Middle East peace process. However, initial steps were tentative, conditioned largely by domestic political factors in both Israel and the USSR. Within Moscow, strongly entrenched opposition on geopolitical and nationalist grounds, still existed towards the Jewish State. 'Arabists' within the Soviet Foreign Ministry, including Aleksandr Dzasokhov, former ambassador to Syria, and Vladimir Polyakov, one-time head of the Foreign Ministry Middle East section and latterly ambassador to Egypt, opposed any approach to Israel at the expense of erstwhile Arab allies in the region.[101] Strong opposition was also voiced by the Soviet Defence Ministry, which placed continued loyalty to states such as Syria and Libya above and beyond any rapprochement with Tel-Aviv:

> For many of them, this was part and parcel of their general dissatisfaction with *perestroika* and new thinking, policies which had led to such events as the virtual break-up of the Warsaw Pact and arms agreements that they perceived as having seriously weakened the Soviet Union in military terms, to the benefit of the United States.[102]

Further opposition to increased overtures to Israel emanated from Russian nationalist organizations such as Pamyat. Virulently anti-Semitic, Pamyat (Memory) linked domestic problems afflicting Soviet, and in particular Russian, society to the sanguine and less partial approach adopted by Moscow towards the Middle East in general, and Israel in particular. This theme was repeated by the Public Committee Against Zionism, the Public Committee Against Resumption of Diplomatic Relations with Israel, and AKSO, all of which argued for ties to be strengthened with the Arab world at the expense of any moves towards Tel-Aviv.[103]

The position and influence of those opposed to both ties with, and the very existence of, the Jewish State covered a broad range of Soviet public opinion. Never the less, all appeared to oppose Gorbachev's reforms, because they either undermined Moscow's superpower status and ideological base, or, particularly in the view of Pamyat, threatened to erode a once-proud Russian cultural heritage. Therefore, unlike other regional conflicts, the Arab–Israeli dispute touched upon the dynamics of internal Soviet politics.[104]

However, implementation of NPT towards regional conflict allowed those advocating a more pliant stance towards Israel to dictate effectively a new agenda. Accordingly, the Public Committee for Renewal of Diplomatic Relations with Israel was established, designed not only to facilitate ties with Tel-Aviv, but to counter the influence of anti-Israel associations. Proponents of this approach included *Izvestia* journalist Aleksandr Bovin; Georgy Mirsky, Middle Eastern analyst at Moscow's Institute of World Economy and International Relations (IMEMO); Oleg Derkovsky, assistant chief of the Soviet Foreign Ministry's Middle East Department; Deputy Foreign Minister Aleksandr Belonogov; and Yevgeny Primakov, a Middle East specialist at the Foreign Ministry, who, as early as 1972, had urged Moscow to undertake a fundamental review of its belligerent policy towards Israel. Crucially, however, a fresh approach towards the Arab–Israeli dispute was increasingly advocated by Aleksandr Yakovlev, one of Gorbachev's closest advisors. Yakovlev, chief ideologist to the CPSU and a member of the Politburo, was largely responsible for the theoretical revision behind the implementation of NPT.[105]

With advocates of Gorbachev's reform programme occupying such influential positions within the Soviet government and foreign policy apparatus, the way was now open for an initial approach to be made towards Tel-Aviv. Consequently, the issue of Soviet Jewry was to play a vital role, affecting Moscow's relations with Washington and other states throughout the Middle East.

The first substantive meeting between Soviet and Israeli diplomats took place four months after Gorbachev had assumed office in March 1985. In July, a meeting took place at the Paris home of Israeli pianist Daniel Barenboim between the Soviet Ambassador to France, Yuli Vorontsov, and his Israeli counterpart, Ovadia Sofer. The issues discussed were subsequently leaked to the Israeli media and broadcast over Israel national radio, Kol Y'Israel:

> The Soviets, under a fresh, new administration, are hinting about a package deal for the emigration of Jews. They are ready for a compromise over the Golan Heights. There is a hint about the renewal of diplomatic relations, and a genuine chance for high-level meetings.[106]

The reported package deal concerning the future emigration of Soviet Jewry involved a unilateral Israeli cessation of overtly hostile anti-Soviet propaganda; moreover, it was conditional on all Jews migrating to Israel, not to the United States. Vorontsov's comments on the Golan Heights, indicating that a partial, rather than total, Israeli withdrawal would satisfy the basic criteria for the renewal of diplomatic ties were welcomed by Israel. This in itself represented a substantial shift away from insisting upon total Israeli withdrawal from all territories occupied following the June 1967 war. Above all else, Vorontsov signalled a Soviet intention to play a major part in determining the future of the moribund Middle East peace process. While Moscow denied that any conclusive agreement was reached, the content and direction of the Paris meeting helped illuminate future Soviet intent towards relations with the Middle East in general, and Israel in particular.[107]

Given that *glasnost* was viewed initially as firmly establishing Soviet Jewry on an equitable basis within Soviet society, the prospect of Moscow endorsing large-scale migration was remote. More likely, Vorontsov's comments, if officially endorsed, were a feint, designed to exert at least some Soviet influence over Tel-Aviv. Certainly, the prospect of large-scale migration from the USSR posed a dilemma for Shimon Peres, the then Israeli Prime Minister. All previous Israeli governments cited the renewal of diplomatic ties as a prerequisite for any Soviet participation in the peace process. Now, faced with the potential of mass migration, Peres stated that Moscow's implementation of such a policy would remove any objection held by Tel-Aviv to full Soviet participation in the peace process.[108]

However, Peres failed to establish a cabinet consensus for this position within the Israeli government, composed as it was of an uneasy alliance between the Labour and the Likud parties. Following a meeting with Karen Brutents, deputy director of the International Department of the CPSU, in April 1987, Peres, now Israel's Foreign Minister, hinted strongly that concessions by Moscow over emigration had paved the way for the imminent convening of an international peace conference. Immediate controversy ensued. Likud leader and Israeli Prime Minister Yitzhak Shamir rejected any linkage between Soviet Jewish emigration and Moscow's participation at such a conference. Indeed, the exodus of Soviet Jewry was viewed as a humanitarian issue, totally divorced from the wider dynamics of Middle Eastern politics. But, more importantly, Shamir wanted to avoid a conference in which undue pressure would be exerted upon the Jewish State to make concessions over the Occupied Territories.[109]

Consequently, Peres was unable to implement any plans he may have had for an international conference, and was forced to back down in the absence of sufficient cross-party support in the Knesset for his proposals. Yet while little progress was made in Moscow's attempts to convene a conference, Soviet Jewish emigration began to increase substantially from 1987 onwards.

Two factors emerge to explain this upsurge: the political and social liberalization of Soviet society and the worsening economic crisis throughout the USSR. Of the two, the latter carried greater weight since the need to enlist Western aid required the establishment of a liberal emigration policy. A constant theme throughout superpower summits continued to be the issue of Soviet Jewry, President Reagan once more calling for a marked increase in the numbers allowed to leave the USSR during the Reykjavik Summit of October 1986.[110]

With preference still resting with *glasnost* to provide a panacea for Moscow's Jewish problem, Gorbachev failed to respond to United States' pressure. However, economic necessity forced the issue. In March 1987, Morris Abram, president of the American based National Conference on Soviet Jewry, and Edgar

Bronfmann, president of the World Jewish Congress, arrived in Moscow for talks with Soviet officials. The two Jewish leaders received 'assurances', listed in the form of nine points, detailing the future of Soviet Jewry. These points included concessions by Moscow on rights of emigration for those previously denied under internal security legislation, and a commitment to resolve all refusenik cases. In addition, all those in possession of exit visas for Israel would in future now travel via Rumania during transit to the Jewish State, not Vienna or Rome.[111]

In return, Moscow hoped that the two Jewish leaders would be able to coax Washington into revising its position towards the Jackson–Vanik and Stevenson Amendments. The activities of Abram and Bronfmann neatly highlight the role that individuals, representing a non-government organization, can play in facilitating a dialogue between states, in this particular case, the United States and the USSR. According to Robert O. Freedman the main purpose behind Soviet concessions on Jewish emigration was the removal of political opposition within the United States to an agreement on scrapping intermediate-range nuclear weapons. They clearly did not wish the issue to complicate the arms control process as had previously been the case with Senator Jackson and his opposition to SALT 2.

From this, two important points stood out. First, Moscow still viewed emigration as a function of superpower politics and was willing to make concessions on the issue of Soviet Jewry, if subsequent economic and strategic benefits were forthcoming. Indeed, the rally held in Washington on the eve of the December 1987 superpower summit by 250,000 Americans, both Jews and non-Jews, in support of Soviet Jewry only reinforced for the Soviet leadership the emotive power that the issue held in American politics.[112] Secondly, to facilitate American economic aid, the Soviet leadership took an increasingly positive attitude towards Israel, Washington's staunchest ally in the Middle East. This was reflected in the more sophisticated analysis of the Israeli political scene presented in the Soviet media. Zionism was no longer seen as a monolithic concept but a movement comprising several ideological strands.[113]

Washington, in concert with the Israelis, had stated that only the re-establishment of direct ties between Moscow and Tel-Aviv would allow Soviet participation in any Middle Eastern peace process. By gradually increasing the range and scope of contacts with the Jewish State, Moscow went some way to removing a regional obstacle to increased co-operation with the Americans. While still far short of full diplomatic relations – internal opposition demanded that Gorbachev adopt an incremental approach towards ties with Israel – the restrained Soviet reaction to the outbreak of the Palestinian *intifada* or uprising in December 1987 suggested a profound reassessment in Moscow's foreign policy towards the region. While condemning the excessive use of force by Israel throughout the West Bank and Gaza, Gorbachev noted that the PLO had yet to address itself fully to the legitimate security fears of Tel-Aviv.[114]

Throughout 1988, the exodus of Jews from the Soviet Union continued to increase. Though in part a response to the domestic pressures unleashed by *glasnost*, continued calls from Washington linking increased trade benefits to new Soviet legislation on rights of emigration forced the issue. During a visit to Paris in May 1989, Soviet Foreign Minister Eduard Shevardnadze, stated that the Supreme Soviet would soon pass a law granting the right of free exit from the Soviet Union.[115] Although this was not to be passed for another two years, the law merely codified existing Soviet practice. This included strict Soviet compliance with provisions laid down in the Helsinki Final Act, governing the denial on grounds of national security of exit rights.[116]

At the beginning of 1989, Washington began to review the linkage that it had made between concessions on trade with Moscow and the issue of Soviet Jewish emigration. At his holiday retreat at Kennebunkport, Maine, the new United States President, George Bush, was advised by a number of leading American academics on Soviet affairs to suspend the provisions of the Jackson–Vanik Amendment linking MNF status to Soviet Jewish emigration.[117] But having removed the obstacle of Jewish emigration rights, Washington continued to withold financial credits in response to Soviet sanctions against Lithuania. Only with the need to secure Soviet support in the United Nations against the Iraqi invasion of Kuwait did the United States acquiesce in the issue. In December 1990, following representations from the American-based National Conference on Soviet Jewry, President Bush announced that he would partially waive the Jackson–Vanik Amendment, thereby allowing the Soviets access to $1 billion in aid for the purchase of foodstuffs.[118]

Although the resumption of full diplomatic ties between Israel and the USSR remained problematic - Moscow insisting upon Israeli participation in an international peace conference, whereas Tel-Aviv demanded the resumption of formal relations without pre-conditions – political and cultural contacts flourished. Consular level delegations were exchanged during the course of 1988 that helped facilitate this process. In July 1989, agreement was reached permitting Israelis to visit the USSR on tourist visas, while in September 1989, the Bolshoi Ballet made its first ever visit to Israel. Tel-Aviv was also making diplomatic inroads into individual Soviet republics: in August 1989, a trade delegation from Georgia reached agreement, in principle, on the establishment of joint companies involved in the trading of agricultural produce and medical equipment from the Jewish State. Similarly, it was also reported that Moscow wished to harness Israeli expertise in food production, desert reclamation, and solar energy as well as promoting tourism between the two countries.[119]

The blossoming of relations throughout 1989 came in the aftermath of the Trans-Siberian railway disaster of June 1988, and the Armenian earthquake in December of that year. In both cases Tel-Aviv dispatched specialist medical aid and search and rescue teams, badly needed given the paucity of Soviet relief efforts.[120] Israel's standing could only have been further increased following the hijacking of a Soviet airliner to Ben-Gurion airport in December 1988. Having negotiated a peaceful conclusion to the drama, the Israeli authorities, at the request of Moscow, promptly extradited those responsible back to the USSR, even though no formal extradition treaty existed between the two countries.[121]

By the end of 1989, Israel found itself in an extremely advantageous position in its relationship with Moscow. In the absence of formal diplomatic ties with Tel-Aviv, the Soviet Union could exert little influence in attempting to convene an international peace conference, an event totally anathema to Israeli Prime Minister Shamir. Moreover, the issue of Soviet Jewish emigration remained largely divorced from the wider Soviet–Israeli relationship. Indeed, it continued to be primarily a function of superpower politics, a position that suited the ideological perspective of the Likud government under Yitzhak Shamir. With Tel-Aviv applying pressure upon Washington to introduce stringent immigration controls, Israel seemed set to become the net beneficiary of the mass exodus of Soviet Jewry.

The United States, Israel and Soviet Jewish Emigration: 1987–1989

In 1988, a total of 18,965 Jews left the USSR on exit visas for Israel. However, with barely 11 per cent finally arriving in the Jewish State, the *noshrim* factor once more appeared to decide the fate of migrating Soviet Jews. Unable to tackle adequately the negative social and political perceptions held by *noshrim* regarding Israel, Tel-Aviv tried to implement policies that would isolate Jews in transit, forcing them at least to set foot on Israeli soil.

As early as February 1987, Prime Minister Shamir had urged Washington to 'deny refugee status' to Soviet Jewish émigrés.[122] Rebuffed initially by the Reagan Administration, the Israelis examined the feasibility of denying Soviet Jews the use of Rome and Vienna, the two main transit points en route to Israel. It was here that most Jews dropped out, opting instead to try and start a new life in the West, principally in the United States of America.

On 17 August 1988, agreement was reached in the Israeli cabinet, authorizing the transit of Soviet Jews via Romania. Moscow agreed to issue Jews with exit permits for Bucharest only, where, upon arrival, the migrants would be given visas for Israel. This removed the influence of American-Jewish aid agencies, which had previously played a large part in deciding the ultimate destiny of the majority of Soviet Jews, and left Israel as the only viable alternative.[123] However, the Dutch Embassy, still formally charged with representing Israeli interests in the Soviet Union, continued to issue visas for the Jewish State via the original transit points. In arguing that emigration was a humanitarian rather than a political, issue, the Dutch scuppered Tel-Aviv's only viable strategy for overcoming the *noshrim* factor.[124]

Despite this setback, a review of standing immigration policy was initiated in Washington once the potential scale of Soviet Jewish emigration was realized. The old policy whereby Soviet Jews were viewed as political refugees was revised because, it was argued, *glasnost* had undermined the claim by the majority of the migrants to be political refugees on the basis of a fear of persecution. On 6 December 1988, the day prior to Gorbachev's historic speech to the United Nations, the US State Department announced that it intended to impose heavy restrictions on the entry of Jews from the Soviet Union.[125]

The State Department had estimated that anything up to 100,000 Soviet Jews would apply for permission to emigrate to the United States in 1989 alone. However, the limit for *all* refugee admissions for that financial year was 85,000. Bush raised the number of Soviet Jews allowed to enter under this quota by 2,500 to 43,500, but it became clear that Soviet Jewish emigration threatened to overwhelm the annual quota for refugee admissions and the annual budget set for refugee absorption. The US Refugee Act of 1980 required that each refugee be provided with housing, medical care, and employment or retraining if necessary. The indefinite costs that continued classification of Soviet Jews as political refugees entailed forced a re-evaluation of that policy, and one that severely curtailed Soviet Jewish emigration to the United States.[126]

Therefore, it was internal financial constraints within the United States, rather than any effective pressure from Tel-Aviv, that forced the growing numbers of Soviet Jewish migrants to opt for a new life in Israel. Reform to the law governing refugee status had its origins in a memo drafted by Attorney General Edwin Meese. This had suggested that all applicants for refugee status should, from now on, demonstrate a real fear of persecution in their country of origin. Thus, the onus of proof of persecution rested with the would-be refugee, rather than an automatic presumption that persecution existed in his or her place of origin.[127]

In addition, United States law required that the migrant who applied for refugee status should satisfy the US Immigration and Naturalization Service officials that no other country was prepared to accept them. Clearly, this closed the option of migration to the United States for most Soviet Jews given Israel's 'Law of Return'. The issue was particularly vexed for those American Jewish organizations that had campaigned for unrestricted Soviet Jewish immigration to the United States. Although the Reagan administration had allowed an expansion of the 'parolee' refugee category that allowed immigrants to enter if their needs were met from private guarantors, the huge financial burden that Soviet Jews admitted under the present quota system represented, soon became apparent to the American Jewish community. American Jewry had traditionally spent $5,000 on each new Soviet immigrant, irrespective of whether or not that person was in receipt of government aid. The prospect of over 100,000 Soviet Jewish immigrants coming to the United States, necessitating the direct expenditure of half a billion dollars, was clearly beyond the capacity of American Jewry. Indeed, during the course of 1989, efforts to raise $75 million for the resettlement of Soviet Jews in the United States and Israel produced only $13 million in hard cash.[128]

These financial constraints undermined the position of immigrant aid groups such as HIAS. In hearings before the US Senate in September 1989, HIAS conceded the need for government restrictions to be placed on the number of Soviet Jewish immigrants. Consequently, with strict quotas coming into force on 1 October 1989, the United States closed its Soviet Jewish refugee centres in Vienna and Rome. From now on, those Soviet Jews who wished to emigrate to the United States had to apply directly to the American embassy in Moscow. Given Washington's new immigration regime, Israel now remained the only viable alternative for the vast majority.[129]

In ending its blanket guarantee of refugee status to Soviet Jews, both the Reagan and Bush administrations placed the blame on budgetary constraints. Yet Washington still continued to intensify pressure on Moscow to ease restrictions further on the exit of Soviet Jews. The new American guidelines on immigration produced benefits for both Washington and Tel-Aviv: the United States could continue to claim the moral high ground on human rights without the social and economic costs of absorption, but Israel would receive a much needed boost to its population. This all but solved the problem of the *noshrim*, reflecting as it had done on the efficacy of Zionism as the ideological base of the Jewish State. For the Soviet Jews, the decision was made for them: if they wished to leave an increasingly turbulent USSR, only Israel offered the prospect of a new life.

Soviet *aliyah* remained relatively small compared to overall Soviet Jewish emigration up until October 1989. Of 21,000 migrants, only 2,000 emigrated to Israel during the course of this period.[130] However, Washington's immigration quotas began to take effect from October 1989 onwards. By the end of 1989, 71,196 Jews left the Soviet Union. Of these, 12,923 arrived in Israel, representing the vanguard of an immigration wave that was to reach over 400,000 by June 1992. The absorption of these *olim* strained the fabric of Israeli society, and thus, altered the wider political landscape.

Conclusion
Throughout the 1970s and 1980s, Moscow's policy towards its

Jewish citizens was largely dictated by the condition of bilateral relations with Washington at any one time. Accordingly, the issue of Jewish emigration became a barometer by which to gauge the state of superpower relations during the course of this period. Yet while the Brezhnev era witnessed selective emigration – a process designed to correlate external needs to internal demands – the reforms of Mikhail Gorbachev undermined any criteria for emigration quotas based on communal origin.

It was the implementation of *glasnost* that proved decisive in provoking a new and overwhelming exodus of Soviet Jewry. Although designed to justify the radical reforms to the Soviet economy by allowing free critical appraisal of the past, it unleashed a tide of sentiment that appeared set to threaten the very liberties that Gorbachev's reforms had bestowed on Soviet Jewry. When coupled with the increasing inability of *perestroika* to satisfy even the most basic needs of the Soviet consumer, Soviet Jews began to fear yet again the rise of popular anti-Semitism; they were stigmatized once more as scapegoats in a society that had never fully accepted them as Soviet citizens even though levels of acculturation, particularly among Ashkenazim Jews, were exceptionally high. Such foreboding, real or imagined, created a critical mass of Jews who wished to leave the Soviet Union: Gorbachev's reforms merely produced the means for them to do so.

The increase in Soviet Jewish emigration from 1987 through to 1989 showed, however, that the growing preference for the United States over Israel, a process that marked Soviet Jewish emigration between 1974 and 1980, seemed set to continue. Low levels of cultural and religious identity among Ashkenazim Jewry; the negative image of Israel and Zionism that had dominated Soviet media coverage of the Middle East; tales of social and economic hardship involved in the process of making *aliyah*; and the activities of American Jewish organizations, all these help to explain the predilection of the emigrants in their choice of final destination.

Yet it was internal financial constraints, both on Washington's refugee programme and the largesse of the American Jewish community once the magnitude of Soviet Jewish emigration as a transnational flow came to be realized, that forced the issue in favour of Tel-Aviv. From October 1989, the Bush administration enforced strict limitations on the number of Soviet Jews it was now prepared to admit. By reinterpreting, and stringently applying, the definition of who was a political refugee,

Washington effectively sanctioned Israel as the only viable destination for those Jews who wished to leave the Soviet Union. This policy decision was not only to have a profound effect upon the social and political dynamics of Israeli society, but, by extension, to expose the state elite to the pressures and constraints of both domestic and international politics. This ultimately provided a catalyst for change in the wider Arab–Israeli conflict.

NOTES

1. From the speech of Mikhail Gorbachev to the 43rd session of the UN General Assembly, *The Guardian*, 8 Dec. 1988.
2. Figures from an official Soviet census showed that those registered as being Jewish totalled 2,150,000 in 1970.
  By 1979 this figure had dropped to 1,810,000 for the whole of the USSR. See David Lane, *The End of Social Equality? Class Status and Power under State Socialism* (London: Allen and Unwin, 1982), p.83.
3. Michael Wolffsohn, *Israel Polity, Society and Economy 1882–1986* (NJ: Humanities Press International, 1987), pp.102–3.
4. Jerome M. Gilison, 'Soviet Jewish Emigration, 1971–80: An Overview', in Robert O. Freedman (ed.), *Soviet Jewry in the Decisive Decade* (Durham, NC: Duke University Press, 1984), p.5.
5. William Korey, 'Soviet Decisionmaking and the Problems of Jewish Emigration Policy', *Survey*, Vol. 22, No. 1 (1976), p.113; Victor Zaslavsky and Robert J. Brym, *Soviet Jewish Emigration and Soviet Nationality Policy* (London: Macmillan, 1983), p.44.
6. Gilison in Freedman (ed.), op. cit., p.6. Two of the hijackers, Eduard Kuznetzov and Mark Dymschitz, were eventually exchanged in 1979 for two Soviet agents convicted of espionage in the United States.
7. Korey, op. cit., p.114.
8. Ibid., p.115.
9. Jerry Goodman, 'The Jews in the Soviet Union: Emigration and Its Difficulties', in Freedman (ed.), op. cit., p.21.
10. Mike Bowker and Phil Williams, *Superpower Detente: A Reappraisal* (London: Sage/RIIA, 1988), pp.196–8.
11. Figures supplied by Soviet Jewry Research Bureau, National Conference on Soviet Jewry, New York. See Appendix.
12. Bowker and Williams, op. cit., p.196.
13. Mike Bowker, 'The Soviet Union and *Detente*', in Richard Crockatt and Steve Smith (eds), *The Cold War: Past and Present* (London: Allen and Unwin, 1987), p.136.
14. See Appendix A.
15. Bowker and Williams, op. cit., pp.170–84.
16. See figures cited in Annex 2 in Freedman (ed.), op. cit., p.150.
17. Raymond Garthoff, *Detente and Confrontation: American–Soviet Relations from Nixon to Reagan* (Washington, DC: Brookings Institution, 1985), pp.738–9.
18. Ibid., pp.731–2. See also Zvi Gitelman, 'Moscow and the Soviet Jews: A Parting of the Ways', *Problems of Communism*, Vol. XXIV (Jan–Feb 1980), p.31; Mike Bowker, 'The Soviet Union and *Detente*', in Crockatt and Smith (eds), op. cit., p.136.
19. Goodman in Freedman (ed.), op. cit., p.22. See also Appendix A.

20. Gilison in Freedman (ed.), op. cit., p.3.
21. *Izvestia*, 5 Dec. 1966. Cited by Thodore Friedgut, 'The Welcome Home: Absorption of the Soviet Jews in Israel', in Freedman (ed.), op. cit., p.69.
22. Thomas E. Sawyer, *The Jewish Minority in the Soviet Union* (Boulder, CO: Westview Press, 1979), pp.185–6.
23. Gilison in Freedman (ed.), op. cit., p.6.
24. Sawyer, op. cit., p.203.
25. Gilison in Freedman (ed.), op. cit., p.6
26. Sawyer op. cit., pp. 203–4.
27. Zaslavsky and Brym, op. cit., p.124.
28. Korey, op. cit., p.118. For example, In January 1971, Moscow contained one-quarter of the scientific workers in the USSR, a total of 233,641. Of these, ten per cent or 25,023 were Jewish. Figures taken from Mordechai Altshuler, 'Some Statistical Data on the Jews Among the Scientific Elite of the Soviet Union', *The Jewish Journal of Sociology*, Vol.15, No.1 (1973), p.48.
29. *Krasnaya Zvezda*, 16 Jan. 1970. Cited by Zachary Irwin 'The USSR and Israel', *Problems of Communism*, Vol.XXXVI (Jan-Feb 1987), p.43; Wolffsohn, op. cit., p.103.
30. Korey, op. cit., p.120; Sawyer, op. cit., pp.202–4.
31. Korey, op. cit., p.121.
32. Ibid., p.127.
33. Arthur J. Klinghoffer and Judith Apter, *Israel and the Soviet Union: Alienation or Reconciliation?* (Boulder, CO: Westview Press, 1985), p.112.
34. Gitelman, op. cit., p.31.
35. Ibid., p.31.
36. Ibid., p.27.
37. Gilison in Freedman (ed.), op, cit., p.11.
38. Ilya I. Lekov, 'Adaptation and Acculturation of Soviet Jews in the United States: A Preliminary Analysis', in Freedman (ed.), op. cit., p.117.
39. *Izvestia*, 10 Nov. 1976. Quoted by Gilison in Freedman (ed.), op. cit., p.7.
40. Ibid., p.10. For a detailed examination of Soviet attitudes towards Jewish nationality see Gitelman, op. cit., p.20.
41. Gilison in Freedman (ed.), op. cit., p.13; Sawyer, op. cit., p.209.
42. Gilison in Freedman (ed.), op. cit., p.13.
43. Klinghoffer and Apter, op. cit., p.109.
44. For a full analysis of the Helsinki Final Act see Garthoff, op. cit., pp.473–9.
45. In particular, Soviet involvement in a number of Third World conflicts did much to erode support for *détente* among both Republicans and governing Democrats in Washington. Zbigniew Brzezinski, President Carter's National Security Advisor, appeared to express a widely held public sentiment when he declared that *detente* had become, 'buried in the sands of the Ogaden'. See Bowker and Williams, op. cit., p.179.
46. Sawyer, op. cit., p.203. The Soviet figure for the total number of Jewish emigrants between 1948 and 1970 was 21,000. This was 3,000 less than the Western figure of 24,000.
47. Friedgut in Freedman (ed.), op. cit., p.68.
48. Ibid., p.69.
49. Ibid., p.70. The actual breakdown of Soviet Jewish *aliyah* between 1971 and 1974 is as follows: 12,819 (1971), 31,652 (1972), 33,477 (1973), 16,816 (1974).
50. Bernard Avishai, *The Tragedy of Zionism* (New York: Farrar, Straus and Giroux, 1985), p.261.
51. For a historical analysis of the discrimination encountered by Oriental Jews in the first wave of *aliyah* after 1948 see Tom Segev, *The First Israelis* (New York: Free Press, 1986), pp.96–155. See also Adam Keller, *Terrible Days: Social Divisions and*

Political Paradoxes in Israel (Amstelveen: Cypres, 1987), pp.53–61.
52. Gilison in Freedman (ed.), op. cit., p.71.
53. Conor Cruise O'Brien, The Seige: The Saga of Israel and Zionism (London: Weidenfeld and Nicolson, 1986), p.355.
54. Professor Erik Cohen, quoted in Ibid., p.355.
55. Avishai, op. cit., p.261.
56. Marin Blatt, Uri Davis, and Paul Kleinbaum (eds), Dissent and Ideology in Israel (London: Ithaca Press, 1975), p.164.
57. Friedgut in Freedman (ed.), op. cit., p.71.
58. Ibid., p.71.
59. Ibid., p.72.
60. Ibid., p.72.
61. Keller, op. cit., p.57.
62. Friedgut in Freedman (ed.), op. cit., p.73.
63. Ibid., p.73. The author went on to state that 'Some professions, such as nursing, were much in demand and posed little difficulty as far as an adjustment of standards. Half of the immigrant nurses from the USSR were certified after one month of training, and 80 per cent by the end of six months.'
64. Ibid., p.74.
65. Korey, op. cit., p.121; Gitelman, op. cit., p.32.
66. Friedgut in Freedman (ed.), op. cit., p.76.
67. Goodman in Freedman (ed.), op. cit., p.22.
68. Ibid., pp.22–3.
69. Zvi Gitelman, 'Soviet Jewish Immigration to the US: Profile, Problems, Prospects', in Freedman (ed.), op. cit., pp.90–1.
70. Fabian Kolker, 'A New Soviet Jewry Plan', in Freedman (ed.), op. cit., pp.84–5. HIAS was a privately funded American-Jewish organization which, none the less, enjoyed widespread support from Washington for its activities. It established transit camps for emigrants in Rome and Ostia in Italy which housed the *noshrim* while their documentation was processed.
71. Goodman in Freedman (ed.), op. cit., p.18. See Appendix for figures.
72. Laurie P Salitan, Politics and Nationality in Contemporary Soviet-Jewish Emigration, 1968-89 (London: Macmillan Press, 1992), p.96.
73. Ibid., p.97.
74. Nora Levin, The Jews in the Soviet Union Since 1917 (London: I.B. Tauris, 1988), pp.753–6.
75. S. Sergeyev, 'Reactionary Theories of Political Zionism', Zionism – Enemy of Peace and Social Progress, Issue 2, (Moscow: Progress Publishers, 1983), pp.5–38.
76. Salitan, op. cit., p.38.
77. 'The Soviet Anti-Zionist Committee Press Conference', Zionism – Enemy of Peace and Social Progress, Issue 4, (Moscow: Progress Publishers, 1985), pp.5–25.
78. Stephen Green, Living By the Sword (London:Faber and Faber, 1988), p.223.
79. Robert O. Freedman, Soviet Policy Toward Israel Under Gorbachev (New York: Praeger/Center for Strategic and International Studies, Washington, DC, 1991), p.6; O'Brien, op. cit., pp.638-9.
80. Salitan, op. cit., pp.54–5.
81. Ibid., p.55.
82. Ibid., p.56.
83. Levin, op. cit., pp.733–7.
84. Salitan, op. cit., p.62.
85. Ibid., pp.56–9.
86. Ibid., pp.63–4.
87. Ibid., p.64.
88. Freedman, op. cit., p.26.

89. Salitan, op. cit., pp.98-9.
90. Ibid., pp.65-6.
91. Freedman, op. cit., p.33.
92. Salitan, op. cit., p.100; Galia Golan, *Moscow and the Middle East: New Thinking on Regional Conflict* (London: Pinter/RIIA, 1992), pp.18-19.
93. Salitan, op. cit., p.101.
94. Johnathan Steele, *The Guardian*, 14 March 1990.
95. Artyom Borovik, *The Hidden War* (London: Faber and Faber, 1990), p.280. According to Borovik, Moscow's disastrous invasion of Afghanistan was popularly blamed upon undue Jewish influence within the Kremlin.
96. Salitan, op. cit., p.65. For a full discussion of the impact of the nationalities issue on the internal cohesion of the Soviet Union, see Timothy Lawrence, 'The Soviet Nationalities Question: Disintegration in the 1980s and 1990s', *Manchester Papers in Politics* (Manchester: Dept. of Government, University of Manchester, 1991), pp.3-8.
97. Margot Light, *The Soviet Theory of International Relations* (Brighton: Harvester Press, 1988), pp.294-315; Allen Lynch, *The Soviet Study of International Relations* (Cambridge: Cambridge University Press, 1989), pp.xv-xxxviii.
98. Freedman, op. cit., p.12.
99. Light, op.cit., p.297; Celeste Wallender, 'Third World Conflict in Soviet Military Thought: Does New Thinking Grow Prematurely Grey?', *World Politics*, Vol. XXXVI (1989), p.37.
100. Alexandre Bennigsen, Paul B Henze, George K. Tanham and S. Enders Wimbush, *Soviet Strategy and Islam* (New York: St. Martin's Press, 1989), pp.57-63.
101. Golan, op. cit., p.14.
102. Ibid., p.14 and p.88.
103. Salitan, op. cit., pp.62-3.
104. Golan, op. cit., p.16; Elena Barikhovskaya, *The Guardian*, 24 July 1991.
105. Golan, op. cit., p.15 and p.86.
106. Freedman, op. cit., p.16.
107. Ibid., pp.17-18.
108. Ibid., p.17.
109. Ibid., pp.36-7.
110. Ibid., p.29.
111. Ibid., pp.34-5. The nine points agreed upon were the following: 1) Soviet Jews with exit visas for Israel would travel via Romania; 2) Refuseniks and their families would be allowed to emigrate within one year except for those with access to particularly sensitive information; 3) First degree relatives of those already abroad could leave within an established time frame. Flexibility would be shown over the meaning of 'first-degree'; 4) Those refuseniks refused permission to leave indefinitely would have their cases reviewed; 5) Unrestricted access to Jewish religious literature from abroad would be allowed; 6) Where there was a clear need, synagogues would be allowed to open; 7) Soviet Jews would be allowed access to rabbinical training overseas; 8) A review of the teaching of Hebrew in schools would begin; 9) The opening of a kosher restaurant in Moscow would be allowed.
112. Robert O. Freedman, 'Jewish Emigration as a Factor in Soviet Foreign Policy Toward the United States and Israel in the Gorbachev Era', Unpublished Paper, 1992, p.6.
113. Golan, op. cit., p.18.
114. Robert O. Freedman, *Soviet Policy Toward Israel Under Gorbachev* (New York: Praeger/Center for Strategic and International Studies, Washington DC, 1991), p.44.
115. 'Soviet Foreign Minister on Shamir's Election Plan, Jewish Emigration', *BBC*

Summary of World Broadcasts (hereafter BBC-SWB), ME/0471 i, 1 June 1989.
116. Salitan, op.cit., pp.66–8.
117. Michael R. Beschloss and Strobe Talbott, *At the Highest Levels: The Inside Story of the End of the Cold War* (London: Warner Books, 1994), p.23. The academics included Adam Ulam, Marshall Goldman, Stephen Meyer, Robert Pfaltzgraff and Ed Hewett.
118. Robert O. Freedman, 'Jewish Emigration as a Factor in Soviet Foreign Policy Toward the United States and Israel', Unpublished paper, 1992, p.34.
119. 'Israeli Travel Agency to Issue Visas to USSR', *BBC-SWB*, ME/0522 A/5, 31 July 1989.
120. 'Soviet Envoy Says Aid from Israel will Bring Two Peoples Closer', *BBC-SWB*, ME/0334 A/7, 14 Dec. 1988.
121. 'Israel Foreign Minister Praises Soviet Decision on Jewish Emigration', *BBC-SWB*, ME/0325 i, 3 Dec. 1988; 'Israel: Peres Refers to Significant Changes in Relations with the USSR over Hijacking Incident', *BBC-SWB* ME/0327 A/4, 6 Dec. 1988.
122. Robert O. Freedman, *Soviet Policy Toward Israel Under Gorbachev* (New York: Praeger/Center for Strategic and International Studies, Washington DC, 1991), p.31.
123. Salitan, op. cit., p.53; 'Plan Agreed on Flight for Soviet Jews via Romania', *BBC-SWB*, ME/0234 A/8, 19 August 1988.
124. Salitan, op. cit., p.53.
125. Hella Pick and Martin Walker, 'US Curbs Entry of Jews from Russia', *The Guardian*, 7 Dec. 1988.
126. Geoffrey Aronson, 'Soviet Jewish Emigration, the United States, and the Occupied Territories', *Journal of Palestine Studies*, Vol.19, No.4 (Summer 1990), pp.32–3.
127. Ibid., p.33.
128. Avishai Margalit, 'The Great White Hope', *New York Review of Books*, Vol.XXXVIII, No.12 (27 June 1991), p.19; Aronson op. cit., p.34.
129. Aronson, op. cit., pp.35–6.
130. 'Israel: Shamir Says Election Plan Important for Publicity', *BBC-SWB*, ME/0494 A/5, 28 June 1989.

3 The Political and Ideological Context of Soviet Jewish Migration to Israel

On the 14 January 1990, in a speech before a gathering of Likud party veterans in Tel-Aviv, Israeli Premier Yitzhak Shamir stated that the growing Jewish *aliyah* from the Soviet Union required the retention of the Occupied Territories since: 'We need the space to house all the people. Big immigration requires Israel to be big as well ... we must have the Land of Israel and we have to fight for it , struggle for it.' He went on to add:

> Just when many among us were saying that time is working against us, time has brought us this *aliyah* and has solved everything. In five years we won't be able to recognise the country. Everything will change – the people, the way they live – everything will be bigger, stronger. The Arabs around us are in a state of disarray and panic. They are shrouded by a feeling of defeat, because they see that the *intifada* doesn't help.They cannot stop the natural streaming of the Jewish people to their homeland.[1]

A clear continuity in Likud ideological thinking was evident throughout Shamir's address, an ideology based on the historical premise that the West Bank and Gaza Strip constituted the integral core of the Jewish State. Nevertheless, the existence of some two million Palestinian Arabs in Judea, Samaria, and Gaza – terminology used mainly by right-wing Zionist parties to describe the Occupied Territories – had precluded the outright annexation of these areas by successive Israeli governments, since such action necessarily entailed conferring democratic rights upon the Palestinian inhabitants. Given the perceived demographic threat caused by a higher Palestinian birth-rate, those advocating retention of the territories had to reconcile pursuit of ideological orthodoxy with the democratic norms of Israeli society, an untenable position given the dilution of the Jewish character and, by extension, Jewish majority of the State of Israel involved in any formal annexation of the territories.

Furthermore, arguments concerning the strategic worth of the West Bank were used by all sides across the Israeli political spectrum to justify either retention of, or compromise over, land conquered by Israel in the June 1967 war. The West Bank provided Israel with a defensive depth it had previously been denied, enabling the Israeli Defence Force (IDF) to exploit the topographical features of the region – such as the mountains overlooking the Jordan valley – to dominate the border with the Hashemite Kingdom of Jordan. Indeed, the official rationale given for the establishment of a series of agricultural settlements contiguous with the River Jordan, the so-called Allon Plan devised by the former Israeli Deputy Prime Minister, Yigal Allon, was premised upon the need to provide a readily defensible barrier in the event of any renewal of hostilities with Amman.[2]

However, following the election of the Likud to power in 1977, the security debate became a means, and not an end in itself, to legitimize Israel's control and development of the Occupied Territories. According to Benyamin Begin, Likud's interpretation of Zionism rested upon two criteria: total Jewish sovereignty over *Eretz Y'Israel*; and the fundamental right of the Jewish people to national security. The synthesis of the two became the dominant strand in the Likud political agenda, 'to prevent the establishment of any foreign sovereignty west of the River Jordan'.[3]

The onset of mass Soviet Jewish immigration offered the human potential to negate any movement towards Palestinian self-determination, and would lead, according to the leader of the Democratic Front for the Liberation of Palestine, Nayif Hawatmeh, to 'more settlement on our Palestinian land at our expense [adding] to the human potential of the Israeli military machine'.[4] Accordingly, as a transnational flow, Soviet Jewish migration was viewed largely as a means to bolster the conceptions of security held by the existing Israeli state elite, in this case the Likud coalition government of Yitzhak Shamir. Yet the sheer volume of the Soviet *aliyah* proved to have a profound impact upon Israel, exacerbating ideological cleavages inherent within the concept of Zionism as well as creating massive social and economic dislocation throughout the Jewish State. Therefore, an understanding of the effect of Soviet *aliyah* has to be placed within the wider debate on Zionist ideology; a debate in which demographic and security concerns – the latter fused with a religious and historical determinism – came to dominate the Israeli political scene.

Soviet Jewish Aliyah: The Ideological Context

Before the sudden and overwhelming influx of Soviet Jews, the State of Israel faced the very real problem of emigration itself. Between 1985 and 1987, 12,000 Israelis left annually, and in 1988 this figure reached 14,500. Of these, over 60 per cent were aged between 21 and 34. The increasing inability of the Jewish State to retain large numbers of its own youth was cited by one politician as revealing the 'ideological bankruptcy of Israel as a Zionist State'.[5] Indeed, it was estimated that by 1990, 400,000 Israelis, some ten per cent of the total population, were resident abroad.

This crisis of confidence afflicting Israeli society was the very real expression of political, social, and economic cleavages that had bedevilled the Jewish State since its inception in 1948. Most visible of the political problems was the Palestinian uprising or *intifada* which had led to a widening rift between those who regarded the concept of Greater Israel – *Eretz Y'Israel* – as sacrosanct, and those who believed that territorial compromise over the territories captured in 1967 was necessary if some semblance of peace was to be attained.[6] These divisions existed before the outbreak of the *intifada* in December 1987 and had their root cause in the different emphasis accorded to the concept of Zionism over a period of 60 years. A brief analysis of the development of Zionist ideology reveals four main schools of thought: Messianic Zionism, Spiritual Zionism, Labour Zionism, and Revisionist Zionism. Of these, the last two have continued to dominate the contemporary Israeli political landscape.

Messianic Zionism was moulded as an ideological force by Rabbi Yitzhak Hacohen Kook, who argued that the attainment of *Eretz Y'Israel* was of 'supreme importance in the redemption of the Jewish people'.[7] Kook stressed the concept of the land as being pre-eminent among the three traditional components of Judaism: Land, Torah, People.

> *Eretz Y'Israel* is part of the very essence of our nationhood; it is bound organically to its very life and inner being... Jewish original creativity, whether in the realm of ideas or in the

arena of daily life and action, is impossible except in *Eretz Y'Israel*.[8]

However, it was to be his son Rabbi Zvi Kook who used his father's writings to add theological legitimacy to the use of force in order to achieve and maintain the unity of *Eretz Y'Israel*. His writings found a receptive audience amongst settler organizations such as Gush Emunim (Bloc of the Faithful) which combined a potent mixture of religious zealousness with a pioneering spirit of settlement throughout the Occupied Territories. The writings of Zvi Kook delivered a *carte blanche* to the followers of Gush Emunim since they divorced settlement activity from any moral or humanistic constraints. They pursued a policy of direct action in building settlements on the West Bank, often without official permission but with the tacit consent of the Likud government.[9]

Comprising both religious and secular Jews, advocates of Spiritual Zionism gave precedence to their interpretation of the Torah in defining Zionism. Spiritualists set out to establish a Jewish community of 'exceptional moral character' in Palestine at the beginning of the century. Based upon the teachings of Ahad HaAm (Asher Ginsberg), Spiritualists argued that the survival of the Jewish people as an entity within the diaspora lay in adherence to the power of the Jewish spirit as opposed to recourse to 'the Sword'. However, the latent anti-Semitism that continued to permeate so-called enlightened European society convinced Spiritualists that a probable solution lay in some form of settlement in Palestine.

HaAm was acutely aware of the potential for confrontation between Arab and Jew. This concern resulted in the formation of Brit Shalom (Covenant of Peace) and later the Ihud group under Dr Judah Magnes and the philosopher Martin Buber. Throughout the 1930s, Ihud campaigned actively for a bi-national state but dropped this position in the aftermath of the 1948 War of Independence. However, Spiritual Zionists continued to maintain that Israel had to lay claim to a spiritual quality above and beyond that of other nation-states. This could not be achieved in the face of continuing Israeli rule over nearly two million Palestinians in the West Bank and Gaza Strip following the outcome of the June 1967 war. Thus, Spiritual Zionists advocated a strong ethical code that would govern Israeli domestic and foreign policies. Consequently, Spiritual Zionists such as the renowned bio-chemist and Judaic scholar, Professor Yeshayu Leibowitz, continued to campaign for a small, Jewish democratic Israel.[10]

Initially, Labour or Socialist Zionism focused upon the emancipation of Jewish labour, particularly in Imperial Russia and Eastern Europe, where workers were subjected to both anti-Semitism and capitalist exploitation. The overriding need to escape this two-dimensional oppression meant that Palestine became an increasingly attractive proposition. This awakening of Jews into believing that they constituted a viable entity dovetailed with the ideas expressed by Theodore Herzl in his pamphlet, *Der Judenstaat*.

The first Zionist Congress at Basle in 1897 endorsed Herzl's strategy for achieving a Jewish 'homeland' in Palestine. Ostensibly, permission and support were to be sought from the great European powers which could exact concessions from the Ottoman Empire, allowing Jewish settlement in Palestine. Yet while Herzl originally insisted upon political agreements prior to Jewish emigration, the groundswell of Socialist Zionism outstripped Herzl's diplomacy. In 1898, the second Zionist Congress established the 'Jewish Colonial Trust', a financial body which facilitated Jewish migration from Russia and Eastern Europe without waiting for the political pre-conditions previously required.[11]

Increasingly, the Zionist Congress came to be dominated by secular left-wing Zionists, drawn mainly from the five million-strong Russian Jewish community. These representatives established the three pillars that became the genesis of the Israeli state: the Kibbutzim, the Haganah (army) and the Histadrut (Trade Union Federation). While imbued with a strong sense of socialism, Labour Zionism did not, however, develop into a homogeneous political party. It comprised a mosaic of several left-wing and Marxist parties that came to be dominated by Mapai, the democratic socialist party of David Ben Gurion. In 1969, Mapai allied itself with the smaller and more radical Mapam to form the Labour alignment. It was this Labour coalition that dominated the Israeli political scene between 1948 and 1977. However, the alignment had already sown the seeds of its own undoing between 1948 and 1952 over the integration of Jewish immigrants from North Africa and Asia.

Revisionist Zionism was born out of a dispute over the tactics and strategy employed by the socialist-dominated Zionist movement of the 1920s. Whereas Ben Gurion was willing to accept British decisions to restrict Jewish settlement, regarding these as temporary setbacks, the Revisionists argued that such tactical concessions were anathema to the historical legitimacy of Jewish settlement throughout *Eretz Y'Israel*. Under their chief mentor, Vladimir Jabotinsky, the Revisionists also took exception to Ben Gurion's policy of refusing to define the State of Israel, lest it annoy Britain and inflame Arab opinion. Revisionist Zionists opposed the UN partition plan of 1947, accepted by Ben Gurion, and continued to agitate for the unity of *Eretz Y'Israel*, including the East Bank of the Jordan. The heirs of the Revisionists, the Herut Party and, latterly, the Herut-led Likud coalition of Menachem Begin and Yitzhak Shamir, continued to argue that, following the June 1967 war, no Israeli government would surrender any part of the Land of Israel. Indeed, many within the Likud argued that Israel had already ceded enough territory by dropping its claim that Jordan form an historical part of *Eretz Y'Israel*.[12]

These four main schools of thought have all claimed that a Jewish state should be established. But the exact parameters and dimensions of that state have never been resolved. To this day, Israel has not defined its boundaries; nor has it a written consitution or bill of rights because no consensus has ever been reached over the exact nature of Zionism as a single ideology. By the time Israel achieved independence in 1948, the four main ideological strands had evolved into two political blocs. The Spiritualists merged with the Labour Zionists to form the dominant state élite in Israel from 1948 to 1977. The Revisionists, however, were initially the political pariahs within the new state, but a fundamental shift in the make-up of the Israeli population was to have long-term effects from which the Likud reaped the rewards.

The election of 1977 produced a new state élite that was to exercise an intellectual and ideological hegemony over the political discourse in Israel for the next 15 years. The establishment of a Likud government under Menachem Begin was made possible by the massive support it received from Jews of Oriental origin. Israeli society was, and still is, dominated by Jews of European origin, the Ashkenazim, who provided the original basis of support for the Labour alignment. The first great wave of *olim* to arrive in Israel following independence came from North

Africa, Iraq, and Yemen. The majority of these Jews were conservative, uneducated, and religiously observant. Consequently, they entered Israeli society at the bottom of the economic and social scale. Indeed, new housing, originally earmarked for Oriental Jews, was, at the behest of the Ashkenazim-dominated Jewish Agency, given to Jews from Europe.

The first generation of Oriental Jews supported the Labour alignment. Yet they were seen and treated by government agencies charged with absorption as second-class citizens. They were largely confined to resettlement centres or *ma'abarot* longer than European *olim*, sent to isolated frontier and development towns that often lacked basic facilities, and employed as low-paid menial labour, mostly in agriculture and construction.[13] This treatment at the hands of Israel's dominant Ashkenazim establishment, coupled with the strident secularism of the Labour alignment, produced a shift towards the revisionist Herut and later Likud-led coalition. By 1987, 60 per cent of all Israelis were of Oriental origin. It has been estimated that 70–75 per cent of Likud support in 1987 came from the Oriental community, compared to approximately 25–30 per cent for Labour. Given that the population growth for Oriental Jews outstripped that of the Ashkenazim, it appeared that Likud domination seemed set to continue.[14]

However, while the Likud inherited a legacy of poverty and under-investment in the development towns from successive Labour administrations, it failed to address the chronic social and economic ills that dogged these urban developments located mainly in the north of Galilee and in the arid Negev desert. Development towns were first established under the Mapai-dominated governments of David Ben Gurion. Initially they were part of a deliberate policy to disperse the growing Israeli population away from the coastal strip. These new towns also served to strengthen the Jewish presence in predominantly Arab areas still within Israel, particularly in the Galilee. Some of these towns prospered; a few such as Kiryat Gat and the port of Ashdod actually evolved into well-planned cities. Yet in seeking to establish as many towns as possible, insufficient account was taken of the economic and social costs involved.

The majority of the first inhabitants of the development towns were drawn mainly from the Oriental community and were not consulted before being dispatched to their new environs. Often the main source of employment centred around one or two factories, reliant upon low-skilled and low-paid labour, mostly in textiles. It was argued that such an infrastructure produced few incentives to attract either skilled or highly educated people, while those young people who did obtain a university education remained in the big coastal cities of Tel-Aviv and Haifa. Consequently, the development towns remained stagnant, offering few opportunities for a higher standard of living outside the coastal strip. The capture of the West Bank only exacerbated the sense of alienation and deprivation felt by the development towns. In the 1970s and 1980s, government funds for development favoured the establishment of settlements in the West Bank. Because of its proximity to the coastal plain, few Israeli entrepreneurs were willing to invest in the development towns, particularly when the establishment of 'Development Zones' in the Occupied Territories offered government subsidies to first-time investors.[15]

Indeed, economic, rather than religious or strategic, settlement of the West Bank was responsible for Israel's informal attempts at annexing the area. The tendency of all big cities to expand was harnessed to the development of the Occupied Territories following the 1967 war. Both Labour and Likud governments provided inducements for the building industry to invest in construction projects beyond the Green Line, Israel's pre-1967 border with Jordan. The immediate result of this policy meant that new housing within the Green Line became an increasingly scarce commodity throughout the 1980s.

> Thousands of Israelis responded to the tempting advertisements, offering plush villas for a down payment of a mere three thousand dollars, with promises that the government would cover the balance of the costs... [yet] emphasis was put on the new settlements' proximity to an urban centre, so the prospective settlers could commute to work inside Israel.[16]

The new generation of settlers were therefore far removed from the popular image of the religious Jewish pioneer. Indeed, the new settlers were labelled 'Yuppies', able to commute into cities such as Tel-Aviv without having to endure the cramped living conditions of Israel's premier city. These considerations coupled with tax incentives and interest-free house loans weighed more heavily with these new settlers than the vexed question of whether it was right to extend Israel's sovereignty beyond the Green Line.[17]

The decision to annex informally the Occupied Territories through economic settlement also had an adverse effect on Israel's agricultural sector. By 1987, the moshav and kibbutz movements, the main producers of food throughout Israel, faced a massive economic crisis. Interest alone on their combined debt was running at a million dollars each day. While much blame could be placed upon the actual structure and investment decisions taken by individual kibbutzim and moshavim, their problems were compounded by an austerity package designed to bring down Israel's hyperinflation. This might have been acceptable to the co-operative farms had it not been for the continuing development of settlements on the West Bank. Many regarded government apathy towards the agricultural sector as stemming from an historical vendetta conducted by the Likud coalition. Moshavim and kibbutzim, traditionally Ashkenazim-dominated, formed a major part of the Labour alignment's support, and had provided the ideological and structural basis around which the nascent Israeli State had evolved. By decreasing subsidies and allowing market forces to exact their toll, it was felt that Likud could erode an important pillar of Labour alignment support throughout Israel.[18]

Thus, from 1967 onwards, settlement of the West Bank and its gradual integration into the Jewish State after 1967 dominated the Israeli political agenda. The 1982 war in Lebanon was designed to accelerate this process. By depriving the Palestinians in the Occupied Territories of any external political leadership it was argued that subservience to Israel's political will would ensue. The poverty of such thinking was revealed not only in the failure of the invasion's objectives (the destruction of the PLO in Lebanon and the establishment of a benign Christian-dominated regime in Beirut), but by the outbreak of a widespread insurrection in the West Bank and Gaza in December 1987: the *intifada*.[19]

The *aliyah* of Soviet Jews therefore offered the ruling Likud coalition, particularly from June 1990 onwards, an alternative means to achieve its ideological goal. In March 1990, Israel's National Unity Government, an uneasy alliance of the Likud and Labour alignment, collapsed. Disagreement centred around Labour's proposal to initiate elections in the territories, which would lead to a 'limited form' of autonomy for the Palestinians. Although these proposals circumvented any participation by the

PLO, they proved unacceptable to Yitzhak Shamir, who promptly sacked the Labour leader and Finance Minister, Shimon Peres. After much internal political manoeuvring, it was Shamir who successfully formed the most right-wing government in the history of the Jewish State. On 18 June 1990, Shamir proclaimed that the Soviet *olim* were to become his government's top priority.[20] However, the dispute with the Labour alignment again highlighted the disagreements that still existed over the scope and dimensions of Zionism, a contention reflected in the demographic and security debates surrounding the mass influx of Soviet Jewry.

The Demographic Debate
The internal cleavages and divisions facing Israeli society, coupled with the external security dilemma, resulted in increasing numbers of young Israelis seeking to leave the Jewish State. Taken against this background, Moscow's decision to relax emigration controls, coupled with Washington's new immigration quotas, appeared to offer the government of Yitzhak Shamir an all-embracing panacea for Israel's problems. Certainly, Ron Nachman, mayor of Ariel, the biggest settlement in the West Bank, believed that the mass influx of Soviet Jews removed any need for territorial compromise.[21] Yet this view was vigorously challenged by the former veteran mayor of Jerusalem, Teddy Kollek, who, responding to Shamir's speech of 14 January, stated that: 'I agree with his statement except that my Greater Israel is not measured in additional square kilometers but rather in content and spirit. I am definitely against holding on to Occupied Territory.'[22]

The debate was further complicated by controversy over the exact numbers expected to migrate from the Soviet Union. Yaakov Feitelson, head of Ariel municipal council, suggested that the Galilee and the Negev had the capacity to settle two million migrants, but considered retention of the territories essential since he envisaged a far higher level of *aliyah*.[23] Other estimates at the beginning of 1990 envisaged the need to absorb 750,000 *olim* over a three-year period, even though the original budget presented by the National Unity Government in January 1990 allocated funds sufficient for the absorption of just 40,000 Soviet Jews for the whole of that year. The shortfall in government projections was revealed following the announcement by the Jewish Agency that 43,000 immigrants had arrived in the period January to May 1990.[24]

Political and Ideological Context of Soviet Jewish Migration 67

Yet while *aliyah* continued to rise, the arrival of even 750,000 *olim* was deemed insufficient to address Israel's demographic inferiority in the territories or provide a solid foundation from which outright annexation could be implemented. According to *The Economist*, the influx of 750,000 Jews would hold the Jewish–Arab ratio throughout Israel and the Occupied Territories at 60:40. But, as the journal went on to declare:

> The territories themselves, where some 70,000 Jews live amongst a sea of 1.7 million Arabs will never feel part of Israel. To extend the majority that Jews at present enjoy in Israel proper (80:20) through the West Bank and Gaza would need the immigration of some 8 million Jews – virtually the whole of the diaspora – by the year 2000. And that would produce a Greater Israel of 12.7 million Jews and 3.2 million Arabs, still a pretty explosive mixture.[25]

Increasingly, concern was expressed that the logical consequence of any annexation would be either an erosion of the dominant Jewish character of the state, or more likely, given the higher Palestinian birthrate, the withdrawal of democratic rights in order to safeguard that self-same character. Consequently, it was argued that incorporating all new *olim* within the pre-1967 borders would maintain both the Zionist and the Jewish character of the Israeli state without having to endure a situation increasingly reminiscent of South Africa. Shamir's remark that 'large scale *aliyah* required a large Israel' was challenged by demographer and town planner Eliashu Efrat. He calculated that Israel's three largest cities, Tel-Aviv, Haifa, and Jerusalem, had the potential to absorb 1,780,000, with the coastal strip between Hedera and Gedeira having the capacity to absorb a further 1,209,000. This forecast did not even include the sparsely populated areas of Galilee and the Negev within Israel proper.[26]

Rates of fertility between Arab and Jew did indeed lend weight to those advocating the settlement of any new *olim* within Israel proper. The Palestinians had a higher proportion of children and youths at 58 per cent of the total Arab population compared with 38 per cent for the Jewish population.[27] Furthermore, concern was voiced that areas firmly within the Green Line already boasted an Arab majority, most notably in the Galilee. Even the Bedouin of the Negev appeared to be on the threshold of surpassing the resident Jewish population of the area. Failure to address this pressing issue through a concerted settlement programme in these areas would, according to one source, lead Israel's Arab community to 'put forth demands for autonomous states, or perhaps something even more far-reaching, in the Galilee or Negev'.[28] Accordingly, the Soviet *aliyah* had to be used to establish a Zionist *fait accompli* within Israel proper, and not to dilute the demographic impact of this immigrant wave by using it to settle the Occupied Territories.

Restricting settlement construction within Israel's pre-June 1967 borders proved antithetical to the core component of Likud ideology: the historical claim of the Jewish people to its Biblical home. While considerable latitude was exercised by some Likud members concerning the Palestinian question – Shlomo Lahat, former Likud mayor of Tel-Aviv, openly proposed the establishment of a Palestinian state in the Occupied Territories – eventual Jewish sovereignty and therefore continued settlement were non-negotiable.[29] Most entrenched in this view was the settlers' movement Gush Emunim, which combined a theological determinism with Likud's historical claim to the disputed territories. The belief that the Jewish people were 'chosen' by God to inhabit the 'promised land' negated any claims to nationhood on the part of the Palestinian people in the West Bank and Gaza. Consequently, the belief that 'Judea and Samaria' constituted hallowed ground abrogated any government concessions, democratic or otherwise, over the future status of the territories.[30]

This reliance upon an acute interpretation of Jewish theology and law, usurping as it did the democratic basis of Israeli society, provoked former Israeli Foreign Minister, Abba Eban, to declare that Tel-Aviv's continuing rule over the West Bank and Gaza was 'corrupting our political culture, our intellectual sanity, because it encourages mystical, Biblical illusions. It is incompatible with prophetic Judaism and classical Zionism'. Warming to his theme, Eban went on to discount the overt military threat facing the Jewish State:

> There is a greater danger to Israel from our own rule of the territory, than there is from the Soviet Union, PLO, or from Syria or from any external threat. We are not under any external threat: Egypt is out of the war, Jordan was never in the war, Lebanon isn't a threat except from terrorist incursions, the Syrian threat can be contained – it would be laughable to say there is a military threat from outside to Israel's existence.[31]

However, despite Eban's dismissal of any tangible external threat to Israel's existence, the strategic worth of holding on to the Occupied Territories was a potent argument in justifying the ideological position of the right wing in Israel. Nevertheless, the failure to establish any consensual base regarding the settlement of the West Bank and Gaza was repeated in the debate regarding the military utility of the area. Nowhere was this more apparent than within the High Command of the IDF.

The Occupied Territories: The Strategic Debate
The arguments in favour of Israel's retention of the West Bank comprised a potent mix of strategic logic and historical and ideological determinism characteristic of the right wing in Israeli politics. According to Dan Horowitz, Israel has enjoyed a national consensus concerning the strategic importance of the Occupied Territories, particularly the West Bank and Golan Heights. This was based on two, purely military, criteria: first, that Israel deny the deployment of enemy offensive weaponry, or the construction of facilities such as airfields that could threaten its security; secondly, that Israel should be able to deploy its military forces in the event of an attack from the east and establish a solid line of defence. Yet as Horowitz himself concluded:

> In this context, it is important to note that the consensus among those with a high level of security and political consciousness vis-à-vis Israel's eastern border is based only on the need to prevent the West Bank from becoming the source of a military threat to the existence of Israel.... However, it does not address three fundamental issues: the size, location, and status of the territories required to ensure successful Israeli self-defence if attacked from the east. Nor does it suggest a rejection of a return of territories to a sovereign Palestinian entity.[32]

If the West Bank were to be an effective buffer against large-scale armed incursion from across the River Jordan, control of the highland plateau running along its spine became a necessity. But for Lieutenant Colonel Michael Ratzner, a Likud party member, control of this strategic asset merely reinforced Israel's Biblical claim to the disputed area. Accordingly, security was defined not only in terms of an external threat, but also in terms of proscribing the national aspirations of the Palestinian people that challenged the very basis of Revisionist Zionism adhered to by Ratzner. This position received strong support from the former Israeli Chief of Staff Rafael Eitan who, on 11 May 1978, and with the tacit support of Prime Minister Begin, issued a public statement that supported Israeli rule over the West Bank on strategic *and* ideological grounds. In sum, Eitan favoured an aggressive policy towards settlement construction throughout the territories, a policy fully in line with the aims and aspirations of Begin and the then Israeli Minister for Agriculture responsible for settlement construction, Ariel Sharon.[33]

For the Likud, security was defined as the maintenance of *Eretz Y'Israel* – an ideological goal – as much as the core defence of Israel proper. This position was endorsed by Major General Matan Vilnai, the commanding officer of Israel's southern region, who concluded that the IDF could not effectively defend the Jewish State against an adjacent Palestinian State created from the West Bank and Gaza Strip.[34]

Other senior IDF commanders took issue with these arguments, some calling for total Israeli withdrawal, while others adopted a minimalist approach that still required a limited Israeli presence throughout the territories. One survey of senior IDF officers conducted by the Jaffee Centre for Strategic Studies of Tel-Aviv University, revealed a majority in favour of territorial concessions, a position seemingly at odds with both lower ranks within the IDF and the Israeli public in general.[35] The belief that territorial compromise was possible, and indeed desirable, was based upon a broader interpretation of Israel's security needs. Those adhering to Likud's ideological stance dismissed the aspirations of the Palestinians to national self-determination, consciously diluting their political claims since these clearly undermined the whole concept of *Eretz Y'Israel*. Consequently, reliance upon 'the Sword' to maintain Israel's position throughout the territories had increasingly come to dominate the security debate.

By contrast, there was a clear recognition amongst those charged with the defence of the Jewish State that security was as much political as strategic. This definition implied the need for greater flexibility on the part of Tel-Aviv regarding territorial compromise. A clear proponent of this position was General Amram Mitzna, the former officer commanding Israel's central region that included the West Bank. Stating that the IDF could defend any border, Mitzna declared:

Whatever the political solution will be, the IDF will always find a way of defending Israel. It does not matter what agreements are reached. Consequently, I do not think that we ought to go by the military perspective concerning the importance of the territories for Israel's security.... there can be no military solution to the [Palestinian] problem. And once this has been understood, the next step can be taken.[36]

Others within the Israeli military establishment went further. Lieutenant General Dan Shomron, Israeli Chief of Staff between 1987 and 1991 – the IDF's most senior officer – maintained that national security, achieved under the auspices of a comprehensive peace agreement, was possible without retaining 'Judea, Samaria and Gaza'.[37] Furthermore, according to another former IDF General, Matityahu Peled, fears of Arab control of the West Bank were ill-founded, dismissing as they did Arab perceptions of the area's strategic worth. According to Peled, Jordan viewed the West Bank as a strategic incubus, surrounded on three sides by Israel, with the Jewish State able to cut off the region from Amman at will.[38]

Nevertheless, Iraq's invasion of Kuwait in August 1990 brought into sharp relief for many Israelis the strategic advantage of continued rule over the West Bank. At a stroke, the agenda shifted away from the internal challenge presented by the Palestinian *intifada*, to the external threat presented by a nation-state whose leader had threatened in April of that year to burn half of Israel.[39] Furthermore, the reluctance exhibited by successive Israeli governments to countenance meaningful concessions over the West Bank appeared justified by two factors: the benign relationship between Baghdad and Amman; and the previous involvement of Iraqi forces in military operations west of the River Jordan in 1948 and 1967.[40]

However, the Iraqi missile attacks against Israeli targets between January and February 1991 created fresh divisions regarding the strategic worth of the territories. Israel's urban areas were clearly vulnerable to attack, undermining the argument that control of the West Bank placed the densely populated coastal plain beyond the range of Arab artillery. But return to the pre-1967 borders required Israel to accept a nine-mile waistline at its narrowest point between the Green Line and the Mediterranean sea, reawakening fears that a determined thrust could divide the country in two. Though very much a 'worst case scenario', this argument did at least provide a sound strategic basis for those who adhered to the concept of *Eretz Y'Israel*.

Since 1948, a preoccupation with military security had marked the development and discourse of daily political life in the Jewish State. But the inherent cleavages within the whole concept of Zionism, and, most notably, the exact dimensions of the Jewish State, created a situation in which Israel's security was measured against a sliding scale of ideological priorities dictated by successive governments. This in turn masked the fundamental source of tension throughout the region: the Palestinian quest for national self-determination. Thus arguments over demographics and security were subservient to a basic fault within Zionist ideology: its failure to define its territorial borders and, by extension, the limits of any Palestinian entity. As one commentator noted:

> The basic reality of this land is the conflict of two nations and two cultures. Without a political settlement, the ongoing conflict, whose roots would be fundamentally unchanged, would remain. This is the reality with which we must deal, unless peace itself is to remain a myth.[41]

Conclusion

In the aftermath of the June 1967 war, Israel justified its control over the Occupied Territories mainly in terms of security. This rationale became increasingly subservient to the the concept of *Eretz Y'Israel* following the election of Likud to power in 1977. In pursuing its historical claim to sovereignty over the disputed territories, Israeli policy was conditioned according to strict criteria: no to negotiations with the PLO, no to a Palestinian state, and no to land for peace.[42]

Yet while the Labour alignment was prepared to condone the principle of land for peace, its political isolation from a large section of Israeli society continued to undermine the broad support needed to pursue meaningful negotiations with the Arabs in general, and the Palestinians in particular. Indeed, having brought down the government of National Unity in March 1990 over the issue of peace negotiations, Shimon Peres failed to form a government geared towards territorial compromise. By contrast, Yitzhak Shamir succeeded in forming a Likud-led government, the most right-wing in Israel's history and one independent of any support from the Labour alignment. The continued dominance of Likud ideology thus seemed set to determine the role that the mass *aliyah* of Soviet Jewry would play in shaping the future of the Jewish State.

Presenting his new government before the Knesset on 11 June 1990, Yitzhak Shamir declared that the Soviet *aliyah* and the successful absorption of *olim* into Israel was to be his main priority. Yet this declaration of intent was conditional upon a continuing commitment to *Eretz Y'Israel*, since this represented 'a value and not just a piece of land'.[43] Clearly, seen through the prism of Revisionist Zionism, the new *olim* represented a human means to consolidate an ideological end. This demographic windfall, with all its concomitant arguments regarding security, was therefore set to become a potent factor in that most crucial of debates: the dominance of a single interpretation of Zionism sufficient to determine the borders of the Jewish State.

NOTES

1. *The Guardian*, 16 Jan. 1990.
2. Conor Cruise O'Brien, op. cit., pp.460—1.
3. Elfi Pallis, 'The Likud Party: A Primer', *Journal of Palestine Studies*, XXI, No.2 (Winter 1992), p.45.
4. *The Guardian*, 25 Jan. 1990.
5. Emmanuel Sussman MK, 'Hamediniyut Le Idud Aliyah' (The Policies that Encourage Emigration) *Ha'aretz*, 1 March 1990.
6. *The Jerusalem Post Magazine*, 12 March 1982.
7. Michael Jansen, *Dissonance In Zion* (London: Zed Books, 1987), pp.4—5.
8. *Ibid.*, p.4; Bernard Avishai, op. cit., pp.67—98.
9. David Newman and Tamar Hermann, 'A Comparative Study of *Gush Emunim* and Peace Now', *Journal of Middle Eastern Studies*, Vol.28, No.3 (July 1992), pp. 511—12. See also Ehud Sprinzak, 'The Politics, Institutions, and Culture of Gush Emunim', in Laurence J. Silberstein (ed.), *Jewish Fundamentalism in Comparative Perspective* (New York: New York University Press, 1993), pp.117—45.
10. Contemporary advocates of Spiritual Zionism express their views through organizations such as Oz Ve Shalom (Courage and Peace) which use biblical arguments in debates with Israeli settlers over the legitimacy of continued Israeli rule over the territories captured in 1967. For a fuller account see David Hall-Cathala, *The Peace Movement in Israel 1967-87* (New York: St Martin's Press, 1990), pp. 146—55.
11. For a detailed account of the roots and dynamics of Zionism see Colin Rubenstein, 'Zionism: The National Liberation movement of the Jewish People', in Christine Jennett and Randal G. Stewart (eds), *Politics of the Future: The Role of Social Movements* (London: Macmillan Press, 1989), pp. 262—89.
12. Lenni Brenner, *The Iron Wall: Zionist Revisionism from Jabotinsky to Shamir* (London: Zed Books, 1984),pp.72—84.
13. See Adam Keller, op. cit.
14. Jansen, op. cit., p.12.

15. Keller, op. cit., pp.43-5.
16. Ibid., pp.43-5.
17. Ian Murray, 'Bombings Boost Resolve of the Hilltop Yuppies', *The Times*, 24 Aug. 1987.
18. Ian Murray, 'Farmers with a Crop of Cash Worries', *The Times*, 25 Aug. 1987.
19. See Schiff and Ya'ari, op. cit., for a definitive account of Israel's invasion of Lebanon.
20. 'Shamir's Address to Knesset Presenting New Government', *BBC-SWB*, ME/0789 A/1-2, 13 June 1990.
21. *International Herald Tribune*, 29 Jan. 1990.
22. *The Independent*, 20 Feb. 1990.
23. Yaakov Feitelson, 'Milkhama Batuakh', (War is Inevitable) *Ha'aretz*, 1 Aug. 1990.
24. Ian Black, 'Israel Strains to Absorb the New Arrivals', *The Guardian*, 22 June 1990.
25. 'Dosvidania and Shalom', *The Economist*, 3 Feb. 1990.
26. Elisha Efrat, 'Ha Demographia Ha Motay Shel Shamir', (Shamir's Faulty Demography), *Ha'aretz*, 13 February 1990.
27. Arnon Sofer, ' Ha Im Ano Be'met Koshvim She Yesh Kano Monopol al Ha Adama Eretz?' (Do We Really Think That We Have a Monopoly on Loving the Land?), *Ha'aretz*, 8 March 1990.
28. Joseph Alpher, 'A Strategy for *Aliyah*', *The Jerusalem Post*, 15 March 1990.
29. Pallis, op. cit., p.49; Don Peretz, 'The Impact of the Gulf War on Israeli and Palestinian Political Attitudes', *Journal of Palestine Studies*, XXI, No.1 (Autumn 1991), pp.25—6.
30. Newman and Hermann, op. cit., p.512.
31. Interview with Abba Eban, *International Assignment*, BBC Radio 4, 5 June 1987.
32. Dan Horowitz, 'The Israeli Concept of National Security', in Avner Yaniv (ed.), *National Security and Democracy in Israel* (London: Lynne Rienner Publishers, 1993), pp.27—8.
33. Yoram Peri, *Between Battles and Ballots: Israeli Military in Politics* (Cambridge: Cambridge University Press, 1985), p.268.
34. Ken Schachter, 'Strategic Scenarios', *The Jerusalem Post Magazine*, 29 April 1988; *The Times*, 5 March 1990.
35. 'Ktznim Bekhirim Yutar Yonot Mein Ha Tzibor' (Senior Officers are More Dovish than the Public), *Ha'aretz*, 24 Oct. 1990.
36. 'Mefaked Ha'Shtachim Sha'ava Omer: Tzahal Yekhol Le Hagen Khol Gvul' (Former West Bank Commander: IDF Can Defend Any Borders), *Ma'ariv*, 15 March 1990.
37. John Bulloch, 'US Land for Peace Deal Splits Israel', *Independent on Sunday*, 24 March 1991.
38. Ken Schachter, 'Strategic Scenarios', *The Jerusalem Post Magazine*, 29 April 1988.
39. For a detailed account of Israel's behaviour during the Gulf War, see Laura Zittrain Eisenberg, 'Passive Belligerency: Israel and the 1991 Gulf War', *The Journal of Strategic Studies*, Vol.15, No.3 (Sept. 1992).
40. Dore Gold, 'A Conflict That Will Solve Nothing', *The Guardian*, 25 Jan. 1991.
41. Allan Shapiro, '*Aliyah* Won't Solve the Problem', *The Jerusalem Post*, 3 Jan. 1990.
42. Avi Shlaim, 'Rabin Versus Shamir: Rivals on a Road to Nowhere?', *The Guardian*, 22 June 1992.
43. 'Israel: Shamir's Address to Knesset Presenting New Government', *BBC-SWB*, ME/0789 A/1, 13 June 1990.

4 Absorbing the Soviet Aliyah: Practicality versus Ideology

Presenting his new government before the Knesset on 11 June 1990, Prime Minister Yitzhak Shamir declared the successful absorption of the Soviet *aliyah* to be his main priority. The establishment of a viable economic system able to create the necessary conditions for the successful absorption and integration of the *olim* into the fabric of Israeli society – most notably housing and employment – required, according to Shamir, the will to 'break conventions and adopt changes, even if they have an adverse effect on parties with a vested interest'.[1]

However, the national euphoria that greeted the onset of mass migration to the Jewish State belied serious difficulties in Israel's ability to cope with this *aliyah*. Not least among these was the capacity to determine immigration levels accurately, a prerequisite given the enormous fiscal expenditure required to meet the social needs of the new *olim*. The Ministry of Immigrant Absorption had, in 1986, produced a strategic plan for the absorption of Soviet Jewry, based upon the premise of some 50,000 arrivals per year.[2] Yet throughout 1990 Israeli government forecasts for immigration were consistently revised upwards, ranging from 100,000 to 250,000 *olim*, with one US State Department official suggesting that the figure for the year alone could be as high as 500,000 immigrants.[3] The difficulty in providing a comprehensive plan, able to reconcile the number of immigrants to a fixed *aliyah* budget, was highlighted by Amos Rubin, an advisor to Shamir:

> How can we build a long-term ordered plan if the number of *olim* who will come here is unknown? If in December [1989] we expected a figure of 40,000 *olim*, the rate is now 150,000 and who can guarantee that this rate will not increase?[4]

Yet the ideological importance of *aliyah* as the defining feature of Zionism, and hence the *raison d'être* of the Jewish State, outweighed any reservations that may have been held concerning Israel's ability to cope with mass migration. Consequently, the Jewish Agency – traditionally charged with facilitating *aliyah* throughout the diaspora – was reported in February 1990 to be sending 150,000 invitations per month to Jews throughout the Soviet Union to emigrate to Israel. Indeed, by August 1991, it was reported by the Jewish Agency that over one million Soviet Jews had requested the necessary documentation for obtaining a visa for the Jewish State.[5]

However, the national consensus that surrounded the onset of mass *aliyah* dissipated once the internal political and economic upheaval involved in absorbing the new immigrants came to be realized. Deep unease, both in Israel and abroad, had met Prime Minister Shamir's speech of 14 January 1990 regarding the Jewish State's need to retain the Occupied Territories because of mass migration. Therefore, Shamir's settlement policy had to strike a balance between the external constraints and the internal pressures towards using migration to strengthen Israel's control over the West Bank, Gaza Strip, and Golan Heights. The failure of Shamir to adhere to the conceptual basis of *Eretz Y'Israel* would have undermined his position within his own coalition and party, but direct placement of Soviet Jews in the territories would have invoked international condemnation. Thus, while stating that any Jewish citizen had the right to live anywhere within *Eretz Y'Israel*, Shamir added that there was no government policy to settle the new *olim* over the Green Line.[6]

Yet with increasing numbers of immigrants arriving, it was hoped that the *aliyah* would create a situation within Israel where increasing numbers of its citizens would look to the West Bank to escape the pressures of life along the coastal plain. Consequently, there was an initial reluctance by the government to sanction large-scale building projects within the pre-1967 border.[7] From the outset, therefore, the new immigrants were viewed as a political means to achieve an ideological end. In practical terms, it mattered little if a Soviet or Israeli Jew settled in the territories. But the resulting shift in the population of native Israelis would allow the Shamir government to dilute any criticism from Western governments and continue the gradual annexation of the West Bank. Speaking before a gathering of Likud party veterans in Tel-Aviv in November 1990, the Israeli premier reaffirmed his commitment to the Likud ideal of a Jewish State encompassing the

Occupied Territories, declaring that this was significant 'for future generations and the mass *aliyah*'.[8] Thus, settlement remained the focal point of Likud government policy, outweighing the social and economic costs to both Israelis and Soviet *olim*.

In presenting his new Cabinet before the Knesset, Shamir announced that Ariel Sharon, as the new minister for housing and construction, was to be appointed head of a new *aliyah* 'cabinet' with powers to co-ordinate the whole absorption process. A right-wing hawk opposed to any form of territorial compromise, Sharon set out to use his new powers to establish as many 'Jewish faces' throughout Occupied Territories and along the Green Line as possible. By deliberately manipulating the envisaged displacement of native Israelis, it became clear that Sharon was seeking to dilute the concept of any Palestinian entity on the West Bank.

Paradoxically, however, it was this very desire to harness mass *aliyah* to consolidate Israeli rule over the territories that proved so fatal for the Likud coalition. While Sharon's tenure as Housing Minister witnessed large-scale expansion in construction activity throughout Israel and the territories, this was often done without prior financial authorization from Finance Minister Yitzhak Mo'dai. Consequently, funds for such building projects were often withheld pending a ministerial compromise. Structural problems inherent within Israel's archaic building industry also retarded the completion of housing units, while tales of nepotism and corruption surrounding building contracts did little to endear the Likud government to either the new *olim* or native Israelis.[9]

Because of such bureaucratic in-fighting, the *aliyah* cabinet never concluded a detailed strategy for absorption able to meet the growing demand for housing and employment throughout the Jewish State. Indeed, Shamir's failure to 'break conventions and adopt changes', particularly regarding the closed nature of Israel's economy, coupled with the scale of Soviet immigration forced Tel-Aviv to approach Washington for aid in the form of loan guarantees. Therefore, the state elite in Israel, unable to meet the costs of absorption through accommodational changes in its relationship with society, was forced to adopt an international strategy, a process that required overtures to other states and international financial organizations.

Although initially forthcoming in accepting an Israeli request for $400m, primarily as a reward for Israel's restraint throughout the Gulf crisis, the Bush administration attached conditions to a further request for $10bn that proved unacceptable to the ideological predisposition of the Likud government: a total cessation of building activity throughout the Occupied Territories including East Jerusalem. The financial enormity of Israel's request underlined the economic burden that faced it as it struggled to cope with the social problems accompanying the mass migration of Soviet Jewry. Yet in rejecting the linkage entailed in Washington's conditions governing the loans, the Likud government clearly signalled its intent to adhere to its main ideological goal: eventual Israeli sovereignty throughout the West Bank and Gaza. This superseded the practical need to fund adequately the absorption of some 400,000 immigrants, a decision that had a profound impact across the whole spectrum of Israeli society.

Organizing the Soviet Aliyah: The Role of the Jewish Agency
Traditionally charged with facilitating emigration to Israel throughout the diaspora, the Jewish Agency possessed a multi-faceted role in the absorption of Soviet Jewry. Although financially independent from government funds – the agency depends upon the largesse of Jewish communities worldwide – it had nevertheless retained close links with successive Israeli governments since *aliyah* remained *the* common denominator among all Zionist parties. In October 1989 the Jewish Agency began to fund education projects throughout the USSR, designed to negate decades of official hostility to Zionism previously endorsed by the Soviet authorities.[10]

However, its main task remained the logistical expedition of Soviet Jewry to Israel. In pursuit of this enterprise – termed 'Operation Exodus' by agency officials – the financial resources of the Jewish Agency became severely stretched, bringing the agency chairman, Simcha Dinitz, and head of its '*Aliyah* and Absorption Department', Uri Gordon, into conflict with state bureaucracies, particularly the Ministry for Immigrant Absorption and Prime Minister Shamir.

Initially the agency stated that transportation costs for 1990, based on airlifting some 150,000 Soviet Jews, would amount to $150 million, or $1,000 per person. In addition, the agency was also responsible for funding up to half of the estimated $500 million for 1990, needed to cover the costs of direct absorption for each immigrant. Yet with a gross income of just $377 million from the financial year 1988–89, the Jewish Agency clearly had insufficient funds required to meet such commitments.[11]

The medium- to long-term solution lay in raising the level of voluntary contributions throughout the diaspora paid to the United Jewish Appeal (UJA), the American fundraising arm of the agency. The activities of the UJA provided a clear example of Peterson's argument that societal actors could operate transnationally in support of a foreign state, in this case Israel.[12] Dinitz launched an appeal in the United States designed to double the income of the agency in the financial year 1990–91 to $606 million. None the less, this did little to alleviate the immediate financial crisis facing the agency, particularly since the level of *aliyah* appeared set to exceed the figure of 150,000 immigrants. Moreover, it became apparent that the UJA was somewhat circumscribed in the amount it readily raised for the Jewish Agency. Although it had transferred $128 million to Israel by October 1990, the UJA was under increasing pressure from American Jewry to spend more on its own Jewish communities, following the large cuts in federal spending on welfare programmes under Ronald Reagan.[13]

As a result, the Jewish Agency, albeit somewhat reluctantly, sought a sharp reduction from the Likud coalition government in the amount it paid towards the costs of direct absorption. This reluctance stemmed from fears that any role the agency had in actually settling and integrating the *olim* throughout the country would eventually become the prerogative of the Ministry for Immigrant Absorption. A convocation of absorption responsibilities had already been suggested by a government appointed committee as far back as 1972, a point seized upon by Israel's State Comptroller, Miriam Ben-Porat, who declared that:

> Experts and commissions over the years have reached the conclusion that the present administrative structure is an impediment to absorption and a waste of funds. The immediate establishment of a central authority for absorption is necessary.[14]

The establishment of the *aliyah* cabinet under the stewardship of Ariel Sharon in June 1990, composed of the Ministries of the Interior, Immigrant Absorption, Education, Housing, Finance, and Labour, as well as representatives of the Bank of Israel and the Jewish Agency, was an attempt to provide such a central authority.

None the less, the agency continued to view the Ministry for Immigrant Absorption with suspicion, fearful that its scope of activities within Israel, and hence its ability to attract revenue from the diaspora, would be severely curtailed.[15]

Even before the magnitude of the financial crisis facing the Jewish Agency became apparent, it had already clashed with Yitzhak Shamir following his 'Greater Israel' speech of 14 January 1990. The international response that met this brash declaration, including a statement by Washington linking further aid to a freeze on new settlements in the Occupied Territories, convinced the Israeli Prime Minister that strict military censorship on all reports concerning Soviet Jewish immigration to Israel should be imposed. This included accurate data on numbers of arrivals, the scale and location of construction activity, as well as detailed figures regarding the financial expenditure incurred by the mass *aliyah*. Censorship, imposed on 1 March 1990 and only partially lifted afterwards, was justified on grounds of national security and, in particular, on fears of Arab terrorist attacks against the new *olim*. This was a complete *volte-face* on the part of the Likud dominated National Unity Government, which had viewed the onset of mass *aliyah* as a welcome media distraction from the ongoing Palestinian *intifada*.[16]

The Jewish Agency, dependent on its ability to raise funds abroad by providing accurate figures on the scale and economic costs of immigration, viewed the imposition of censorship as an unwarranted development that could only add to an already overstretched budget. None the less, Shamir remained impervious to the demand of Simcha Dinitz that the censorship ruling be lifted.[17]

In spite of this, the Jewish Agency continued to release general figures detailing the growing pace in the exodus of Soviet Jewry. Indeed, following the disclosure of approximate figures for Soviet Jewish emigration to Israel in the *New York Times*, the military censors quietly allowed Shamir's ruling to fall into disuse.[18] In September 1990, Uri Gordon revealed that 17,500 Soviet Jews had migrated to Israel throughout August, the highest monthly total for 39 years. By the end of that year, with Soviet immigration having reached a total of 185,000, Dinitz announced that some 1.2 million Soviet Jews now held valid visas for Israel. Clearly, the Jewish Agency had exceeded its immediate financial ability to cope with the growing pace of 'Operation Exodus'.[19]

Therefore, if the agency was to fufil its main role – furnishing the necessary logistical support required for mass migration – the scope of its mandate had to be reduced. In March 1991, the board of the Jewish Agency approved a plan turning the grant given by the organization to new *olim* as part of the policy of direct absorption, into a loan repayable over ten years. Even this proved controversial, with Gordon arguing that such benefits be withdrawn altogether, allowing the agency to focus more resources on simply facilitating *aliyah* from the Soviet Union.[20]

The agency was, however, forced to abandon several other projects throughout Israel much to the ire of Shamir as it struggled to finance mass migration. It transferred all social service responsibilities it had previously undertaken in Israel's cities and development towns amongst new *olim* to local municipal control. This infuriated government officials who had little alternative but to increase funding to such councils from an already overburdened state budget. Futhermore, many cited the agency's insistence on continuing to duplicate services already run by the Ministry for Immigration and Absorption – *ulpanim*, retraining courses, and information centres – for new *olim*, as evidence of the bureaucratic dogmatism and financial inefficiency that plagued the organization.[21]

While an element of truth existed in such criticism – the agency clearly rejected a purely external role – the duplication of services was more an indictment of the *aliyah* cabinet's failure to adopt and enforce an integrated absorption strategy. Nowhere was this more evident than in the economic challenge facing Israel, culminating in the political struggle with Washington over the loan guarantees.[22]

Financing Immigration and Absorption
On 29 January 1990, Shimon Peres, the Labour alignment leader and Finance Minister within the Likud-dominated government of national unity, announced that for the financial year 1990–91, one billion New Israeli Shekels (US$1 = NIS2) were being allocated to the funding of immigration. This figure, double that of 1989–90, was based on the arrival of some 40,000 *olim*. Yet with the pace of immigration exceeding most forecasts, officials at the Israeli treasury admitted that increasing the Israeli budget deficit above the projected NIS3.8 billion for the coming fiscal year remained the only choice if increased numbers of migrants were to be catered for.[23]

Peres was somewhat limited in the immediate options available for raising additional revenue to finance absorption. Servicing of the national debt and Israel's defence spending already accounted for some 58 per cent of the NIS64 billion budget for 1990-91. Yet he was reluctant to impose increases in direct taxation, given the cross-party support within the cabinet for moves to liberalize Israel's closed economy. Such action would have curtailed the private sector growth necessary to alleviate an unemployment rate that stood at nine per cent even before the immigrants had begun to compete in the labour market. This clearly limited the scope of any accommodational strategy that the government could impose on Israeli society in its attempts domestically to fund immigrant absorption.[24]

The immediate response of Peres was to authorize a six per cent devaluation of the shekel in February 1990, a clear attempt to promote an export-driven expansion of the economy, while increasing value-added tax by one percentage point to 16 per cent. Yet as Michael Bruno, governor of Israel's central bank, readily admitted:

> Economic uncertainty is greater now than at any other time I remember. Currently, about 5,000 (immigrants) are arriving each month, but the figure is predicted to climb to 19,000 taking the total for this year to 230,000. The changing estimates have raised concerns that Israel, facing the Palestinian uprising and a growing shortage of housing and jobs, will be unable to cope with the influx. If the latest estimate is correct, the government will have to raise up to NIS10 billion.[25]

Concern for the stability of the Israeli economy was further voiced by the International Monetary Fund, which urged either a further devaluation of the shekel, or a complete liberalization of the Jewish State's capital and labour markets if Israel were successfully to absorb the wave of immigrants. This would have meant a sharp reduction in state subsidies given to government corporations including El Al, Israel Chemicals, and Israel Aircraft Industries, as well as to companies affiliated to the Histadrut trade union federation. The accompanying job losses such action would have entailed, coupled with fears of widespread industrial unrest if such stringent measures were enforced, prevented serious discussion of such measures within the National Unity Government.[26]

However, the government had already decided in 1989 that the private sector should play a greater role in the process of absorption. This was to be accomplished through 'direct absorption', a measure driven by both financial and social considerations. Even before estimates for the number of expected immigrants began to be revised upwards, it was clear that Israel's absorption centres lacked sufficient capacity to cope with the influx. Short of constructing additional centres, an option fraught with the difficulty of matching supply to an uncertain demand, the only alternative lay in reliance upon private sector accommodation. In theory at least, this strategy appeared prudent. It allowed a free housing market to adjust to and absorb the fluctuations in immigrant numbers, thereby absolving the government from incurring extra financial expenditure. Although small groups of *olim* with special needs continued to be placed in absorption centres, the majority, already displaying a high level of socio-economic acculturation, immediately entered the housing market.

Until July 1990, each immigrant family received a joint grant from the Immigrant Absorption Ministry and Jewish Agency on arrival in Israel. The grant, dependent on family size and payable in monthly instalments, was designed to cover the costs of living in Israel for the first year, while immigrants adjusted to their new environment. However, the sheer volume of *aliyah*, coupled with easy access to large sums of money throughout the housing market, resulted in rents more than doubling in the first six months of 1990 alone. Undoubtedly, part of the problem arose from property owners exploiting the immediate situation, but the clear tendency for the *olim* to gravitate towards towns and cities along the coastal plain in search of employment only served to exacerbate the problem.[27]

With the collapse of the National Unity government in March 1990, no decisive action could be taken to ameliorate the glaring distortions in the housing market, already reminiscent of the similar crisis that faced Golda Meir in the 1970s. Not until Shamir succeeded in forming a new Likud-led coalition in June 1990 was the problem addressed. On 1 July, it was announced that funding for new immigrants would take the form of an 'absorption basket', which, for a family of three amounted to $10,000. A quarter of this sum was given on arrival in Israel with the rest presented in monthly cheques. The basket also included generous tax breaks on consumer durables, free health insurance and favourable mortgage rates. Although in receipt of the same benefits, it was hoped that the new system would force *olim* to 'economise as much as possible on rent, so as to have more money left for other purposes'.[28]

With 40,500 Soviet immigrants having made *aliyah* in the first five months of 1990, it was clear that the original absorption budget of NIS 1 billion was insufficient. Not only was pressure on the absorption basket expected to increase, but it had become clear that the private sector alone could not meet the national demand for housing created by Soviet immigration. Already, the government had approved plans to construct 70,000 housing units for immigrants, a move that forced a clear revision of the original absorption budget.[29]

This was condoned by the new *aliyah* cabinet following Shamir's successful formation of a Likud-led coalition government – the most right-wing to date in Israel's history – on 11 June 1990. Nine days later, a new absorption budget totalling $2.3 billion and based on the need to absorb 150,000 immigrants for the year was approved. Of this $1.4 billion was set aside to pay for the 70,000 housing units, although one source suggested that such large-scale construction would require at least $4 billion.[30] By September 1990, over 100,000 Soviet Jews had migrated to Israel, forcing government officials once more to revise expenditure plans in line with the increased volume in *aliyah*. The initial ceiling of 150,000 immigrants for 1990 was revised upwards by a further 100,000, requiring expenditure on absorption activities of some $22 billion – half of Israel's gross national product – if the perceived needs of the *olim* were to be successfully met.[31] But given the high level of defence expenditure and the continuing need to service the national debt, additional revenue had to be raised without negating growth in the economy or fuelling an inflation rate already approaching 20 per cent. Clearly, hopes of funding absorption through an accommodational strategy had proven beyond the immediate resource capability of Israel's existing economic infrastructure.

Immediate consideration was given to the wholesale privatization of state-owned companies in what amounted to pursuit of a restructural strategy. It was hoped this would allow the government to appropriate the revenue raised from privatization and direct it towards the funding of immigrant absorption. This strategy, however, carried inherent political risks, not least the threat of large-scale unemployment among blue collar workers as companies, previously used to substantial government subsidies, struggled to compete in a free market. Government ministers were all too aware that the social costs of embracing the free market would fall mainly upon the Oriental Jewish community, traditionally the bedrock of Likud Party support. Clearly, societal constraints were apparent in deciding the efficacy of a restructural strategy in coping with this *aliyah*. Therefore, while advocating the liberalization of Israel's foreign currency and capital markets to attract overseas investment, Yitzhak Moda'i stopped short of fully embracing free market economics as the panacea to financing Soviet Jewish immigration. Instead, the Likud cabinet sought to increase domestic revenue by imposing 16 per cent value added tax (VAT) on selected foodstuffs; removing subsidies on bread and reducing those on chicken and margarine; a 20 per cent tax on savings accounts, insurance policies, and pension plans; plus imposition of a new 15 per cent tax upon the tourist industry.[32]

By October 1990, it was becoming clear that the financial challenge presented by Soviet immigration was having a fractious effect amongst the composite members of the *aliyah* cabinet. Absorption Minister Yitzhak Peretz charged Moda'i with undermining his plans for integrating new *olim* into the Israeli work force, following the refusal by the Finance Ministry to allocate $12.5 million for new immigrants to start their own businesses. Given the modest sum involved, the Finance Minister's refusal to countenance the project appeared hard to understand, particularly as Moda'i concurrently announced the need to build 250,000 new homes and create 500,000 new jobs 'in the next few years given the present level of *aliyah*'.[33]

Instead, the Likud cabinet sought to boost employment by the simple expedient of reducing the number of work permits issued to Palestinian Arabs, a measure designed to produce a gradual dependency on Jewish labour and create 60,000 vacancies at little or no extra cost to the government.[34] Nevertheless, having eschewed reliance upon privatization as the primary means of both funding construction and creating employment, Moda'i was forced to adopt plans that appeared incongruous with stated Likud party policy: a reduction in defence expenditure for the fiscal year 1991 and increased co-operation with the Labour dominated Histadrut.

The budget presented by Moda'i envisaged government expenditure of some NIS66.47 billion ($33 billion) for the year, with NIS12.3 billion earmarked for the absorption of 300,000 new immigrants. This figure, double the total for 1990, necessitated a three per cent cut in defence expenditure, a move that angered the IDF high command since it adversely affected the research and development of the 'Arrow' anti-ballistic missile system, a project designed to negate any future Arab missile attacks upon the Jewish State.[35]

However, faced with growing unemployment levels amongst both Israelis and new immigrants and with the acute shortage of available housing, Moda'i had little option but to increase the absorption budget. Moreover, reliance upon the Histadrut to offset mass unemployment now overcame the entrenched ideological antipathy in which the organization was traditionally held by the Likud. Although the Histadrut was a legacy of the historical affiliation between the workers' movement and the Labour party, the Likud nevertheless recognized that as the largest employer within the economy, the Histadrut was best placed to both help, and hinder, the immediate task of absorption. Consequently, the agreement reached with Histadrut President Yisrael Kessar, in May 1991, allowed for the creation of 'thousands' of new jobs through infrastructure projects directed by Histadrut-owned construction companies.[36]

By August 1991, however, 160,000 Israelis and *olim* were registered as unemployed, representing ten per cent of the workforce. Clearly, attempts to raise sufficient internal revenue to meet the social and economic demands placed upon Israeli society by Soviet *aliyah* had faltered, belying Shamir's pledge to 'break conventions and adopt changes'. The problems stemmed in part from the sheer volume of immigration in so short a period of time, undermining the political will to introduce economic reform lest this provoke industrial unrest throughout the Jewish State. Yet Israel still expected one million Soviet Jewish immigrants to have arrived by 1995, requiring the economy to create 600,000 vacancies, 150,000 of these for native Israelis alone. According to Arnon Gafni, a former President of the Bank of Israel, this required an investment of some $25 billion over a four-year period. This sum could only be realized domestically through an increase in the level of direct taxation, an unpopular measure likely to negate both economic growth and employment opportunities in the private sector. Therefore, the only viable alternative lay in massive borrowing on the international money markets, the third strategy according to Michael Barnett's model and a measure Gafni freely admitted was fraught with difficulty:

> The amounts we need are far higher than anything we have raised before. They will be hard to get for three different reasons: the competition for financial resources we face from others in need, such as Eastern Europe and East Germany; the growing caution exercised by Western banks following the huge losses they have suffered in the international arena; and the uncertainty over the size of the immigration wave and the growth rate it will fuel.[37]

To these reasons should be added a fourth: the growing realization that Likud's continued settlement of the Occupied Territories was incompatible with Washington's new Middle East agenda following the removal of Moscow as an overt military and ideological threat. Indeed, the seismic changes wrought by Gorbachev's attempts to reform the Soviet political system proved to be a double-edged sword for Israel. While reaping the immediate demographic reward presented by this transnational flow of people to Israel, the Likud government was unable to mobilize the Israeli economy to meet the financial challenges presented by the growing volume of Soviet *aliyah*. The subsequent attempts to realize additional funds from the United States clearly illustrated the disparity in foreign policy objectives between Washington and Tel-Aviv, a disparity that eventually forced the Likud coalition government to choose between ideological orthodoxy and economic expediency.

Israel, the United States, and the Loan Guarantees
The limitations upon Israel's ability to finance mass migration were acknowledged at an early stage by Shimon Peres. In the Autumn of 1989, while still Finance Minister in the Government of National Unity, Peres had appealed for support from the United States Congress in backing an Israeli bid for $400 million in housing loan guarantees. Loan guarantees in themselves did not constitute direct aid yet they allowed the recipient nation to borrow money from commercial banks at preferential rates of interest. In presenting the request before a Congressional committee, Peres admitted that housing would be built for new immigrants in the Occupied Territories.[38]

This statement of intent was clearly at odds with the policy of United States Secretary of State, James Baker, who, in an address before the powerful American Israel Public Affairs Committee (AIPAC) in May 1989, called on Israel to 'lay aside, once and for all, the unrealistic vision of a Greater Israel'.[39] That Washington was openly able to challenge the core precept of Likud's political doctrine was clear testimony to the changed international and regional environments concurrent with the demise of the bipolar system. As one commentator noted:

> The end of the cold war [also] shattered the political marriage between the American neo-conservatives with their messianic cold war agenda, and the Likud government with its vision of Greater Israel. It had been these partners that had successfully pressed upon Washington and Jerusalem the 'strategic alliance' idea.[40]

With the removal of regional superpower rivalries, the ideological veil under which settlement activity had been tacitly condoned during the Reagan presidency was dropped, heralding a dependency relationship in which the financial aid required to absorb the Soviet *aliyah* was increasingly used by the United States to exact political concessions from Tel-Aviv. Direct US aid to the Jewish State at the beginning of 1990 stood at some $3 billion per annum sanctioned by Congress. However, Israel was also the recipient of indirect aid or grants that were not based on laws passed by Congress. These grants included money already earmarked for the absorption of Soviet Jews as well as a further $180 million in strategic co-operation between the two nations for the development of advanced weapons technologies. By March 1990, Israel's total debt to Washington stood at $11 billion. This dependence upon American largesse had already been challenged by Republican Senator Robert Dole, who had proposed a five per cent reduction in aid to Tel-Aviv, allowing money to be released for redevelopment programmes in Eastern Europe.[41]

The link that the Bush Administration now made between granting the $400 million in loan guarantees and continued settlement activity in the Occupied Territories became clear during the presentation of the loan guarantee bill before Congress. On 1 March 1990, speaking before the House Subcommitee on foreign aid appropriations, James Baker raised the issue of 'fundibility' – the belief that such aid could release other funds for construction activity in the territories – if the loans were approved. The US Secretary of State went on to add that the President would only approve Israel's request once it had received clear assurances from Tel-Aviv regarding a freeze on all settlement activity.[42]

The position taken by the Bush Administration was a clear riposte to Shamir's 'Greater Israel' speech, an address that clearly undermined ongoing attempts by Baker to convene a regional peace conference that included Palestinian representation. Indeed, the President's proclamation of 3 March, opposing settlement construction in all the Occupied Territories including East Jerusalem provoked a sharp response from Shamir. Reaffirming the view that all Jerusalem – including the east of the city captured in 1967 – remained the sovereign capital of the Jewish State, Shamir declared that he wanted as many Soviet immigrants to settle in East Jerusalem as possible.[43]

The clear dissonance between Washington and Tel-Aviv regarding the loan guarantees rapidly exposed cleavages within the National Unity Government. Labour Party leader and Finance Minister Shimon Peres remained amenable to an American framework for an Israeli–Palestinian dialogue, a process in which Peres supported the participation of Palestinian representatives from East Jerusalem. The Likud rejected this outright, believing that any such representation from the Eastern half of the city enforced Palestinian claims to *Al-Quds* (East Jerusalem) as capital of an independent Palestinian entity, a position anathema to the conceptual basis of Likud ideology.

On 15 March 1990, the Government of National Unity collapsed, unable to reconcile the competing positions of Peres and Shamir. The ensuing battle of political attrition that marked both leaders' attempts to form a stable government resulted in the issue of loan guarantees remaining unresolved, despite the growing volume of Soviet *olim* and the concomitant economic strains. Yet following the successful formation of a new Likud-led coalition government in June 1990 under Yitzhak Shamir – an arrangement dependent upon the support of the Tehiya, Tsomet, and later Moledet parties, all of which embraced the concept of *Eretz Y'Israel* – the impasse reached between Washington and Tel-Aviv over the loan guarantees appeared set to continue.

However, the Iraqi invasion of Kuwait on 2 August 1990 forced the Bush Administration to adopt a more benign attitude towards Israel's request. Anxious to placate Israel lest it undermine America's attempts to form a broad-based Arab coalition against Baghdad, Washington tacitly accepted continued settlement activity throughout the territories, providing that the guarantees were not used to house new immigrants over the Green Line, including East Jerusalem. In effect, James Baker conceded the issue of fundibility, even though the application of American aid still had to be seen to be politically correct from Washington's perspective.[44]

In a letter written to the US Secretary of State, dated 2 October 1990, the Israeli Foreign Minister, David Levy, pledged not to settle Soviet immigrants in East Jerusalem or the Occupied Territories in return for the loan guarantees. But within the Israeli cabinet, Levy had failed to establish a consensual base regarding the issue of Jerusalem, provoking the Israeli Housing Minister, Ariel Sharon, to announce that construction of 15,000 housing units for the eastern half of the city would begin at once. Faced with the hostility of his own government, Levy retracted the pledges given to Baker on 2 October, declaring on 18 October that the wording of the original letter was incorrect. Levy stated that Israeli assurances regarding the settlement of Soviet Jews, rather than encompassing all the Occupied Territories, applied to 'Judea and Samaria' only, and did not include East Jerusalem.[45]

This volte-face on the part of the Israeli Foreign Minister increased the atrophy in bilateral relations with Washington, coming as it did ten days after the killing of at least 17 Palestinian Arabs on the Temple Mount in Jerusalem. The Bush Administration took immediate diplomatic action, sponsoring a UN Security Council resolution condemning the action taken by Israeli security forces, and recommended the prompt dispatch of a UN mission to investigate the circumstances behind the shootings. Now, with Sharon having raised the ante, Baker made it clear that any such construction was a clear violation of the original letter received from David Levy. Conscious of the heightened symbolism surrounding the status of East Jerusalem and its potential to derail effective action against Saddam Hussein, the United States reaffirmed its view concerning the settlement of Soviet Jews, a position that clearly excluded their direct placement in the eastern half of the city.[46]

Over this issue, the Likud government refused to compromise, regarding submission to the conditions set by Washington for the release of the guarantees as undermining Israel's claim to sovereignty over the whole of the city. That Israel needed the loans urgently was not in doubt. Finance Minister Moda'i, having announced plans to build 'tens of thousands of housing units', then proceeded to admit that initial reliance on the private sector to provide sufficient housing had actually reflected bad planning.[47]

Ironically, it was Iraq's missile attacks on Tel-Aviv and Haifa that allowed Shamir eventual access to the guarantees. Israel accrued significant political capital in Washington following its restrained response to these strikes, thus ensuring the continued stability of the US-led coalition ranged against Baghdad. Under pressure from both Houses of Congress as well as from the intensive lobbying of AIPAC, the Bush Administration eventually released the $400 million at the beginning of March 1991. However, the State Department made it clear that any future Israeli request would be dependent upon receiving precise information on government expenditure on housing and other services in the territories .[48]

This constituted a clear signal to Tel-Aviv: the issue of fundibility would largely dictate the administration's attitude towards any future Israeli petition for immigrant aid. Indeed, on 21 January 1991, barely six days into the air war against Baghdad, Finance Minister Moda'i had been dispatched to Washington in an effort to prise $13 billion from the United States at the conclusion of hostilities: $3 billion in direct compensation for missile damage and $10 billion in loan guarantees for the continued immigration and absorption of Soviet Jewry. This new Israeli request was met with dismay in the White House. In particular, it was deemed insensitive and lacking in gratitude, not least because United States forces were engaged in removing the most potent Arab military threat to the Jewish State. Nevertheless, even though Moda'i was told to present the request at a more opportune moment, the size of Israel's application – meant to fund immigrant absorption over a five-year period – proved ample testament to Israel's inability to self-finance Soviet *aliyah*, and thus its reliance upon an international resource strategy.[49]

Washington now sought to exploit Israel's evident financial dependency upon American largesse, hoping to pressure it into pursuing a more tangible approach towards Middle East peace negotiations. Having enforced UN resolutions against Baghdad, the United States could no longer apply asymmetrical standards regarding Israeli non-compliance of resolutions 242, 338, and 425 if its new found prestige throughout the Middle East were not to be tarnished. Accordingly, Secretary of State James Baker embarked upon a total of eight trips to Israel and its Arab neighbours between March and October 1991 in an effort to convene a Middle East peace conference.

From the start, the Bush Administration made it clear that continued Israeli settlement throughout the Occupied Territories remained the 'biggest obstacle' to peace throughout the region. Therefore, acceptance of Israel's $10 billion request was made conditional upon a total cessation of Israeli settlement construction across the Green Line. Such conditions angered the Shamir government for one main reason: it challenged the whole premise upon which Likud ideology was based, thus presenting the cabinet with a clear choice between the immediate social and economic security of Israelis and immigrants alike, or maintaining and expanding Israeli control throughout the West Bank, Gaza Strip, and Golan Heights. By June 1991, the degree of atrophy in bilateral relations was such that Shamir signalled his marked reluctance to accept any further visits from Secretary Baker.[50]

Despite the explicit stand made by the Bush Administration over this issue, Shamir continued to hope that the loans would indeed be forthcoming without compromising ideological orthodoxy. By arguing that *aliyah* was a humanitarian and not a political issue, many felt that Washington's official endorsement of Soviet Jewish migration dating back to the *détente* period, along with the restrictions imposed upon Soviet Jewish emigration to the United States, would place a moral obligation upon the Bush Administration it could no longer ignore. This was the argument used by both AIPAC and pro-Israeli Congressmen who maintained that the United States should at least uncouple $1 billion of the loan guarantees from the linkage that had been made by the White House.[51]

Thus, contrary to explicit warnings from the US State Department, Israel's ambassador to Washington, Zalman Shoval, submitted his government's request for the $10 billion in loan guarantees on 6 September 1991. At the same time, President Bush stated that he would ask Congress to defer action on the Israeli request for 120 days at which time the planned peace conference in Madrid would be underway. If Congress failed to approve his request, Bush threatened to exercise his presidential veto, a move according to one commentator that was tantamount to a declaration of 'a political war against Israel'. Eleven days later, Baker, increasing the pressure upon Tel-Aviv, let it be known that under no circumstances would the United States release the guarantees until all settlement construction in the Occupied Territories had ceased.[52]

Despite previous warnings from Shoval – the ambassador had already warned Shamir in June that Israel would have to decide between settlements and loan guarantees for immigrant absorption – the Israeli premier was shocked by Washington's stand, not least because Israel had already agreed to attend the Madrid conference. Furthermore, palpable discontent with the Likud government's stand over the guarantees was evident amongst the Israeli populace. One opinion poll suggested that 57 per cent of Israelis were in favour of a freeze on settlement construction if this would release the guarantees. This represented a clear rebuff to the guiding principle of Likud ideology while indicating a growing sense of economic unease associated with the costs of absorbing the Soviet *aliyah*. Clearly, growing numbers of Israelis felt that the state élite was failing to provide a definition of security commensurate with the economic and social needs of society.[53]

None the less, the United States maintained its tough stance against Israel in lieu of any formal acceptance by Tel-Aviv of conditions set by the Bush Administration. Accordingly, two weeks prior to the Madrid conference, Washington rejected outright an Israeli request for a further $200 million in military aid. Consequently, many within the Likud coalition government, as well as extra-parliamentary organizations such as Gush Emunim, called on all Israelis and diaspora Jewry to raise the necessary sums for immigrant absorption, thus severing economic dependence upon Washington and political servitude to its dictates. This only demonstrated that the pursuit of an ideological goal had prejudiced the international resource strategy of the Likud coalition government, forcing it to turn once more to Israeli society for the mobilization of resources deemed necessary to meet the needs of its own agenda. As one leader of Israeli settlement in the Occupied Territories, Israel Harel, noted:

> In our opinion, the main economic effort when it comes to absorbing the immigrants can and must be made by the

citizens of Israel and not by the citizens of the United States. The view of most Israeli opinion makers which is that the State of Israel is incapable of carrying most of this burden, is both untrue and immoral. If the citizens of Israel were called upon by the government with a vision and with ministers, administrators and advisers willing to set a personal example, to join the national effort of immigrant absorption, we could raise far more than the $2 billion per annum that the government is currently trying to borrow.[54]

While it is questionable whether this clarion call for greater economic self-sacrifice carried much weight − aside from the polarized nature of Israel's political scene, no government would condone the drastic reduction in living standards entailed in Harel's proposals − some on the left did share this scepticism over Shamir's need to obtain the guarantees. Sever Plotzker, writing in *Yediot Aharanot* on 13 September 1991, noted the fact that Israel had accumulated $7 billion in foreign currency reserves, largely due to reparations and military aid paid to the Jewish State in the aftermath of the Gulf conflict, as well as money accompanying the mass *aliyah* to Israel. Furthermore, with the rate of immigration lower than forecast for 1991 − just over half of the 300,000 immigrants expected for the year had arrived by the end of September − a budget surplus was predicted for 1992. For Plotzker 'greater budgetary restraint, a modest reduction in living standards, more serious devaluations, incentives for savers, faster privatization, higher taxes, and a small rise in inflation and unemployment', would alleviate any dependency upon the loan guarantees.[55]

Yet given the structure of the Israeli economy, such recommendations remained outside the political remit of the Likud coalition government. In September 1991, Shamir authorised the Histadrut-owned Koor industrial concern, a major employer throughout the Oriental Jewish community, to be subsidized to the tune of $150 million. Unwilling to reform Israel's domestic economic structure, while committed to the concept of *Eretz Y'Israel*, Shamir had no alternative but to pursue an international resource strategy and thus the loan guarantees.

Restricted by its self-imposed ideological straitjacket, the Likud government was unable to accept the conditions laid down by Washington for the release of the loan guarantees. Indeed, under

Housing Minister Sharon, the pace and scope of settlement construction throughout the West Bank increased rapidly following the opening of the Madrid peace conference. This was clearly designed to undermine further negotiations by provoking the territorial sensibilities of the Arab delegations in general, and the Jordanian-Palestinian delegates in particular.[56]

However, considerable friction existed between Sharon and Moda'i over the consistent failure of the Housing Ministry to work within financial parameters set by the Treasury. All new government housing starts required the financial backing of Moda'i following detailed discussion within the *aliyah* cabinet. Faced with the need to derail the Madrid peace process, Sharon exhibited a growing disregard for this bureaucratic mechanism, preferring to gain the necessary finances once construction was in progress.[57] Such practices led to the Housing Ministry exceeding its annual budget for 1991 by some NIS 1.5 million, which together with allegations of bribery and malpractice within the ministry, led Moda'i to submit a complaint concerning its finances to the Israeli Attorney General.[58]

Such fiscal irregularities only added to the growing strain on the Israeli economy. Aware that Israel would not receive the loan guarantees, Moda'i announced that Tel-Aviv had an alternative plan to raise money in the world capital markets, but refused to elaborate further, explaining that he did 'not want to give the Americans an excuse not to give us the loan guarantees'. This rather amorphous statement disguised the belief widely held throughout the Knesset that Israel would have difficulty in raising even $5 billion in loan guarantees itself.[59] Already, Moda'i had approved a report, subsequently appended to Israel's loan guarantee request, detailing Israeli economic needs in the five years between 1992 and 1996. Working on the premise that Israel could expect some 200,000 *olim* per annum over this fixed period, the report concluded that Israel required $26.5 billion to absorb one million immigrants.[60]

Once again, senior public figures called for drastic measures to be taken by the government. On 18 March 1992, Ya'acov Frenkel, Governor of the Bank of Israel, publicly called on the government to change its national priorities, an overt reference to Likud's continued commitment to its ideological ethos over economic necessity. Warming further to this theme, Frenkel stated on 28 May that Shamir's government had failed either to generate sustainable economic growth, or to create enough jobs for both Israelis and immigrants alike. Moreover, the Governor endorsed widespread privatization and concomitant cuts in social welfare and defence spending, a policy designed to attract the inward investment needed if Israel was to cope with mass *aliyah*.[61]

Unable to comply with such recommendations or to acquiesce in American conditions, Tel-Aviv approached foreign commercial banks, most notably in Japan, in an effort to circumvent the restrictions placed on access to the loan guarantees by Washington. The response from Tokyo was unequivocal: Israel was considered a high financial risk and, as such, unattractive to large-scale business investment. In presenting his response, the Japanese Ambassador to Israel stated that 'only after progress was made in the peace process and agreements against double taxation were signed' would such investment be forthcoming.[62]

Such remarks neatly illustrate the dilemma faced by the Likud government. Taxation was an immediate means to raise revenue, but negated the very growth needed to expand the economy and attract overseas investors. Furthermore, domestic political and economic structures precluded effective use of available resources to offset the cost of *aliyah*, compelling reliance upon foreign aid. Access to such aid remained dependent upon compliance with conditions diametrically opposite to stated Likud Party policy. That Shamir chose to condone continued settlement construction, despite an increasing inability to fund such projects, says much about the conceptual efficacy of *Eretz Y'Israel* as the primary objective of Shamir's Likud-led coalition government. The mass exodus of Soviet Jewry as a transnational flow provided a convenient means to achieve this ideological end. Nowhere was this more clearly demonstrated than in the construction programme initiated under the auspices of Housing Minister Ariel Sharon.

Soviet Aliyah, Construction, and the Double Agenda
Since 1977, settlement of the West Bank and its gradual integration into the Jewish State has dominated the Israeli political agenda. The 1982 war in Lebanon had been designed to expedite this process but had resulted in the total failure of Israel to achieve its war aims.[63] The *aliyah* of Soviet Jews, therefore, offered the ruling Likud coalition an alternative means to achieve their objectives. Having received strong warnings from both

Washington and Moscow regarding the direct placement of immigrants into the territories, Shamir's settlement policy had to strike a balance between the external constraints and the internal pressures towards settlement over the Green Line. The failure of Shamir to adhere to the concept of *Eretz Y'Israel* would have undermined his own coalition, but direct placement of Soviet Jews onto the West Bank invited Moscow, already the subject of much Arab vilification, to impose severe restrictions on the exit of its Jewish citizens. Thus, while stating that any Jew had the right to live anywhere within the Land of Israel, Shamir added that there was no overt government policy to settle Jews on the West Bank.[64]

It was, however, hoped that the *aliyah* would create a situation within the Green Line where increasing numbers of Israelis would look to the West Bank to escape the pressures of life along Israel's coastal plain. This scenario explained the continuing reluctance of the Israeli government to sanction large-scale building projects within the Green Line. From the onset of the Soviet *aliyah*, therefore, the new immigrants were viewed as a political means to achieve an ideological end. In practical terms, it mattered little if a Soviet or Israeli Jew settled in the West Bank. But the resulting shift in the population of native Israelis enabled the government of Yitzhak Shamir to dilute any criticism from Western governments and continue the gradual annexation of the West Bank. Thus, construction and settlements remained the focal point of Israeli policy, to the detriment of the social and economic needs of both *olim* and Israelis alike.[65]

In June 1990, Ariel Sharon, as the new Minister for Housing, was invested with the power to co-ordinate the whole of the absorption process. As head of the newly formed *aliyah* cabinet, Sharon was charged with alleviating the immediate housing crisis by co-ordinating the activities of the various ministries charged with absorption. Under this arrangement, Sharon inherited control of the Israel Lands Administration (ILA), an organization responsible for the sale and lease of state land throughout Israel and the Occupied Territories. Announcing the immediate construction of 3,000 housing units before the cabinet in July 1990, the Housing Minister declared his intention to confiscate 'all privately owned land required for the building of immigrant housing, wherever it is required'.[66]

This was seen by one commentator as signalling mass land expropriations from Israel's own Arab citizens since most Israeli land is owned by the state. Arabs who did not flee the new-born Jewish State in the Galilee had managed to retain the rights of private land ownership. In addition to this, Sharon announced plans to import 45,000 mobile prefabricated houses. While ostensibly a short-term solution to the growing overcrowding along the coastal plain, it was pointed out that the very mobility of such housing units would allow whole 'prefab' neighbourhoods to appear overnight on the hills of the West Bank. These provided the 'facts' onto which more permanent structures could be grafted.[67]

Irrespective of the political ramifications of such homes for the Israeli–Palestinian conflict, reliance upon such accommodation served to highlight the failure of Israel's initial dependence on the private sector. However, emergency housing powers granted to Sharon on 1 July 1990 to expedite mass construction projects were revoked by the Israeli High Court 16 days later. The ruling effectively undermined the very *raison d'être* of the *aliyah* cabinet which had been set up to circumvent the cumbersome bureaucracy involved in immigrant absorption. The court's decision stipulated that Sharon, in future, had to formulate building plans in accordance with regular Knesset channels, such as sub-committees on housing and construction, which were subject to cross party scrutiny. Therefore, any hopes that the Likud had of circumventing close inspection of construction patterns in Israel and the Occupied Territories were somewhat curtailed by this judgement.[68]

By November 1990, acute paralysis afflicted efforts to deal with the housing crisis. Construction on less than ten per cent of the 45,000 housing units approved for that financial year had actually been started, while none of the mobile homes ordered by the *aliyah* cabinet as a stopgap measure had yet arrived. Behind this malaise lay the limited financial grants given to new immigrants and in the outdated work practices of Israel's own construction industry. Building contractors were reluctant to engage in large-scale programmes because mortgages offered to *olim* – $37,000 for the coastal plain and $57,000 for the Negev and the Galilee – proved insufficient to pay for new apartments. Furthermore, immigrants were reluctant to buy private accommodation without having acquired full-time employment.[69]

Compounding the situation was the nepotism and inefficiency rife throughout Israel's construction industry. According to a British architectural consultant, Melvin Cohen, standards on building sites were extremely poor:

A tour of local construction sites reveals why Israel's building industry is not meeting the challenge of the Soviet *aliyah*. Most sites are dirty and disorganized and show signs of under mechanization and waste of expensive materials and labour. As a result, construction is slow and inefficient with high costs and low standards of workmanship.[70]

Moreover, the building industry relied predominantly on cheap Palestinian and Arab Israeli labour. The withdrawal of this workforce, either because of the closure of the territories or in Palestinian support for the *intifada*, further inflamed the situation.[71] In response, the *aliyah* cabinet adopted a carrot-and-stick approach towards the building industry in an effort to increase construction activity. The government offered to buy apartments off contractors if after one year they had not been sold, while, concurrently, Sharon issued threats to open up the Israeli housing market to foreign contractors in an effort to accelerate construction activity. Yet, according to Housing Ministry planner Uri Soshani, even the planned 45,000 units would take at least two years to build, by which time the volume of *aliyah* would have exhausted this extra housing capacity.[72]

Far more serious, however, remained widespread allegations that the Housing Ministry was rife with corruption. Rather than promote open competitive bids for government construction work, the ministry allocated contracts on a closed basis, prompting speculation that a building cartel with close ties to members of the ruling state élite was manipulating the *aliyah* as a means to exact maximum profit from the housing crisis.[73] Any challenge to this monopoly proved difficult, as the case of Amutah illustrates.

Unable to finance the mortgages necessary to purchase apartments from the state-owned Amidar construction company, a group of Soviet *olim* pooled their resources to form Amutah (literally meaning protest or protest group), an immigrant housing co-operative established in 1991. By enlisting the help and advice of independent surveyors, contractors, and architects, Amutah calculated that it could build individual housing units at 40 per cent below official government costing estimates.

Yet hopes of building cheap, affordable housing were dashed by the Housing Ministry and Amidar for one main reason: it would signal the demise of a monopoly in which fixed prices yielded large profit margins. With the introduction of free and fair competition, the disparity between cost and profit would have been lost. Accordingly, a process of official subversion of Amutah was instituted. Under Israeli law, all land earmarked by the ILA for development should be subject to competitive tender. However, this due process was denied Amutah as the ILA accepted closed bids only from private contractors or Amidar, thereby denying Amutah the opportunity to compete on the open property market.

Outraged by such policies, Amutah tried to enlist legal aid to challenge this patently illegal practice. However, government officials informed Amutah that legal aid was dependent upon government solicitors fighting its case, clearly a tactic to dilute the strength of the co-operative's argument. None the less, the Likud government, believing that court proceedings would quickly ensue, sanctioned legal aid of some NIS2,000 to each of Amutah's 250 members.

Instead of bringing its case to court, however, Amutah used its legal aid to prove the viability of its project. On land acquired privately outside of Haifa near Kiryat Yam, Amutah constructed a model housing unit for NIS155,000, undercutting Amidar construction costs and demonstrating the viability of its project. This represented a visible challenge to the government-controlled construction apparatus. The Housing Ministry obtained a court order that declared the building project to be illegal since its construction was financed by misappropriated funds. This ruling compelled Amutah to destroy the building, thus removing a potent symbol of the ongoing corruption inherent within the construction industry. Somewhat ironically, the inflated costs levied by Amidar, a state company run in conjunction with the Jewish Agency, only reinforced Israeli dependence upon the loan guarantees, a position that undermined the very concept of Zionism that Housing Minister Ariel Sharon sought to promote.[74]

Doubts surrounding the closed nature of housing construction also extended to the purchase of prefabricated houses. Originally, the Housing Ministry had ordered 5,000 caravans as an immediate response to the housing crisis. However, Sharon disclosed in December 1990 that such structures cost 60 per cent more than was actually budgeted for them, resulting in only 3,500 of the 5,000 approved by cabinet actually being ordered. Furthermore, the Housing Minister announced that some 4,000 extra housing units were needed to meet the present levels of *aliyah*. In deciding to opt for mobile homes, most of which were imported by contractors under licence from the United States, the Housing Ministry dismissed bids from Israeli architects such as Shlomo Gur, who designed cheap wooden structures that could be constructed and assembled in Israel. The damning report issued by Israel's State Comptroller, Miriam Ben-Porat, in May 1992 concerning the Ministry's response to the housing crisis, lent some weight to allegations of financial malpractice between Ministry employees and those contractors involved in importing the mobile homes.[75]

None the less, with 185,000 immigrants having made *aliyah* in 1990, reliance upon mobile homes remained Sharon's preferred option. With NIS800 million set aside for the purchase of such housing for the coming financial year, the Housing Ministry announced that 3,000 caravans had been bought from the United States with a further 30,000 mini-caravans on order. Of these 1,300 would be placed across the Green Line.[76] But in lieu of such projects maturing, the social strain caused by the housing shortage was beginning to tell. In Qatzrin, Upper Nazareth, and Carmiel, development towns in northern Israel, local councils exhausted their capacity to absorb new immigrant families. No new housing was being built in Qatzrin, while in Upper Nazereth 350 families were packed three or four at a time into apartments designed for one. Although it was earmarked for a new housing development, it was calculated that 1,000 families within the municipality would remain homeless. Increasing strain was placed upon other services: schools became overcrowded and water supplies, already a precious commodity in Israel, came under severe strain. Carmiel, a town which had absorbed new families at the rate of five every week since the wave of *aliyah* began, imposed a block on further absorption. Already, 370 Soviet Jews, having completed their *ulpanim*, found themselves unemployed.[77]

Stung by Absorption Minister Peretz that new immigrants would have to be accommodated in makeshift tent encampments, Sharon announced plans to attract 10,000 foreign construction workers, a measure designed to accelerate the number of building starts. The Gulf crisis exposed Israel's reliance upon cheap Palestinian building labour; it was hard for contractors to recruit workers form the territories following their closure by the IDF. As a result, Sharon calculated that the construction industry was working at 20 per cent of its stated capacity.[78]

Sharon's proposal met with fierce resistance from both the Histadrut, concerned at the wider ramifications of wage settlements, and the Ministry for Labour and Social Affairs, a key portfolio within the *aliyah* cabinet. Menachem Porush, a deputy minister at the department, ignoring the 8 months required to train a single construction worker adequately, suggested the placement of new immigrants in tents while they helped to construct their own homes, thus alleviating an ever growing level of unemployment. Faced with such entrenched resistance, Sharon's attempts to circumvent the withdrawal of Palestinian labour came to nought.[79]

Irrespective of the immediate impediments to large-scale construction projects for new *olim*, Likud policy continued to place emphasis on the steady ingestion of the Occupied Territories into *Eretz Y'Israel*. Although the government was circumscribed in openly placing Soviet immigrants across the Green Line, every encouragement was made for Israelis to do so. According to the West Bank Data Base Project (WBDBP) in Jerusalem, special loans and aid were already available for first-time buyers without a home, loans that were biased in favour of settlement in the territories rather than in Israel's development towns. Thus in the West Bank settlement of Ma'aleh Adunim, interest-free loans from the Ministries of Housing and Absorption ranging from $9,750 to $21,600 were readily available, representing on average $2,000 more than comparable loans for settlement within the Green Line.[80]

With increased demand for accommodation in and around Israel's main conurbations, it was hoped that many Israelis – anxious to escape the cramped conditions of the coastal plain but not its proximity – would locate to the West Bank. Between January and September 1990, some 7,000 Israelis moved to 'Judea and Samaria' attracted by the generous subsidies, a visible slackening in the *intifada*, and the perception that Likud would not relinquish control over the territories. Thus a clear correlation existed between the volume of Soviet *aliyah* and plans to attract substantial numbers of Israelis to migrate across the Green Line. Given the continuing pace and scope of immigration, steady expansion of the 90,000 strong Jewish community throughout the West Bank appeared inevitable.[81]

Clear proof of this emerged in March 1991 with the announcement by Sharon that 13,000 new homes would be built in the coming two years. Expanding on this theme, the Housing Minister readily admitted that acceleration of construction activity across the Green Line, despite the housing malaise throughout the rest of Israel, had been prompted by Washington's attempts to promote a Middle East settlement based on the traditional formula of land for peace. Furthermore, evidence existed of plans to place 20 per cent of the caravans, and ten per cent of the mini-caravans, in and around existing settlements throughout the West Bank specifically for the purpose of accommodating Soviet immigrants. According to the Ratz MK, Ran Cohen, the plan, detailed in 'Housing Ministry Comprehensive Report No. 21', represented a *de facto* policy of encouraging both immigrants and Israelis alike to settle in the Occupied Territories.[82] Indeed, the Israeli pledge not to place immigrants beyond the Green Line was, according to Meron Benvenisti, former head of the WBDBP, merely an exercise in diplomatic semantics.

> Arik [Ariel] Sharon laughed his head off when there was all that fuss about the Russians settling in the West Bank – so he gave out the figures: one per cent here, 1.5 per cent there. But it's meaningless. He says he will not direct immigrants to settlements. And he doesn't direct them. If they go, they just go. But what is an immigrant anyway? After a year they're not immigrants but ordinary Israeli citizens. Sharon was born here but David Levy [Israel's Foreign Minister] is an immigrant. And what is a settlement? Ma'ale Adunim, Ariel? [Names of Israeli settlements on the West Bank][83]

The expansion of existing settlements came to mark Sharon's tenure as Housing Minister. Ariel, the second largest settlement on the West Bank, had quickly developed an infrastructure comparable to a medium sized town. It comprised 2,500 houses and with a further 1,000 apartments under construction; a population of 10,000 and growing; a 300 room hotel; and an envisaged university totalling some 1,500 students. Such construction was in violation of both the Hague Convention of 1907 and the Fourth Geneva Convention that prohibits the occupying power from transferring, by whatever means, parts of its civilian population to areas it controls. Yet according to a Galei Zahal (IDF) radio broadcast of March 1991, 'an accelerated development process for the Jewish population in the territories is involved. Nearly all the settlements in the territories have been engulfed in the momentum for some months now'.[84]

Attempts to elicit the exact scale and cost of settlement construction from the Housing Ministry proved to be fruitless. According to Ratz MK Dedi Zucker, a vehement opponent of Israeli settlement beyond the Green Line, Ariel Sharon deliberately gave erroneous figures for the cost of settlement in the Occupied Territories even after 'facts' had been created. No separate budget was kept by the Housing Ministry for construction projects in the territories. Therefore the precise costs to the Israeli taxpayer remained hidden in the overall housing budget. Zucker estimated that, because of this lack of accountability, construction costs for the territories were three times those officially announced by Sharon at the end of March 1991.[85]

The layout and growth of settlements were also far more systematic than the Likud government was willing to admit. Brigadier General Ephraim Sneh, former Israeli military governor of the West Bank, argued that the strategy of the government had been twofold: geographical and political. The geographic objective lay in slicing the area into four mini-cantons, preventing the establishment of any viable Palestinian entity. The increase in population, encouraged by the *aliyah* of Soviet Jewry, would in turn create a strong lobby of Israelis, who for purely economic reasons would wish to maintain control over the territories. With government subsidies available to purchase housing, the Likud would have bought the political allegiance of this new Israeli constituency.[86]

The extent to which Israel envisaged a population explosion on the West Bank was revealed by the Jewish Agency which, announcing an expansion programme for settlements under its jurisdiction, envisaged the Jewish population of the territories expanding to 850,000. However, it was the emergence of the 'Seven Stars Plan' or Stars programme, in addition to ongoing settlement in and around East Jerusalem, that appeared to present the greatest obstacle yet to any negotiated peace settlement between Israel and its Arab neighbours.[87]

The Stars Programme and East Jerusalem
The Stars programme announced by Sharon on 25 October 1990 was the most potent expression of the Revisionist Zionist concept of *Eretz Y'Israel*. The programme called for a line of settlements

along the Green Line, which would stretch from the Latrun enclave up to the Jezreel valley, and through expansion would eventually evolve into a city of 250,000. However, the most important effect of this new construction project was psychological: to break down the 'myth' of the Green Line by building the foundations for these seven new urban areas 50 metres inside the Green Line, but placing the ancillary services and industries just metres across from them on the West Bank. For Israelis, the concept of the Green Line would cease to have any empirical meaning. Work on the infrastructure of the first settlement, at Avney Hafetz, began in August 1991.[88]

Again, the costs of construction were impossible to ascertain. West Bank settlements were totally integrated within the state budget while the housing districts of Tel-Aviv and Jerusalem encompassed building programmes both within and beyond the Green Line. Therefore, Ariel was considered a suburb of Tel-Aviv with the majority of settlers employed, entertained, and cared for by the municipality of Israel's largest city. In October 1991, the foundations were laid for Tzur Yigal, another 'Star' in the programme. At the opening ceremony, Likud Health Minister Ehud Olmert declared that 'in case anybody had any doubts, we must be clear today that since 1967 there has been no Green Line. The Green Line is not the border or the framework of the State of Israel and that has been the national consensus for years'. Yet according to Zucker, the expenditure of some $2 billion on the programme came at the expense of adequate economic and social provision for Soviet immigrants.[89]

While hoping that upwards of 200,000 *olim* would eventually comprise the resident population of the 'Stars' settlements, the Likud government remained concerned at the insufficient numbers drawn towards Jerusalem. Of approximately 83,000 arrivals between January to September 1990, 53 per cent had settled within the municipality of Tel-Aviv; 32 per cent in Haifa and the north, 5 per cent in the Negev and 10 per cent around Jerusalem. According to the Housing Ministry, only 1 per cent of the total *aliyah* had decided to locate directly in the Occupied Territories.[90]

The US State Department was, however, claiming in March 1991 that immigrant settlement over the Green Line was four per cent of total *aliyah*. The disparity in figures was due to the exclusion in Israeli calculations of those *olim* who had settled in

East Jerusalem. According to these figures, 225,000 Israelis had migrated to the Occupied Territories by the beginning of 1991, of whom 100,000 were resident in the West Bank.[91]

Problems in accurately gauging numbers associated with settlement in and around East Jerusalem exacerbated the political dissonance between Washington and Tel-Aviv. Israel had captured and annexed East Jerusalem in 1967 but had failed to elicit recognition of its sovereignty from all Arab and most Western states. To the Palestinians of East Jerusalem it was obvious that the Likud government meant to achieve practical sovereignty through numbers by salami-style tactics: settlements would be established claiming jurisdiction under the municipality of the city which gradually expanded on the West Bank proper. Thus, despite repeated warnings by the Bush Administration to desist from any continued settlement over the Green Line, including East Jerusalem, it was estimated that 120,000 Israelis were resident in the eastern half of the city by the end of 1990. As a transnational flow, Soviet Jews were being used to consolidate Israeli sovereignty over the whole of the city and its immediate environs.[92]

The continued construction of new suburbs was an integral part of the process of creating a Jewish majority throughout the city, thereby usurping any Arab claims to East Jerusalem as part of an independent Palestine. Such construction activity required, according to a report in *Ha'aretz*, the expenditure of NIS two billion over a four-year period and had the 'explicit aim of establishing a *fait accompli* that would make it hard for her [Israel] to enter into a political process at the end of the Gulf war'.[93]

In accordance with such plans, Sharon initiated a large scale road-building programme, able to link large settlements such as Ma'aleh Adunim to Jerusalem and allow the establishment of a 'contiguous demographic strip' that would eventually form a new suburb. To this end, Sharon continued to allocate work to large construction companies, ostensibly to reduce bureaucracy and so speed the construction process. Those firms involved in such work began to receive undisclosed financial renumerations whose total cost remained hidden within the overall housing budget.[94]

The magnitude of Sharon's construction drive – new settlements in Tulkarm, Revava, the Stars programme, as well as the expansion of existing settlements throughout the West Bank,

Gaza Strip and Golan Heights – elicited strong criticism from Yitzhak Mo'dai. Concerned at the deleterious effect such action was having on Israel's loan guarantee request in Washington, the Finance Minister expressed open opposition to the action initiated by Sharon, though not to the legality of Israel's claim to the land west of the River Jordan.[95]

Extracting reliable data from the Likud government regarding Soviet Jewish settlement throughout the territories and East Jerusalem became increasingly problematic. While the Jewish Agency declared that only 275 *olim* had moved to the West Bank and Gaza between April 1989 and July 1990, it readily admitted that 'once they [immigrants] no longer receive monthly absorption allowances from any source, they are free to move without reporting to anyone'.[96] The amorphous nature of gauging the volume of *olim* locating over the Green Line was illustrated by the disclosure by the mayor of Ariel, Ron Nachman, concerning Soviet Jews who had settled there: between February and October 1990, the number of Soviet Jews moving to the settlement had doubled to 900, some 10 per cent of its total population.[97]

The first half of 1990 saw a total of 5,375 immigrants move into Jewish neighbourhoods adjacent to Arab East Jerusalem. By October, however, the disclosure of such precise figures had been curtailed. Insisting that Israeli sovereignty extended over the whole of the city, Shamir declared that the Jewish State had no obligation, legal, moral or otherwise, to justify internal settlement policy to a foreign power.[98] The construction and expansion of the suburbs of Gilo, Ramot, Pisgat Ze'ev, and Neve Ya'acov were a clear attempt to push the issue of Jerusalem beyond diplomatic accountability. Soviet Jewish immigration provided a clear means to accelerate that process.

Yet, expansion of Jewish urban areas throughout East Jerusalem constituted a clear violation of the terms laid down by President Bush, linking appropriation of $10 billion in loan guarantees to a total freeze in settlement construction across Washington's definition of the Green Line. Regarding adherence to such conditions as apostasy, Sharon accelerated the construction of settlements on the West Bank. On 11 September 1991, it was reported that 19,000 housing units – triple the number originally cited to the Knesset for the year – had been built or were presently under construction. Unable to determine the exact scale of construction in the territories from the blanket statistics provided by the Housing Ministry, the civil rights movement Peace Now, adopted the simple expedient of physically counting the number of new units. According to Dedi Zucker, the intensity of such building activity, requiring the investment of NIS2.7 billion, undermined any concerted effort to tackle the growing levels of unemployment among both immigrants and Israelis alike.[99]

Such activity compromised attempts by Moda'i to reach an accommodation with Washington over the loan guarantees and thus conclude a successful international resource strategy. The Finance Minister, unable to adapt the economy to the composite needs of immigration, housing, and employment, had outlined a proposal designed to exact some fiscal support from Washington: if $2 billion was made available over a five-year period, Israel would only draw on the guarantees if 200,000 immigrants arrived per annum. After that period, Israel would accept a phased elimination of all United States aid over the following three years.[100]

Such attempts at establishing a symbiotic understanding were rejected by a Bush Administration only too aware that compromise over an issue in which it had invested large amounts of political capital could derail the nascent Madrid peace process. For Sharon, this represented a collective victory for Arab pressure upon the United States: 'They have made their participation in the peace conference conditional on the deferral of the loan guarantees and the US Administration has capitulated to the Arab demands'.[101]

Irrespective of the Madrid peace talks, however, Shamir clearly announced his intention to sanction continued building in the Occupied Territories. Thus, while Washington had called for a freeze on settlement activity for 120 days, settlement activity continued apace throughout November and December 1991. Moreover, Sharon now called for formal Israeli annexation of the territories captured in 1967, arguing that Israel's attendance at the Madrid negotiations was tantamount to de facto acceptance of Palestinian autonomy in the territories. This would only serve to engender the creation of a Palestinian State and undermine the very concept of *Eretz Y'Israel*. This fear explains the urgency to establish as many 'facts' as possible.[102]

Concomitant with this policy, the budget approved by the Knesset on 2 January 1992 allowed for the provision of NIS200 million for the construction of an additional 5,500 units throughout the Occupied Territories. This budget allocation infuriated Washington. According to State Department spokesman Richard Boucher it was ' hard to understand how a quarter of the housing budget will go to increased housing in the territories when they have many other needs for the money'.[103] This was a veiled reference to the increased strain on Israel as a homogeneous society while it struggled to meet the social and economic problems presented by the Soviet Jewish exodus.

Shamir's endorsement, however reluctant, of the continuing peace talks resulted in the collapse of his coalition government on 19 January 1992. The resignation of Rehavam Ze'evi and Yuval Ne'eman, respectively leaders of the extreme right Moledet and Tehiya parties, was over Israel's participation in a process in which Palestinian autonomy was high on the agenda. This resulted in Shamir's call for a general election, set for 23 June 1992. Realizing that the resignations of Ze'evi and Ne'eman constituted a direct challenge to his own perceived commitment to Revisionist Zionism, the Israeli Prime Minister was quick to signal his intent to continue settlement activity apace, despite 'land for peace' being the central issue of the revived peace process. Speaking at Betar, a settlement south-east of Jerusalem just two days after the cabinet crisis, Shamir loudly proclaimed that 'We see building here and all over Judea and Samaria. This building will continue and no force on earth will halt it'.[104]

Even at this juncture Shamir remained confident that an eventual compromise, forced upon the Bush Administration by AIPAC and pro-Israeli congressmen and senators, would break the impasse over the much needed $10 billion loan guarantees. Such a compromise had been proposed by Senator Patrick Leahy, who suggested that Tel-Aviv receive part of the guarantees. In turn, Washington could reduce the amount in line with the total amount invested by Israel in settlement construction across the Green Line. But while Shamir condoned the proposal – the Lifshitz report had stated that $26.5 billion was needed for immigration over the next five years – it failed to address the central issue of fungibility: the use of US supported loans to underwrite the attainment of *Eretz Y'Israel* through large-scale construction programmes.[105]

While settlements continued to be founded, often, as in the case of Ofarim, initially consisting of 14 caravans, evidence began to emerge that suggested a considerable asymmetry between the numbers of completed units and the number of Israelis choosing to move over the Green Line. In Aley Zahav 'dozens of apartments' remained empty, forcing settlement leaders to launch a sales campaign in a bid to attract the necessary customers.[106] Such disparities indicated the inherent difficulties of dependence upon Soviet Jewish *aliyah* to furnish the intrastate migration needed to justify Likud's economic and ideological investment in the territories.

Hopes that a convocation of competing positions would allow Washington to release part of the $10 billion loan guarantee request proved equally unfounded. Unwilling to comply with the clear linkage set forth by James Baker, the Israeli Defence Minister, Moshe Arens, announced on 17 March 1992 during a visit to the United States that Israel would withdraw its request rather than 'beg or crawl for help'.[107] While continuing to insist that the Bush Administration was effectively denying the Jewish State humanitarian aid it had a moral obligation to provide, the 'Judea and Samaria Council', representing the interests of West Bank settlements, launched a campaign – Operation Heartland – designed to attract 70,000 new settlers to the territories in the space of one year.[108]

In support of the project, a member of the Knesset finance committee, Haim Oren, disclosed that the Likud had condoned a fourfold increase in funding, some $430 million for the rest of the fiscal year, towards the construction of 17,000 new housing units throughout the territories. A further $40 million was to be made available for industrial development contiguous with this planned expansion.[109] While this perhaps represented a defiant political gesture – the Likud party, in the midst of an election campaign, wished to assert clear independence of Washington – the ability to finance construction of such magnitude remained a moot point.

The scale of such proposed investment earned the ire of many municipalities within the State of Israel struggling to cope with the social pressures imposed by mass migration. Shlomo Buchbut, mayor of the northern development town of Ma'alot, claimed that, in total, some NIS4 billion had been spent on settlements across the Green Line, whereas investment proportionate to the social needs of Israelis and *olim* within Israel's pre-1967 border had not been forthcoming.[110]

While it was hoped that mass *aliyah* would provoke increased population movement to the Occupied Territories, the volume of immigrants provided a potent means to dilute the higher Arab birthrate, particularly in the Negev and Galilee, that threatened to usurp the Jewish majority and, by extension, the identity of these regions. Although the flow of immigrants to development towns throughout Israel was encouraged, insufficient account was taken of the accompanying social and economic commitments entailed in such large-scale demographic movement. Thus of 10,000 *olim* who moved to Upper Nazereth between 1990 and 1992, some 50 per cent remained either unemployed or without full-time work. Failure to invest in readily accessible industries for such numbers would, it was felt, herald the exodus of immigrants from the region to the coastal plain, thereby defeating the very objective the government set out to accomplish.[111] Indeed, the emphasis placed by Likud on adhering to ideological orthodoxy rather than promoting the collective economic and social well-being of society, served to alienate growing numbers of Soviet *olim* from the very Zionist ideals that Shamir sought to promote. This failure to understand the nature and characteristics of the mass migration of some 450,000 Soviet Jews between 1989 and 1992 was to prove disastrous for the right wing in Israel.

Conclusion
No Israeli government could have accurately forecast the volume of Jewish migration from the former Soviet Union. Yet the policies pursued by the Likud coalition government did little to assuage growing discontent among both native Israelis and Soviet Jews. This unease resulted from a confluence of factors: the initial reliance upon the free market to provide sufficient accommodation; failure to adjust the structure of the Israeli economy to the needs of *aliyah*; and adherence to an interpretation of Zionism that placed the land above the people.

Diversion of resources from the territories to ease the social dislocation caused by Soviet immigration would not have been enough by itself, but it would have secured much needed financial support from Washington. The failure of the Likud leadership to appreciate the changing nature of the international environment, particularly in the aftermath of the Gulf War, demonstrated the continuing influence of *Eretz Y'Israel* as the ideological prism through which the Likud and its right-wing partners perceived the Middle East. More importantly, given the societal constraints, both economic and political, of a resource strategy located in Israel's domestic milieu, the ideological agenda of Shamir effectively precluded the implementation of an international resource strategy required to meet the needs of immigrant absorption.

Certainly, Israel's attendance at the various rounds of peace talks resulted from the wish to avoid being labelled as an obstacle to peace, rather than from any meaningful desire to relinquish any of the land captured in 1967. Peace for peace, not land for peace, proved to be the proposed Israeli basis for negotiation. However, while the creation of 'facts' did much to erode the concept of the 'Green Line', the timescale required to achieve a substantial increase in Israelis resident in the Occupied Territories fell foul of Washington's new regional security agenda.

The inability of Shamir to formulate an effective resource strategy, and the unwillingness of the Likud coalition government to abandon ideological orthodoxy for the sake of financial expediency, shaped the immediate environment in which the Soviet Jews struggled to establish themselves. This formative experience, in tandem with the profile of this *aliyah*, played a crucial role in changing the political direction of the Jewish State. It raised serious questions regarding communal integration and the relationship between the security conceptions of the state élite and the needs of Israeli society.

NOTES

1. 'Shamir's Address to Knesset Presenting new Government', *BBC-SWB*, ME/0789 A/2, 13 June 1990.
2. Wolf Moskovich, *Rising to the Challenge: Israel and the Absorption of Soviet Jews* (London: Institute of Jewish Affairs, 1990), p.26.
3. The Jewish Agency estimated a total of 230,000 Soviet immigrants for 1990. See 'Immigration to Israel This Year will be Three Times the Expected Figure', *BBC-SWB*, ME/0701 i, 1 March 1990. For the United States estimate of 500,000, see Geoffrey Aronson, 'Soviet Jewish Emigration, the United States, and the Occupied Territories', *Journal of Palestine Studies*, XIX, No.4 (Summer 1990), p.37.
4. Ariel Ben Hanan, 'Takziv Ha' Aliyah Ya'Lay Svevot 4 Billion: Ha'Memshala Itztareich Lakhtzot NIS530 Million', (The *Aliyah* Budget will Rise to Around NIS4 billion; The Government will Have to Cut NIS550 million), *Ha'aretz*, 11 May 1990.
5. 'Israel Reports 150,000 Invitations to Immigrate Sent Monthly to USSR', *BBC-SWB*, ME/0680 A/5, 5 February 1990; Yehuda Ben Meir, 'The Strategic Implications of the Immigration of Soviet Jewry to Israel', in Shlomo Gazit and

Ze'ev Eytan (eds), *The Middle East Military Balance,1990-1* (Tel-Aviv: Jaffee Centre for Strategic Studies, 1992), p.146.
6. 'Shamir's Address to Knesset Presenting New Government', *BBC-SWB*, ME/0789 A/1, 13 June 1990.
7. Adam Keller, op. cit., pp.43-5.
8. '*Aliyah* Activists Attack Remarks by Politicians', *The Jerusalem Post International*, 1 Dec. 1990.
9. 'Sharon Threatens to Halt Building Projects Over Dispute with the Treasury', *BBC-SWB*, ME/1233 A/5, 19 Nov. 1991.
10. Moskovich, op. cit., p.19.
11. Ibid., p.27.
12. Gabriel Sheffer, 'Political Aspects of Jewish Fundraising for Israel', in Gabriel Sheffer (ed.), *Modern Diasporas in International Relations* (London: Croom Helm, 1986), pp.258-93.
13. George E. Gruen, 'Impact of the *Intifada* on American Jews', in Robert O. Freedman (ed.), *The Intifada: Its Impact Upon Israel, the Arab World and the Superpowers* (Florida: University of Florida Press, 1990), p.226.
14. *The Jerusalem Post*, 15 May 1990.
15. Moskovich, op. cit., p.20; Joost R. Hiltermann, 'Settling for War: Soviet Immigration and Israel's Settlement Policy in East Jerusalem', *Journal of Palestine Studies*, Vol. XX, No. 2 (Winter 1991), p.74.
16. Ian Black, 'Israel Censors News of Soviet Influx', *The Guardian*, 3 March 1990.
17. *New York Times*, 15 March 1990.
18. Pnina Lahav, 'The Press and National Security', in Avner Yaniv (ed.), op. cit., p.181.
19. Bill Hutman, 'Security and Economics will Not Stop Soviet Immigrants arriving', *The Jerusalem Post International*, 29 Dec. 1990; *New York Times*, 3 Sept. 1990.
20. Herb Keinon, 'Agency Board Backs Loan Instead of Guarantee', *The Jerusalem Post International*, 2 March 1990.
21. Herb Keinon, 'Immigrants Squalid Hotels Stun MK's', *The Jerusalem Post International*, 6 April 1991.
22. Herb Keinon, Dan Izenberg, and Alisa Odenheimer, 'Unemployment in Some Towns Will Top 20 per cent in 1992', *The Jerusalem Post International*, 7 Dec. 1991.
23. Hugh Carnegy, 'Israel Puts Aside Funds for Soviet Jews', *Financial Times*, 30 Jan. 1990.
24. Hugh Carnegy, 'Soviet Immigrants Put Daunting Strain on Israel's Economy', *Financial Times*, 3 Feb. 1990.
25. Ohad Gozani, 'Israel Economy Drive as Immigration Wave Rises', *The Daily Telegraph*, 2 March 1990.
26. *Financial Times*, 6 March 1990.
27. David Horowitz, 'Soviet Jews Swap Torment for an Uncertain Future', *The Independent*, 1 March 1990.
28. Moskovich, op.cit., p.17; Hiltermann, op. cit., p.73.
29. 'Israeli Cabinet Approves Economic Plan for Absorption of Immigrants', *BBC-SWB*, ME/0765 A/4, 16 May 1990.
30. See the comments of the chairman of the Israeli Contractors Association, Mordechai Yona in *Yediot Aharanot*, 27 June 1990, cited in Moskovich, op. cit., p.27.
31. '*Cent Mille Immigrants Sovietiques Depuis le Debut de l'annee*' (One Hundred Thousand Immigrants Since the Beginning of the Year), *Le Monde*, 13 Sept. 1990.
32. *Financial Times*, 25 July 1990; Moskovich, op.cit., p.28.
33. Herb Keinon and David Rudge, 'A Record 22,000 Immigrants in October', *The Jerusalem Post International*, 10 Nov. 1990.
34. *Financial Times*, 15 Oct 1990.

35. Asher Wallfish, '1991 Budget Blazes Path for Growth', *The Jerusalem Post International*, 5 Jan. 1991.
36. *Financial Times*, 28 May 1991.
37. Arnon Gafni, 'Me Eshalem Et Ha Kleita' (Who will Finance the Absorption of the Immigrants), *Ha'aretz*, 2 June 1991.
38. Aronson, op. cit., p.42.
39. Ibid., p.42.
40. Leon T. Hadar, 'High Noon in Washington: The Shootout over the Loan Guarantees', *Journal of Palestine Studies*, Vol. XXI, No. 2 (Winter 1992), p.77.
41. Shmuel Schnitzer, 'Chai'avim Lilmod Leheot Ble' Artzot Ha'Brit', (We Must Learn to Live Without US Aid) *Ma'ariv*, 19 Jan. 1990.
42. *Washington Post*, 4 March 1990; Hiltermann, op. cit., p.79.
43. *Washington Post*, 6 March 1990.
44. David Makovsky and Allison Kaplan, 'Signs of Truce With Washington over E. Jerusalem Housing Dispute', *The Jerusalem Post International*, 27 Oct. 1990.
45. *New York Times*, 19 Oct. 1990.
46. Hiltermann, op. cit., pp.80–1.
47. Alisa Odenheimer and Larry Derfner, 'Moda'i About Face on Public Housing', *The Jerusalem Post International*, 10 Nov. 1990.
48. Allison Kaplan, 'Housing Loan Guarantees Delayed', *The Jerusalem Post International*, 23 February 1991; Allison Kaplan, Alisa Odenheimer and David Makovsky, 'US Gave Loan Guarantees Without the Facts It Sought', *The Jerusalem Post International*, 2 March 1991; *New York Times*, 21 February 1991.
49. Jeffrey Blankfort, 'Bush Locks Horns with Shamir', *Middle East Report* (Nov.–Dec. 1991), pp.38–9; Peretz Kidron, 'The Sword at Israel's Throat', *Middle East International*, No. 404 (13 Sept. 1991), pp.4–5.
50. *Davar*, 20 June 1991; Ian Black, 'Israel Says Baker Not Welcome', *The Guardian*, 21 June 1991.
51. Martin Walker, 'Israel Risks Losing War for US Goodwill', *The Guardian*, 12 Sept. 1991; 'Shamir Hopes Conditions Attached to Aid Will Be Dropped', *BBC-SWB*, ME/1111 A/9, 29 June 1991.
52. Hadar, op. cit., p.72; *New York Times*, 7 Sept. 1991;
53. 'Israeli Envoy Reproved After Settlement Issue Linked with Aid for Immigrants', *BBC-SWB*, ME/1106 A/6, 24 June 1991; Hanoch and Rafi Smith, 'Most Say Stop Building Settlements to Get US Loans', *The Jerusalem Post International*, 28 Sept. 1991.
54. Israel Harel, 'Aliyah ve Ityashvot Holkhim Yad-be-Yad' (Immigration and Settlement Go Hand in Hand), *Ha'aretz*, 11 Oct. 1991; 'Officials Cited on USA's Rejection of Request for Additional Military Aid', *BBC-SWB*, ME/1197 A/10, 8 Oct. 1991.
55. Elfi Pallis, 'Israel's $10 billion Loan Guarantee: Is It Needed?', *Middle East International*, No. 410 (11 Oct. 1991), p.19.
56. 'Israel Reportedly Unable to Accept US Proposals on Loan Guarantees', *BBC-SWB*, ME/1233 A/6, 27 Jan. 1992; Simon Tisdall and Ian Black, 'Israel Loses Hope of US Loan Deal', *The Guardian*, 18 March 1992.
57. 'Sharon Threatens to Halt Building Projects over Dispute with Treasury', *BBC-SWB*, ME/1233 A/5, 19 Nov. 1991.
58. 'Agreement on Housing Ministry's Budget Deviation but Investigation Continues', *BBC-SWB*, ME/1263 A/19, 24 Dec. 1991.
59. 'Israeli Minister Speaks of Alternative Plan If USA Fails to Provide Guarantees', *BBC-SWB*, ME/1314 A/1, 26 February 1992.
60. 'Official Report Says $26.5 billion Needed for Immigration over Five Years', *BBC-SWB*, ME/1284 A/8, 22 Jan. 1992.
61. 'Bank Governor: National Priorities Need to Change After Loan Guarantees Not

Given', *BBC-SWB*, ME/1334 A/12, 20 March 1992; *Financial Times*, 29 May 1992.
62. 'Japanese Banks Not to Give Any Loan Guarantees Until Progress in Peace Talks', *BBC-SWB*, ME/1405 A/7, 12 June 1992.
63. See Shai Feldman and Heda Rechnitz-Kijner, 'Deception, Consensus and War: Israel in Lebanon', *Jaffee Center for Strategic Studies Paper No. 27* (Tel-Aviv: JCSS, University of Tel-Aviv, 1984).
64. 'Sharon Pledges No *Olim* in Occupied Territories', *BBC-SWB*, 15 May 1990.
65. 'Em Olim Lor Mityashvim ve Shtakhim, Israelim Itzrakho' (Immigrants Don't Move to West Bank but Israelis might Have to), *Ha'aretz*, 14 June 1990.
66. 'Batyim le Olim Ivne al Shetakh Aravi' (Immigrant Housing to be Built on Land of Arab Citizens), *Ha'aretz*, 5 July 1990.
67. Ziva Yariv, 'Ha Tromim Shal Sharon' (Sharon's Mobile Prefabs), *Yediot Aharanot*, 29 June 1990.
68. *New York Times*, 18 July 1990.
69. Abraham Rabinovich, 'Immigrant Housing Fails to Materialize', *The Jerusalem Post International*, 3 Nov. 1990.
70. Melvin Cohen, 'Wanted Now: Builders Who Can Build', *The Jerusalem Post International*, 29 December 1990.
71. Peretz Kidron, 'Knives Make Repression Harder', *Middle East International*, No. 397 (5 April 1991), p.9.
72. Yosef Yaakov, '7,000 Immigrants in a Single Weekend', *The Jerusalem Post International*, 29 Dec. 1990.
73. Bill Hutman and Asher Wallfish, 'Comptroller Blasts Sharon and Misrule by his Aides', *The Jerusalem Post International*, 9 May 1992.
74. Interview with Leonid Kilbert, Netanya, Israel, 3 July 1993. Kilbert, an immigrant from Tashkent is an independent film maker. He produced and directed 'Alphason', a documentary detailing the plight of the Amutah building co-operative. Scheduled to be broadcast by the Israel Broadcast Authority in May 1992, its transmission was postponed because of its political content in the run-up to the Israeli general election. It has yet to be shown to the Israeli public.
75. Interview with Lesya-Shtance Smirnoff, absorption co-ordinator for Ratz(Meretz), Tel-Aviv, 18 Nov. 1992.
76. '200,000 New Immigrants Made Israel Home in 1990', *The Jerusalem Post International*, 5 Jan. 1991.
77. *The Jerusalem Post International*, 3 Nov. 1990. The extra burden that mass immigration would place on Israel's limited water resources was made by Gershon Baskin, 'The West Bank and Israel's Water Crisis', in Gershon Baskin (ed.), 'Water: Conflict or Cooperation', *Israel/Palestine Center for Research and Information*, Vol. II, No. 2 (March 1992), p.5.
78. Bill Hutman, 'Builders Flunking Challenge', *The Jerusalem Post International*, 9 Feb. 1991.
79. Bill Hutman, 'Should We Import Workers?', *The Jerusalem Post International*, 16 March 1991; Bill Hutman, 'Few Requests for Foreign House Builders', *The Jerusalem Post International*, 2 March 1991.
80. Interview with Mayor of Ariel, Ron Nachman, in *Panorama*, BBC-1, 22 June 1992; *New York Times*, 4 March 1990.
81. *Ha'aretz*, 14 June 1990; *New York Times*, 23 Sept. 1990.
82. 'More Jews for Settlements on West Bank', *The Daily Telegraph*, 23 March 1991; Bill Hutman, 'Housing Funds Going to Areas Settlements', *The Jerusalem Post International*, 23 March 1991.
83. Ian Black, 'Rolling Back the Green Line', *The Guardian*, 19 July 1991.
84. 'IDF Radio Reports on Building of Housing in Israeli Occupied Territories', *BBC-SWB*, ME/1015 A/17, 8 March 1991.
85. Interview with MK Dedi Zucker, *File on Four*, BBC Radio 4, 22 Oct. 1991. See also

comments of Knesset members Haim Oron and Dedi Zucker, 'Israel Levniot Batyim be Shtakim be Shovyi Sheqalim 2 Billion', (Israel to Build Housing for NIS 2 Billion in the Territories) *Ha'aretz*, 14 Feb. 1991.
86. Interview with Brig. Gen. (Res) Dr Ephraim Sneh, *File on Four*, BBC Radio 4, 22 Oct. 1991.
87. 'Jewish Population in the Territories of 850,000 Reportedly Envisaged', *BBC-SWB*, ME/1073 A/14, 16 May 1991.
88. Reported in *File on Four*, BBC Radio 4, 22 Oct. 1991; Benjamin Cohen, 'An Insecure Future for Israel's Immigrants', *Middle East International*, No.404 (12 July 1991), p.18; *Wall Street Journal*, 26 Oct. 1990.
89. Jacob Wirtschafter, 'Shamir Breaks Ground for New Town Inside Green Line', *The Jerusalem Post International*, 5 Oct. 1991.
90. Cohen, op. cit., p.18; Hiltermann, op. cit., p.77; Herb Keinon, 'Newest Citizens are Secular', *The Jerusalem Post International*, 3 Nov. 1990.
91. 'Artzot Ha'Brit: Arba Ekhuz Ha Olim Mityashuim Be Shtakhim. Israel: Ruck Ekhuz Ahad', (US: 4 Per Cent of Immigrants Settled in the Territories Israel: Only 1 per cent) *Ha'aretz*, 22 March 1991.
92. Hiltermann, op. cit., p.76. See also Jean François Legrain, 'A Defining Moment: Palestinian Islamic Fundamentalism', in James Piscatori (ed.), *Fundamentalisms and the Gulf Crisis* (Chicago:American Academy of Arts and Sciences, 1991), p.81.
93. *Ha'aretz*, 14 Feb. 1991.
94. 'Israeli Housing Minister Gives Percentage of Immigrants Settled in Territories', *BBC-SWB*, ME/1067 A/6, 9 May 1991; Ian Black,'Sharon Sends in Bulldozers to Build New Barrier to Peace', *The Guardian*, 16 April 1991.
95. 'Finance Minister Opposed to Expedition of Settlement Policy', *BBC-SWB*, ME/1065 A/9, 7 May 1991.
96. Hiltermann, op. cit., p.75.
97. 'Mispar Ha Olim Ha' Mityashvim Be Ariel Hook-Pal' (Number of Immigrant Settlers Doubled in Ariel), *Hadashot*, 26 Oct. 1990.
98. 'Russim Yehudim le Ezor Ha Kavosh Shel Yerushalayim' (Russian Jews Moved into Annexed Part of Jerusalem), *Ha'aretz*, 24 Sept. 1990; 'Shamir lo Imtzor Informatzia al Hityashvot Be Ha Rama ve Yerushalayim le Artzot Ha'Brit' (Shamir Will Not Inform US of Immigrant Settlement in Golan Heights and East Jerusalem), *Ha'aretz*, 14 Oct. 1990.
99. 'Sharon Opens New Neighbourhood in West Bank; Vows Continued Settlement', *BBC-SWB*, ME/1115 A/12, 4 July 1991; 'Israeli Knesset Member Says Building in Territories Triple Reported Level', *BBC-SWB*, ME/1176 A/11, 13 Sept. 1991.
100. *Washington Post*, 26 Nov. 1991. The proposal did not apply to the continuation of US military aid.
101. 'Israel: Sharon Says US Stance on Loan Guarantees a "Danger Signal"', *BBC-SWB*, ME/1176 A/10, 13 Sept. 1991.
102. 'Shamir Tells Settlers that Settlement Activity Will Continue', *BBC-SWB*, ME/1197 A/11, 8 Oct. 1991; 'Shamir Rejects Settlement Freeze Proposal', *BBC-SWB*, ME/1216 A/6, 30 Oct. 1991; 'Sharon Says Israel Needs to Annex Areas Settled by Jews to Offset Autonomy Moves', *BBC-SWB*, ME/1242 A/2, 29 Nov. 1991.
103. David Makovsky and Dan Izenberg, 'US Slams Settlement Funds', *The Jerusalem Post International*, 11 Jan. 1992.
104. Ian Black, 'Shamir Says Settlements Will Continue', *The Guardian*, 21 Jan. 1992.
105. 'Israeli-US Tensions over Wording of UN resolutions and US Loan Guarantees', *BBC-SWB*, ME/1275 i, 11 Jan. 1992.
106. '"Rapid" Rate of Construction of Settlements in Occupied Territories', *BBC-SWB*, ME/1313 A/10, 25 Feb. 1992.
107. David Makovsky and Allison Kaplan, 'Baker Sets Ultimatum: Guarantees or Settlements', *The Jerusalem Post International*, 7 March 1992; Simon Tisdall and

Ian Black, 'Israel Loses Hope of US Loan Deal', *The Guardian*, 18 March 1992.
108. Jon Immanuel, 'Campaign Aims to Attract 70,000 Jews to Areas in 1 year', *The Jerusalem Post International*, 18 April 1992.
109. *Washington Post*, 28 May 1992.
110. Jane Corbin, *Panorama*, BBC1, 22 June 1992.
111. Joel Rebibo, 'Upper Nazareth: A Phoenix Struggles for Rebirth', *The Jerusalem Post International*, 14 March 1992.

5 Absorption of Soviet Jewry: Integration and Dislocation

Mizug galuyot, the successful integration of Jewish immigrant communities into mainstream Israeli society, remained a shared ideal among most Israelis. The means to achieve this ideal, however, remained subject to a number of variables that included the political allegiances of the governing state élite, economic expediency, the composition and nature of the *aliyah*, previous absorption practice, as well as the reaction of composite ethnic groups within Israel.

From the onset of mass immigration in 1989, direct absorption became the preferred method to achieve *mizug galuyot*. A hybrid process born out of free market thinking and the experience of integrating previous waves of *aliyah* – particularly the Soviet immigrants of the 1970s – direct absorption sought to place *olim* with high levels of social acculturation among established communities throughout the Jewish State. By allowing immigrants freedom of settlement it was hoped that alienation from Israeli society could be minimized, while concurrently reducing reliance upon absorption centres that were costly to build and expensive to maintain.

Indeed, experience of Soviet *aliyah* in the 1970s had shown that a dependency culture developed among many *olim* in such centres. Having completed *ulpanim* as well as vocational retraining, many immigrants still exhibited a marked reluctance to compete in the Israeli marketplace independent from the support structures offered by absorption centres.[1] Furthermore, direct absorption appeared to avoid the ethnic and social divisions that had marked the integration of Oriental Jewish communities into an Ashkenazim-dominated Israel between 1948 and 1960.

The hopes placed upon direct absorption were soon to be dashed. The volume of Soviet Jewish immigration soon imposed a severe strain on available accommodation within the pre-1967 borders and, in particular, along Israel's coastal plain. The reliance upon caravan parks to ameliorate the immediate disparity between demand and supply of housing units undermined the conceptual basis of *mizug galuyot*, since such parks were placed outside the physical confines of most Israeli cities.

While the scale of *aliyah* overwhelmed the capacity of the free market to provide sufficient housing and employment within existing population centres, the very nature of the Soviet exodus created cultural and ethnic dissonance that reverberated throughout Israeli society. Unlike the Soviet immigration wave of the 1970s, the *olim* were mostly secular and non-Zionist, and possessed a high level of educational achievement. One intake of 23,000 immigrants at the beginning of 1990 included 11,300 engineers, 2,000 scientists, and 2,600 doctors.[2]

Such a mass profile quickly exacerbated tensions among Israel's disparate interest groups and communities, raising questions concerning the citizenship and loyalty of the Soviet *olim* towards the Jewish State. Aside from increased competition for jobs and housing, many within the Oriental community viewed the Soviet Jews as reinforcing the Ashkenazim dominance of Israeli society, reversing the struggle for equality that marked the development of social patterns and political allegiances for 40 years. Material benefits accorded the new immigrants came to be resented, not least because such treatment appeared incongruous with the apparent absence of Zionist ideals. In short, the new immigrants did not conform to the 'we' identity of the recipient society. However misguided, such sentiments formed the immediate social milieu in which the immigrants had to adapt to their new lives.

This process proved traumatic for scores of Soviet Jews. Able to migrate to Israel under the Law of Return, many found their Jewish credentials challenged by officials from an Absorption Ministry run under the auspices of the ultra-Orthodox Rabbi Yitzhak Peretz. Awarded the portfolio by Shamir as a means to consolidate support from the religious parties for his coalition government, Peretz concerned himself with religious questions regarding Jewish identity rather than the more immediate concerns of housing and employment. The Absorption Minister used his office to portray Israel as a theocratic state to the Soviet *olim*, an interpretation that belied the secular nature of Israeli society.

Such practices proved largely anathema to a community whose

adherence to Jewish customs, laws, and religion had been eroded by decades of official Soviet repression. Indeed, where the Georgian Jews in the 1970s had problems adapting to the secular norms of Israeli society, this wave of *aliyah* faced problems precisely because Israeli society appeared too theocratic. Unable to comprehend fully a political system that prohibited the operation of public transport on Shabbat, many Soviet immigrants, particularly those living in caravan parks and isolated development towns, experienced introversion. This only increased their sense of isolation from the Israeli populace in general, leading many of the *olim* to adopt disparaging attitudes towards the diverse cultural traditions practised throughout the Jewish State.

For a small minority, the sum experience of life in Israel proved too much, resulting in attempts to migrate to Europe and South Africa. These *yordim*, though small in number, did attract critical attention to an absorption process that singularly failed to meet the ideal of *mizug galuyot*. But for the majority, adapting to the pluralism of the Jewish State remained their only viable option. Despite the physical rejection of one monolithic social system involved in the very act of migration, many had become socially conditioned in the Soviet Union to believe in a single truth able to meet their immediate needs. However naive, such assumptions defined the immediate expectations of the Soviet *olim*. The failure of the Likud coalition government to fulfil such hopes, not least because of its continued ideological commitment to *Eretz Y'Israel*, endowed Soviet Jewry with the demographic potential to change the political landscape of the Jewish State.[3]

The Soviet Olim: A Profile
The motives behind any significant migration of an ethnic group can be both multifarious and complex. None the less, any understanding of such patterns remains dependent upon both 'pull' and 'push' factors: the attraction of a new life outside existing national borders; and the need to escape a perceived threat, however diffuse it may appear to the group or individual.[4]

The push factors behind Soviet Jewish migration were readily identifiable. Increased concern at socio-economic instability, combined with a rise in interstate and ethnic tension throughout the USSR, proved incentive enough for many Jews to leave. Far from restructuring the Soviet economy, *perestroika* and *glasnost* destroyed the conceptual basis of the Soviet Union, and allowed resurgent nationalism to dominate the political agenda. Throughout the constituent republics of the Soviet Union, Jews became increasingly concerned at the strength of indigenous nationalism and overt displays of anti-Semitism that accompanied the rise of national movements.[5]

The most visible proponent of anti-Jewish sentiment in the Soviet Union was Pamyat, a neo-fascist organization which openly blamed Jews for the parlous state of the Soviet economy. While it failed to implement a threatened pogrom against the Russian Jewish community in May 1990, many Jews did receive anonymous telephone calls and notes on doorsteps threatening violence on certain days. Such action, though falling short of outright violence, increased the psychological pressure on a community whose collective consciousness recalled all too vividly the pogroms of the nineteenth century. Elsewhere, other Jewish communities were not so lucky. In Audizhan, Uzbekistan, the 5,000 strong Jewish community was attacked. While nobody was killed, women were raped and some 150 privately owned artisans' shops were destroyed. Although physical attacks upon Jews and their property remained the exception rather than the rule, the latent fear of anti-Semitism proved crucial in the decision to emigrate. The activities of groups such as Pamyat were welcomed by some on the right wing in Israel, who believed that the Jewish State could only be a net beneficiary of any rise in anti-Semitic prejudice throughout the USSR.[6]

The momentum behind the initial stages of migration was maintained, and often increased, by the activities of the Jewish Agency's *shlichim*, Israelis who helped expedite the emigration of Jews throughout the Soviet diaspora to the Jewish State. Their activities, however, came to be criticized within Israel once the magnitude of the social and economic burden facing Israeli society came to be realized. *Shlichim* were accused of inflating both the real threat posed by anti-Semitism within the Soviet Union, and the material benefits to be had in Israel once an immigrant had made *aliyah*. According to one journalist, prospective emigrants were told 'that work can be found quickly and is abundant, accommodation is no problem, and that they would learn Hebrew with little difficulty'.[7]

Other push factors helped contribute to the growing exodus of Soviet Jewry. Most notable among these was the ecological catastrophe at Chernobyl, the deleterious environmental impact of which contributed to the growing volume of Jews seeking to leave the Ukraine. In 1990, 59,000 Jews emigrated to Israel from the republic, 12,000 of these coming from the capital Kiev alone.[8] None the less, widespread Soviet Jewish fear of civil disorderdid provide the initial momentum from which Israel appeared set to reap the demographic and political rewards.

If the push factors behind Soviet Jewish emigration were readily apparent, pull factors proved harder to define. That migration to Israel reached overwhelming proportions said as much about the imposition of immigration quotas in the West, particularly in the United States, as the efficacy of Zionism as a potent pull factor.[9] Therein lay the distinctive feature of Soviet Jewish immigration between 1989 and 1992: the low level of political affiliation with the ideological basis of the State of Israel. This was in marked contrast to the 191,618 Soviet Jews who had chosen to migrate to Israel between 1965 and 1989 once the opportunity arose. These immigrants proved to be committed Zionists, able and willing to endure the hostility of Moscow in their attempts to reach Israel, while rejecting the lure of the United States.[10]

Yet such Jews proved to be a minority within their own communities. Until *perestroika* and *glasnost* legitimized the open expression of cultural and political activity for Jews throughout the Soviet Union, most Jewish communities, particularly in the major towns of Russia and Ukraine, were denied access to objective information regarding the nature of the Jewish State. Consequently, once restrictions on emigration were eased, Soviet Jewry came to rely upon the *shlichim* for the dissemination of information on both Israel and Zionism. Such information, however well-informed, often proved contradictory to the immediate experience of those who migrated to Israel. This served to exacerbate both a sense of frustration and disillusion towards a state that promised so much and appeared to deliver too little.[11]

Indeed, the very use of the Hebrew term *aliyah* implied a conscious choice on the part of Jews to migrate to Israel for ideological reasons. Yet according to a poll carried out by Public Opinion Research of Israel amongst new Soviet immigrants in October 1990, only five per cent expressed any form of affinity with Zionist ideals. Clearly, adherence to Zionist ideology proved of limited utility in providing the positive impetus or pull factor for the growing numbers of Soviet Jewish emigrants. Thus, as a transnational flow, Soviet Jewish immigration to Israel came to be defined by its involuntary nature. This migration wave did not make *aliyah* for ideological reasons but for purely pragmatic reasons based on the prospect of a new quality of life.[12]

If concern at domestic socio-economic instability provided a potent push factor behind emigration, it also defined the main rationale behind this *aliyah* of Soviet Jewry: the belief that by coming to Israel they could improve their material well-being and social status, while utilizing skills they had gained in the Soviet Union. As the Israeli author Amoz Oz observed:

> Most of them [Soviet Jews] come hoping to find a mini-America in Israel. The sooner they can get a house and a car – preferably two cars – and a good refrigerator full of good food, the sooner they will become solid citizens. They are survivors of the Marxist fantasy. They come here aspiring to a middle class fulfillment.[13]

Such aspirations were a product of the high educational profile that marked this particular wave of Soviet *aliyah*. Amongst new arrivals up to October 1990, 42 per cent had received a higher education. In comparison, the figure for Israelis stood at 8.5 per cent of the population. Simultaneously, it was estimated that some 500 doctors per month made *aliyah* throughout 1990 to a country that already had the best doctor-to-patient ratio in the world: three per 1000 people.[14] By June 1991, there were proportionally 13 times as many architects and engineers amongst the new *olim* as among Israelis, while some 4,000 immigrants were qualified to undertake research or teach in Israel's universities. Only in skilled and unskilled manual labour did Israel possess a proportionate advantage.[15]

Family structure also distinguished this *aliyah* from the recipient society and previous waves of immigrants. Unlike its predecessor of the 1970s, the contemporary migration of Soviet Jewry represented a 'total exodus' since whole families, rather than individuals, could safely negotiate their passage to Israel. The average size of an immediate family was three compared to four throughout the rest of the Jewish State. This, together with the mean average age of 32 for Soviet immigrants – compared with the Israeli figure of 27 – highlighted the divergent roles of gender among the two communities.

Soviet Jewish women tended to have children much later in life, enabling them to pursue a career unfettered by family commitments. According to figures released in August 1990, some 32 per cent of Israeli women considered themselves housewives against a figure of 1.5 per cent for their Soviet Jewish counterparts. The traditional maternal role performed by many women in Israel, particularly among the Orthodox and Oriental communities, proved antithetical to the secular lifestyle experienced by most Jews throughout the Soviet Union. Many hoped to continue careers or find new employment once in Israel. By the end of August 1990, over half of the Soviet *olim* who had made *aliyah* expected to find employment.[16] Given the failure of Shamir's government to reform the structure of Israel's economy, such expectations could not be easily realized.

Employment and Housing
In November 1990, it was announced by the Ministry of Absorption that of some 83,000 Soviet *olim* who had made *aliyah* between January and September of that year, over 85 per cent had chosen to settle in the coastal conurbations, particularly between Ashdod and Netanya. Over 14,000 had settled in Haifa while another 9,000 immigrants had chosen Tel-Aviv.[17] Such demographic settlement reflected the influence of two main factors in the initial settlement of Soviet Jewry: previous urban experience and employment prospects.

Although most of the 'refuseniks' of the 1970s came from the major cities of the USSR, the main corpus of that *aliyah* had been drawn from economically less developed areas such as Uzbekistan and Georgia. By contrast, contemporary emigration from the Soviet Union was distinguished by its high urban profile, a factor clearly reflected in the numbers of *olim* opting to settle in Israel's coastal cities. Many Jews had been part of the Soviet scientific, academic, and intellectual élite. Therefore, for these immigrants cities represented a secure base in which to seek employment compatible with the needs and aspirations of a highly trained and educated work-force.[18]

Even before the onset of mass *aliyah*, Israel already faced a national unemployment rate of eight per cent in 1989, a figure that increased to 10.6 per cent two years later.[19] More significantly for the Soviet immigrants, Israel already had 6,000 graduates registered as unemployed in October 1990. According to David Mena, head of Israel's Employment Service, unemployment was

Integration and Dislocation

particularly high amongst scientific and technical professions, areas in which a substantial proportion of the *aliyah* were qualified. Every vacancy in a physics related appointment attracted some 61 applications from qualified graduates, while similar asymmetries existed with regard to vacancies in mathematics and statistics.[20]

The problem was even more acute in the medical profession. Of the 400,000 immigrants to have arrived in Israel between 1989 and 1992, one in 36 was a doctor. According to Professor Avi Harell, a doctor at the Ichilov Hospital in Tel-Aviv, and a board member of the Council for Soviet Russian Jewry, only a small proportion of these would ever be able to practise medicine. Apart from the high doctor-to-patient ratio already within Israel, Harell pointed to deficiencies in the technical skill and scientific training of Soviet Jewish doctors. By law, any doctor from the Jewish diaspora wishing to practise medicine in Israel has to pass qualifying examinations set by the government. In 1990 alone, some 70 per cent of Soviet *olim* taking these exams failed to meet the required standard. Furthermore, entrance into Israel's medical institutions was inhibited by language difficulties and a marked shortfall in computer skills. Although the government launched various vocational programmes designed to keep those with a medical training within the profession as radiotherapists, physiotherapists, health officers as well as paramedics, the immediate prospects of employment in appropriate positions still remained bleak.[21]

The Likud coalition government was faced with a paradox it was unable to resolve. Although representing an enormous reservoir of academic and scientific potential, the Soviet Jews faced the immediate prospect of either under- or un-employment. Moreover, failure to utilize or preserve these skills for future benefit merely enhanced feelings of discontent and isolation amongst highly qualified immigrants. By the end of 1990, it had already been reported that companies and academic institutions in the United States and Japan had begun to recruit unemployed scientists among the new *olim*.[22]

Increasingly, any hopes that the Soviet immigrants may have entertained of entering the higher echelons of the Israeli job market became subordinate to economic reality. Cases of an ear, throat, and nose specialist forced to work as a tea lady for the Jewish Agency in Jerusalem or engineers and technicians working as supermarket assistants were not uncommon. A walk down Dizengoff Street in Tel-Aviv or Ben Yehuda Street in Jerusalem is rarely unaccompanied by some form of classical performance, often top class, from immigrant musicians unable to find suitable employment in their chosen profession. In economic terms, Israel had no immediate need for this *aliyah*, nor the financial means with which to cope with its incumbent social demands.[23]

By the beginning of 1992, of nearly 400,000 Soviet Jewish immigrants only 50 per cent had found employment. Of these only 20 per cent worked in their chosen professions. Tales of hunger, despair, and even suicide amongst the *olim* became all too common. Landlords often demanded six months rent in advance, a major slice of an immigrant's initial absorption basket that often left families with insufficient funds to cover the costs of basic essentials such as food and fuel. President Chaim Herzog, shocked by the sight of *olim* scavenging for scraps in Tel-Aviv's Carmiel fruit market, called for the establishment of soup kitchens and argued that everyone should have at least one hot meal each day.[24]

Although the scale and pace of *aliyah* exceeded all official expectation – the figure for 1990 and 1991 of 331,894 easily surpassed the total for Soviet immigration between 1965 and 1989 of 191,618 – the inability of the Shamir government to implement structural reform in the Israeli economy produced a marked decrease in the number of Jews leaving the Soviet Union from the middle of 1991 onwards. While account had to be taken of security fears in the aftermath of the Gulf War, Uri Gordon stated that 'sadly we have to admit the facts. We are on the threshold of losing a great opportunity for immigration because of the dire unemployment situation and because of housing problems'.[25]

This situation was amply reflected in a poll conducted by the Tazpit Research Institute that revealed widespread dissatisfaction amongst the new immigrants over the absorption efforts of Israel's municipal and town councils: over 53 per cent replied that local authorities exhibited little interest in concerning themselves with immigrant problems.[26] Such sentiment was unfair on those municipalities charged with helping to facilitate the absorption process but struggling under the burden of government underfunding, a symptom of the government's failure to implement a coherent international resource strategy. The products of a monolithic political environment, Soviet Jewry had enjoyed both social security and full employment in the USSR. Once in Israel, these two certainties were often removed, leading to confusion and disillusion. This simmering discontent was in marked contrast to the *aliyah* of the 1970s. Although facing similar problems of employment and housing, this wave of immigration had been imbued with a deep Zionist commitment, enabling it to connect psychologically with mainstream Israeli society and accept the initial hardships, including, in the case of the Georgian Jews, adaptation to a secular environment, that absorption entailed.[27]

Yet with reliance upon direct absorption and the free market to achieve *mizug galuyot*, there was little beyond providing free *ulpanim* and vocational retraining that municipal authorities could do. Most *olim*, having completed a compulsory six month language course, had to undertake menial labour, often at a salary well below the national minimum wage. Aware that immigrants' ignorance of employment legislation and limited Hebrew led to their exploitation on the labour market, one group of Soviet Jews formed their own self-help association, *Aliyah* 90, or the All Israeli Federation of Public and Professional Organizations of *Olim* from the USSR, was established to help those immigrants suffering economic hardship and unemployment, but particularly exploitation. A former Soviet Jew who emigrated to Israel in the 1970s used his legal training to defend the rights of new *olim*: he successfully filed and won a lawsuit against a Haifa employer who used the immigrants' ignorance of Israeli law to hire and fire labour without the payment of wages.[28]

A similar service was performed by the Histadrut trade union federation. It set up counselling services in most of its regional offices throughout Israel designed to arbitrate in labour disputes involving new Soviet immigrants and employers. While the federation often provided free legal representation for *olim* in such matters, the importance of their work lay in helping the Soviet Jewish community adjust to the free market. The Histadrut represented a centralized structure that could help immigrants regulate their lives in an alien economic milieu. Although keen to embrace the material benefits of the free market, the desire for protection within this system remained strong. As one Histadrut employee remarked, this was not a desire to return to the socialism of their former homeland but for social security within the capitalist system. For many *olim*, the importance of such organizations was magnified by the failure of their preconceived ideas of the Jewish State – often inflated by the activities of *shlichim* – to equate with the reality of their immediate experience of Israel.[29]

The acute shortage in suitable employment not only forced most immigrants to undertake menial work but also encouraged an alarming growth in levels of prostitution among Soviet Jewish women. Within one year of the start of the Soviet exodus, it was estimated that some 15 per cent of all prostitutes in the major coastal cities of Ashdod, Tel-Aviv, and Haifa were recent Soviet immigrants, some in possession of university degrees.[30] Israel had experienced this social phenomenon before, particularly amongst the wave of immigrants who arrived from North Africa during the 1950s. Yet the motives for becoming prostitutes, particularly amongst women in their late teens and early twenties, had as much to do with material expectations in a consumer society as with the imperative of economic survival.

> Whether they're intelligent or not, they have to live. To eat. To wear clothes. And the Russian immigrants have a much bigger problem. They see the abundance there is in the shops today, see how the Israeli women dress, they want to go into the shops to buy but they can't. It hurts. They want to be like everyone else. That's another reason to make money fast.[31]

Not all new Soviet immigrants, however, experienced a sense of disillusion on arrival in Israel. Predominantly from working-class occupations and often between middle age and retirement, these *olim* possessed a lower level of expectation than those with professional qualifications. Many were more sanguine about their futures in Israel, often just grateful that they had some form of accommodation, however basic.[32] Nevertheless, adjustment to the atrophy of unemployment proved particularly difficult for Soviet scientists, engineers, doctors, and other professionals – people who had based their decision to leave the USSR on the premise of gaining access to a new social élite.[33]

The housing crisis provided the most visible example of the social upheaval that accompanied mass *aliyah*. In theory, the policy of direct absorption – the placement of immigrants directly into existing communities – reduced financial dependence on central government funding, while promoting rapid integration of immigrants into their new environment. The paucity of this strategy was revealed in the inability of the private sector to cope with the magnitude of immigration, particularly in the demand for rented accommodation. The tendency of Soviet *olim* to gravitate towards Israel's main cities in pursuit of work soon exhausted the rented sector of the housing market. Furthermore, without the security of full, well-paid employment, few were prepared to undertake the burden of loans and mortgage repayments required to purchase property. Therefore, even though the Likud coalition government had failed to complete any of the promised 45,000 housing units by the end of 1990, most immigrants in any event possessed neither the will nor the means to sustain such an investment.[34]

To this extent, both underemployment and unemployment had a profound effect on the immediate housing crisis faced by the Soviet *olim*. With severe competition and inflated costs in trying to find rented accommodation, new immigrants began to share flats between families and friends. By the end of 1990, it was estimated that 30 per cent of the 185,000 Soviet Jews who had made *aliyah* that year were housed under such arrangements.[35]

With immigration set to rise throughout 1991, Housing Minister Sharon came to rely upon hotels, hostels, and eventually mobile homes to offset the immediate housing crisis. Conditions in many of these places were often cramped with little provision made for sanitary needs. Whole families were forced to share single rooms in hotels, with detrimental effects on health and hygiene usually the concomitant result.[36]

At the end of March 1991, Sharon announced that the *aliyah* cabinet had reached an agreement allowing the settlement of up to 100,000 *olim* on kibbutzim. Although they had always been ready to accept Soviet immigrants from the beginning, two main factors militated against kibbutzim as a means to alleviate the housing crisis: the prevailing attitude of the new immigrants and the ideological bias of the kibbutz movement itself. Traditionally aligned to the Labour movement and left-of-centre parties, most kibbutzim had endured economic crisis, incurring huge losses but unable or unwilling to adapt to new management techniques and technical skills in order to compete with the dominant private sector. Consequently the retention of youth had become particularly problematic for organizations such as the United Kibbutz Movement (UKM). The UKM viewed Soviet *aliyah* as a means to revive the co-operatives, but only 1,600 immigrants had settled in 90 of the country's 270 kibbutzim by the beginning of 1991.[37]

Such low numbers, despite the acute housing shortage, were not totally unexpected. To many immigrants, kibbutzim were too reminiscent of Soviet collective farms – *kolkhozy* – with all their obvious connotations. While the comparison was unfair, it did undermine the appeal of kibbutz life. Despite the increased diversification of some kibbutzim into light and high technology industries, the image of agrarian-based communes proved unattractive to the largely urban *olim*. In addition, while many kibbutzim ran successful *ulpanim* in a concerted effort to attract new members, many kibbutzniks believed that absorption of Soviet Jews would force the acceptance of waged labour, undermining the social, political, and cultural traditions of the kibbutz. This view was reinforced by the knowledge that economics, rather than ideology, had been the prime motive behind this immigration wave. The pursuit of individual material benefit was anathema to the very ethos of the kibbutz movement.[38]

With congestion along the coastal plain compounded by bureaucratic paralysis and inefficient construction methods, greater emphasis was placed on the use of mobile homes to alleviate the immediate housing crisis. Large caravan parks began to appear on the outskirts of most urban areas, but were particularly prominent around the development towns of the Galilee and the Negev. The decision to direct a steady concentration of immigrants to these areas had a separate rationale: it helped allay fears of a demographic asymmetry that would have favoured Israel's Arab, Druze, and Bedouin citizens. Indeed, estimates released in December 1991 showed just over half of the residents in the Galilee, some 51 per cent, were in fact Jewish. The clear strategy was to use this transnational flow of Soviet Jews once more to consolidate Israeli demographic hegemony over these regions.[39]

Yet the movement of increased numbers of Soviet Jews to caravan parks often resulted in complete isolation from mainstream Israeli society. While such parks offered immigrants cheap rented acommodation, they offered little in the way of immediate employment. Thus having completed their *ulpanim*, most immigrants' job prospects remained bleak, since the government continued to rely on the private sector to provide employment that was simply not forthcoming. As a result, these communities became introverted and disillusioned. Unable to interact with Israeli society through the work place, many immigrants, particularly the middle aged and the old, allowed their Hebrew to lapse, resulting in a self-imposed cultural isolation. According to Moshe Lissak, professor of sociology at the Hebrew University, this was in marked contrast to the *aliyah* of the 1970s. These immigrants had wished to become Israelis, whereas their latter day compatriots wished to retain their own existing identity within the wider milieu of the host society.[40]

Unemployment within development towns caused many immigrants to reconsider their position. Upper Nazareth had managed to provide homes for 10,000 Soviet Jews between 1990 and 1992. But over half remained unemployed, contributing to an overall regional jobless rate of 12.8 per cent. With the absorption basket designed to last over three years and subject to consecutive annual reductions in the amount paid to an immigrant family, many *olim* began to consider the viability of relocating to Israel's coastal conurbations in the search for work.[41] The movement of immigrants to development towns and caravan parks without adequate employment opportunities engendered feelings of isolation among many *olim*. This not only denied many of them access to mainstream Israeli society, but undermined the whole rationale underlying direct absorption: *mizug galuyot*. Against this background, Sharon's construction activity on the West Bank continued apace, preventing access to American loan guarantees that could have been used to alleviate the burden of unemployment throughout Israel. In placing priority on the consolidation of an ideological goal, the Likud coalition government was in effect failing to provide a sufficient level of societal security, most notably in adequate employment opportunities, for the Soviet Jews.

These problems were reflected in the marked decline in the levels of *aliyah*. In 1990, 184,602 Soviet Jews emigrated to Israel. For the year up to October 1992, this figure stood at 58,588 as news of the hardships encountered by friends and relatives began to filter back to the constituent republics of the former Soviet Union.[42] Reflecting the old adage which greeted *aliyah* in the 1970s that 'Israelis love immigration but hate immigrants', Yigal Amitai, a journalist with *Ha'aretz* and himself a former Soviet immigrant, argued that *aliyah* had become the sacred cow of Zionism: nobody wanted to touch it but few were prepared to accept the social and economic consequences that it entailed. Yet if housing and employment remained the more mundane issues determining the lives of Soviet *olim*, larger questions concerning the ethnic, religious, and cultural identity of this *aliyah* proved as efficacious in shaping the immediate political perceptions of the Soviet immigrant community.[43]

Soviet Jewish Identity: Acculturation and Alienation
The Israeli author, Amos Elon, stated that he was glad that there was a gap between the 'official' Israel and the 'real' Israel. The former he defined as theocratic and ethnocentric; the latter was democratic, secular, and above all tolerant. The problem for the Soviet Jews was that access to the 'real' Israel was initially dependent upon the Ministries of Interior and Immigrant Absorption, the portfolios of which were held by Rabbis Aryeh Deri and Yitzhak Peretz respectively.[44]

That Peretz and Deri came to be charged with facilitating immigrant absorption was a result of Israel's complicated system of proportional representation. Although this produced a Knesset that accurately reflected the diversity of political opinion throughout the Jewish State, it usually denied the formation of majority governments on the basis of single party support. Therefore, from 1948 onwards, coalition government had become the political norm in Israel. The government presented by Shamir before the Knesset on 11 June 1990 included seven ministers from parties other than the Likud. Of these, five were from either the Orthodox National Religious Party (NRP) or the ultra-Orthodox Sephardi Tora Guardians Party (Shas).[45]

This very structure enabled parties with vested interests to exact concessions from the dominant party over single issues. In return, allegiance was usually secured for the wider political programme of the dominant party. As Asher Arian, professor of political science at Tel-Aviv University noted, this arrangement suited religious parties whose influence in government proved disproportionate to their actual demographic source of support.

> [T]he major plank of political ideology is to have the State of Israel organize its public life in accordance with Jewish religious law, Halacha. This is the overriding concern of both parties; after that, issues of economic policy, the future of the territories, and all other matters with which a political party

concerns itself are addressed. In these parties the religious lobby and the party are synonymous. They have been successful in at least partially creating in Israel a Jewish State that adheres to orthodox rabbinical law. This has been achieved not through an articulate lobby impressing legislators with its vision but by succeeding in the game of coalition politics.[46]

The formation of the Likud coalition government in June 1990 was no exception. Moreover, cabinet positions were allocated on the basis of their direct bearing on Israeli public life, allowing Orthodox views to be distilled through a largely secular society. Zevulun Hammer of the NRP gained the education portfolio, thus safeguarding the interests of religious education throughout Israel's school system. Similarly, the position of Minister of the Interior, usually the preserve of a religious party member, was awarded to Shas Knesset member, Aryeh Deri. The importance of this ministry lay in its ability to determine the civil and religious status of Israelis, powers that were to have a traumatic effect on the lives of so many Soviet immigrants.

The appointment of Shas MK Yitzhak Peretz to the Absorption Ministry portfolio was not, however, without irony. Shas was founded in 1984, following a split with the non-Zionist Ultra-Orthodox *Agudat Y'Israel* over the latter's refusal to endorse the candidature of sufficient rabbis of Oriental origin in the party list. Despite this ethnic schism, Shas remained a non-Zionist party, upholding the belief that the secularism that had marked the development of Zionism served only to impede the return of the Messiah. Consequently, the application of a theological prism through which Shas viewed Israel allowed it to conclude that most of its inhabitants remained in spiritual exile, irrespective of the physical existence of a Jewish State. Yet while considerable antipathy existed in the relationship between Ultra-Orthodox parties and organizations charged with facilitating *aliyah* – the core precept of Zionism – the structure of party politics within Israel forced Shamir into appointing Peretz to his cabinet. This proved a necessary condition if his political agenda was to enjoy Shas party support.[47]

While ostensibly concerned with integrating Soviet *olim* into Israeli society, the parochial mandate adopted by Peretz over the Judaic legitimacy of this *aliyah* undermined still further the hope of achieving *mizug galuyot*. Being predominantly European and secular, the immigrants carried the demographic potential to limit the political power of both Oriental and Orthodox communities within Israel.[48] In an attempt to dilute this potential, the Minister for Immigration and Absorption used his office to challenge the Jewish character of Soviet *aliyah*, and the secularism that dominated the immigrant perceptions of the Jewish State.

In 1950, two years after the declaration of independence, the Knesset passed the 'Law of Return' which enshrined the right of any diaspora Jew to emigrate to Israel. This civil law defined as a Jew anyone who could claim to be born of a Jewish mother, could provide proof that at least one female grandparent was Jewish, or had converted to Judaism. Furthermore, non-Jewish spouses and children of non-Jewish mothers were entitled to reside in Israel. This definition was challenged by the Orthodox religious authorities whose conceptual approach to Jewish identity remained immutable in accordance with Halachic law. Thus, only direct lineage through the mother or conversion to Judaism in accordance with Halachic practice could define who was a Jew. In 1986, Peretz resigned as Interior Minister over the decision by the Israeli High Court to register as a Jew a woman whose conversion to Judaism had been approved by a Reform rabbi in the United States.[49]

Within the parameters allowed under the Law of Return, the Jewish Agency operated a strict regime in determining the legitimacy of a claimant's right to emigrate to Israel. This required prospective Soviet immigrants to present documentation to Agency officials throughout the USSR which would give proof of Jewish identity or connections. Necessary documents included both birth and marriage certificates, and the presentation of internal Soviet passports that listed Jew as comprising the nationality of the holder. Only then would a visa for Israel and subsequent immigrant status be conferred upon the applicant.

Under the stewardship of Aryeh Deri, however, Interior Ministry officials declared many such documents to be insufficient in determining the Jewish identity of many immigrants. While cases of forged documents did arise, it appeared that the Halachic interpretation of immigrant status exercised undue influence over the absorption process. For some Soviet migrants, the withdrawal of Jewish identity had the most serious ramification: the denial of full Israeli citizenship and attendant civil rights.[50]

The volume of immigration, coupled with the evident

dichotomy between the Law of Return and Halachic practice, brought into sharp relief the authenticity of Soviet Jewry and the sagacity behind the Law of Return. With some 57 per cent of Jewish men and 48 per cent of Jewish women estimated in 1990 to be married to non-Jewish spouses throughout the Soviet Union, Michael Kleiner, chairman of the Knesset Committee for Immigration and Absorption, argued on economic grounds alone that Jewish identity under the Law of Return should be more narrowly defined. Under the existing legislation, a potential 3.5 million Soviet citizens possessed the right to make *aliyah*.[51]

Thus, concern at Israel's financial ability to manage large immigration combined with Orthodox fears over the usurpation of religious values and political power. One month after his appointment as Interior Minister, Deri used his office to question openly the character of the immigrants and declared that the new *olim* should provide additional proof of Jewish identity. Such proof included a knowledge of Jewish traditions and religious customs, problematic for a community whose experience of Judaism was severely inhibited by an ideological system imbued with atheism. By application of a strict Halachic definition of Jewish identity, his colleague, Yitzhak Peretz, managed to cause uproar during a visit to Moscow in November 1990. Speaking during the course of the twelve day visit, the Absorption Minister declared the Law of Return to be 'a bad law because it allows large numbers of non-Jews to come to Israel', estimated by Peretz to have totalled some 40 per cent of total *aliyah* to that point.[52]

Although supportive of incremental reform to the Law of Return, Michael Kleiner, refuting the inflated figure cited by Peretz, claimed the true figure for non-Jewish *olim* was nearer three per cent.[53] None the less, the amorphous criteria applied to questions of Jewish identity suited the needs of the ruling Likud coalition government. Amendment to the Law of Return would have created a schism within world Jewry in general and American Jewry in particular. Most of the 5.5 million Jews in the United States belonged to either Liberal Reform or Conservative Jewish congregations, theologically outside the remit of Halachic jurisprudence. To predicate the Law of Return on the dictates of the Halachic position would have effectively disenfranchised many American Jews from the Jewish State. This demand had been made by religious parties in the Israeli general election of 1988 and had been resisted by both the Labour alignment and the Likud party.[54]

With Israel now requiring the political leverage of AIPAC over the issue of loan guarantees, Shamir could not afford to alienate this most important diaspora community by condoning wholesale reform of the Law of Return. Nor, however, could he ignore the concerns of his religious coalition partners if he wished to maintain their allegiance in government. Therefore a policy of benign neglect was adopted towards the religious-political campaign waged by Peretz and Deri among the new immigrants. As one commentator of Soviet Jewish affairs noted, 'Peretz is not interested in more Jews but in pure Jews'. Shamir's decision was expedient given the need to avoid alienating domestic political support, and to maintain the allegiance of an important non-state foreign societal actor.[55]

The strategy behind this campaign represented a concerted attempt to undermine the secular milieu of Israeli society among the new immigrants. Peretz allowed the dissemination of material to new *olim* upon their arrival in Israel which reinterpreted the very basis of Zionist historiography. Pamphlets in Cyrillic were produced, providing erroneous details concerning the religious blessing bestowed upon Israel's Declaration of Independence on 14 May 1948. In fact no rabbi was present during the historic proclamation by David Ben Gurion in Tel-Aviv. Such attempts to impose a religious-cultural hegemony over a largely non-religious *aliyah* drew the ire of many on the centre and left of Israel's political spectrum. Appalled at the gross misrepresentation of historical data at the taxpayers' expense, organizations such as the International Centre for Peace in the Middle East (ICPME) produced similar pamphlets that stressed the secular origins of the Zionist movement over the eschatological interpretations provided by the Ministry for Immigrant Absorption.[56]

Attempts to disabuse immigrants of any secular identity extended to the spheres of housing and education. Access to new *olim* at Ben Gurion airport remained closed to organizations whose prevailing ethos remained opposed to the religious identity which Peretz hoped to imbue throughout this *aliyah*. Representatives of the Soviet Jewry Zionist Forum, headed by former refusenik Nathan Sharansky, were prevented from helping new immigrants through the initial process of registration at the airport. This, despite an initial shortfall in Absorption Ministry officials proficient in Russian. Furthermore, until the direct intervention of Sharon, representatives from the UKM were prohibited from recruiting Kibbutz members among the new arrivals despite the growing magnitude of Israel's housing crisis. Indeed, Peretz proposed that immigrants be housed temporarily in tents, rather than enter an institution whose secular, socialist structure largely precluded religious influence. As a transnational flow, therefore, the migration of Soviet Jewry impacted upon domestic cleavages that had marked the development of Israel since 1948.[57]

The belief that Judaic piety should determine the absorption process extended to the realm of immigrant education. Religious control over the Ministries of the Interior, Education, and Absorption forced *olim* into *ulpanim* run according to Orthodox strictures. All males, regardless of age or religious commitment, were required to wear skullcaps while attending their six month Hebrew language course. Women, in accordance with the sobriety demanded by Orthodox tradition, had to wear long-sleeved dresses. Such *ulpanim* contained a heavy emphasis upon religious instruction as part of the language curriculum, leading Israelis to label this process 'spiritual absorption'.[58]

Yet this process went beyond the norms of religious instruction to include the personification of good and evil, right and wrong. Non-Jews were portrayed as the embodiment of evil or *Amalekh*, a conceptualization that reduced the complexities of indigenous societies to a uniform anti-Jewish prejudice that was all pervasive. Such views, expressed in pamphlets produced for immigrants on the eve of major Jewish holidays, included overt attacks on the prevailing secular social order within Israel. During celebrations to mark the 1991 Passover, the *Haggada* – a collection of traditional stories surrounding the ancient exodus of the Jews from Egypt, and distributed to new immigrants – provided one such attack.

> One of the passages in the *Haggada* is a fable of four types of sons, among them a wise son and an evil son. In the ministry's *Haggada* the illustration of the wise son is of an Orthodox man with a full beard and a large black skullcap, while the evil son, a clean shaven young executive without a hat, is portrayed as a secular Jew.[59]

Yet the effect of such indoctrination remained limited. Immigrants resented the imposition of religious norms that circumscribed any significant role for modernity in defining their new environment. Moreover, the endeavour to mould an image of Israel based on such norms failed to disguise the all too visible materialism that permeated Israeli society. While economic anomie curtailed immediate access to this society, *olim* felt frustrated at the manner in which religious laws impinged on their everyday lives. For them, denial of public transportation on the sabbath was indicative of an overbearing theocratic influence throughout Israeli society, a situation entirely at odds with their secular upbringing in the former Soviet Union.[60]

Although constituting a minor inconvenience for Israelis, the withdrawal of transport, particularly among those living in caravan parks, only heightened feelings of isolation from the rest of Israeli society. Indeed, the inability to explore their immediate environs on the one free day of the Jewish week meant that a tangible appreciation of Israel's history, culture, and heritage remained outside their limited experience of the Jewish State. The ironic, but somewhat bitter refrain, 'Prisoners of Zion', proved an apt summation of the situation as perceived by many *olim* housed in hastily constructed caravan parks.[61]

The sense of isolation was further compounded for many families by the ambiguity surrounding their exact legal status. Control over the Interior Ministry enabled Aryeh Deri to impose Halachic legal definitions by which immigrants were entitled to be considered as both Jewish and Israeli. On the immigrants' arrival in Israel, Interior Ministry officials were required to register religion and nationality on the basis of documentation that had usually been authenticated by the Jewish Agency. The term Jew was perceived as synonymous with both but only under a Halachic interpretation. Thus a child, entitled to make *aliyah* under the Law of Return if the father alone was Jewish, could not qualify as a Jew, only as an Israeli without religious or civil status.

Only through Halachic conversion could full rights be conferred upon such immigrants, a traumatic process because most immigrants defined being Jewish in terms of race alone, rather than by religious belief or affiliation. In some cases, the Interior Ministry was forced to revoke previous decisions withholding immigrant status, following submissions from lawyers working on behalf of Soviet *olim*. One such lawyer, Marina Heifetz, herself a former Soviet immigrant, used her affiliation to the Israeli civil rights party Ratz as the platform from which to make such representations. Although appeals on an individual basis were upheld, Heifetz believed that the problem of citizenship could only be resolved by a written constitution which enshrined the rights and status of new immigrants according to civil law. Her work did, however, represent a limited success for Soviet Jews in challenging the declared policy of representatives of the state hierarchy.[62]

Yet if the application of Halachic law determined the identity of the *olim*, it also placed restrictions on marriage and divorce. Israel has no civil marriage or divorce procedures that govern relations between Jews. All such matters within the jurisdiction of the Jewish State are dealt with by Orthodox Rabbinical Courts. Therefore, only couples deemed Jewish under Halachic law can be married in Israel. Those unable to meet such conditions, for example, marriage between a Jewish woman and a non-Jewish husband, have to travel overseas, even though this marriage is then accorded legal recognition by the civil courts once the couple return to Israel.[63]

Such strictures produced problems for many *olim* particularly in the area of divorce. One female immigrant, previously divorced in the Soviet Union, found her attempt to remarry blocked by the Rabbinical Court. They ruled that because her divorce had not legitimately been carried out under the auspices of a Rabbinical Court – only civil marriage and divorce existed in the USSR – she was still technically married. Furthermore, even if she went overseas to marry, under religious law any child conceived as a result of this union would always be considered a bastard.[64]

Although cases involving civil status had often appeared before the Orthodox religious authorities, the mass influx of Soviet Jewry brought to a head the anomalies that existed between civil and religious law in Israel. Pressure began to mount for reform of the judicial system that would separate church from state, allowing the civil definition of who was a Jew to be legally binding on all authorities. A leading proponent of such reform was the Labour MK Avraham Burg, himself an Orthodox Jew. During the 1991 Labour party conference, Burg campaigned for the clear separation of church from state to be incorporated as part of the Labour manifesto agenda for the 1992 national election. However, wary of the political bargaining that invariably accompanies the formation of governments in Israel, the Labour party leadership defeated the proposal. This rejection was based upon the belief that the issue of civil rights pertained to a single constituent group, the Soviet Jews, and did not warrant either the political alienation from the Israeli body politic, or the inevitable ostracism from religious party political support, that this proposal was deemed to entail.[65]

Only through fundamental reform of the electoral system could legislation be passed determining who was a Jew according to civil criteria. Given that religious party support would be required for such a transformation – an unlikely event – the anomalies regarding immigrant status remained set to continue. While hard to quantify the social impact of religious norms upon a largely secular identity, the officially sanctioned emphasis on religion did contribute to a tangible sense of dislocation from, and discontent with, the prevailing political order in Israel. 'There [the Soviet Union] we were Jewish. Here we are Russian', proved a bitter but widespread summation among immigrants of an absorption experience that precluded their full social, economic, and civil integration into Israeli society.[66]

Such sentiment was most prevalent among educated immigrants in their forties and fifties. With a dearth of suitable employment opportunities for this age group, the incentive to learn Hebrew to a proficient standard and interact with Israelis remained limited. Increasingly, these *olim* relied upon their own cultural heritage to provide a sense of identity in an alien environment. The culmination of a process that can be termed introverted socialization produced a reawakening of Russian culture that proved particularly strong among the inhabitants of development towns and caravan parks. Regarding themselves as the standard bearers of a rich intellectual heritage that encompassed the writings of Tolstoy and Pushkin, these immigrants expressed considerable antipathy towards a society that was viewed as brash, aesthetically barren, and unduly influenced by synthetic American culture. With the desire at the very least to remain Russian, it was a moot point as to whether this immigrant age group could ever adapt psychologically to their new environment.[67]

The Issue of the Yordim and Noshrim
The rejection by numerous *olim* of the norms and values of their host society received scant attention from the Israeli media, so widespread were immigrant problems. More dramatic, though less widespread, was the issue of the *yordim*, immigrants who emigrated to a third country after less than one year in Israel. The

Integration and Dislocation

issue was important because it became a composite expression of the anomie that mass *aliyah* had produced in Israel: socio-economic dislocation, and ethnic, cultural, and religious discord.

The ability of new immigrants to travel abroad was subject to strict conditions imposed by the Ministries of the Interior and Absorption. Because of the financial burden that the absorption basket imposed upon the state, *olim* were required to spend at least one year in Israel before applying for a passport. Those who needed to leave the country during this period, usually for family reasons, were given *laissez-passer* documents that restricted travel between Israel and the country stated on the documents. Commensurate with the issuing of such documentation was the need to provide four guarantors for debts incurred during the first year's residence in Israel. The terms surrounding guarantors were difficult for immigrants to comply with, ensuring that access to travel overseas remained severely restricted. Guarantors had to be Israelis in full salaried positions. Given the *olim*'s language difficulties and isolation from mainstream Israeli society, finding such guarantors proved particularly difficult. Furthermore, would-be guarantors were themselves dissuaded by the prospect of inheriting a debt should the immigrant fail to return. Indeed, if the guarantor had to leave Israel during the period of absence by the immigrant, he or she remained liable to full repayment of the debt.[68]

Figures released by the Interior Ministry for the year 1991 disclosed that 4,125 immigrants were issued with *laissez-passer* documentation for that year. Of these 1,015 did not return and were classified as *yordim*.[69] Compared to the overall levels of *aliyah*, this figure appeared small yet it effectively disguised one fact: the increasing numbers of immigrants who wished to leave but were prohibited from doing so by the strict Interior Ministry conditions. In November 1990, a poll taken by the Tatzpit Research Institute had shown that 75 per cent of new Soviet immigrants were content with life in Israel. This satisfaction, it was noted, was linked to the availability of housing and employment. A similar poll conducted one year later by the institute, found that 30 per cent wanted to leave Israel, with over half now advising friends and relatives in the former Soviet Union to delay making *aliyah*.[70]

While discontent clearly focused on the dominant socio-economic issues – of 125,000 *olim* available for work in

December 1991, only 45,000 had found employment – the case of some 400 *yordim* who faced extradition from the Netherlands provoked further debate over the criteria for determining immigrant status. Controversy surrounded the case: many stated that they were not Jewish and claimed that they had falsified documents in Moscow in order just to leave the Soviet Union. Such incidents merely strengthened the hand of those who sought to impose the *Halachic* definition of Jewish identity upon the Law of Return.[71]

The inability of Israel to provide sufficient housing to meet the demands of *aliyah* had, by the end of November 1990, raised the spectre that the United States might once more raise the ceiling of its immigrant quota for Soviet Jewry.[72] While such fears were misplaced – Soviet Jewish emigration provided *the* most salient means by which Washington could extract political concessions from Tel-Aviv regarding the peace process – increasing numbers of Soviet Jews did migrate to Germany. Until November 1991 when new regulations came into force, Bonn operated the most liberal immigration regime for Jews outside Israel. During December 1990 and January 1991 an average of 100 Soviet Jews arrived daily. Some 25,000 Soviet Jews were estimated to have migrated to Germany in total by the time new restrictions were imposed.[73]

While not strictly *noshrim* – these emigrants did not hold valid papers for Israel – the reaction of Israel's Foreign Ministry to this lost constituency revealed that *aliyah* as a Zionist ideal had been undermined. By declaring that 'Israel is the natural country of immigration for the Jews', the Foreign Ministry expressed a wider sentiment that applied the label of *noshrim* to these emigrants in all but name.[74] But if numbers of *yordim* and *noshrim* provided a visible focus of protest and discontent at immigrant conditions, it was the incremental decline in immigrant numbers to Israel from 1991 onwards that provided the best barometer to the factors affecting Soviet Jewish migration. From a peak of 200,000 immigrants for 1990, Soviet *aliyah* for the year ending 1992 fell to just under 70,000.[75] The explanation behind this shortfall was, according to Lev Goronetsky, head of the Zionist Federation throughout the former Soviet Union, simply negative feedback. The pace and scope of *aliyah* were now largely dictated by letters and telephone calls to Russia and the Ukraine that gave graphic accounts of the hardships entailed in adjusting to life in Israel.[76]

Yet if socio-economic realities now determined the Soviet

Jewish attitudes towards making *aliyah*, they also produced a marked shift among the Israeli populace towards both the immigrants and the state élite. Although it fulfilled a normative condition of Zionism, the scale and profile of Soviet immigration exposed considerable communal dissonance among Israel's several Jewish identities. Often racist in character, these debates came to reflect fear of the threat posed by Soviet Jews to the ethnic composition and the societal security of the Jewish State.

Soviet Jewish Aliyah: The Popular Response
The rationale behind *mizug galuyot*, the provision of social and economic structures that would cement social cohesion and national identity, placed a heavy burden upon Israelis as the recipient society. While the Likud government hoped to offset the financial cost of immigration to the Israeli body politic through loan guarantees, the particular profile of the immigrants created social and ethnic tensions throughout the Jewish State. In particular, the response of Oriental Jews, concerned at the challenge presented by a highly educated, Ashkenazim-dominated wave of *aliyah*, raised important issues regarding the homogeneity of Israel's disparate communities.

Above all, Oriental Jews feared the demographic usurpation of their political power and status that the Soviet *aliyah* appeared to entail. Moreover, despite social and economic gains, Oriental Jews continued to be under-represented in white collar professions while over-represented in non-skilled labour, the poor and unemployed. The fear existed that the cost of absorption would be at the expense of those that could least afford it.[77] This solicitude found vocal expression in the outspoken comments of some Oriental community leaders. The mayor of one development town remarked:

> I am beginning to hear new tunes. Some of the mayors of development towns are afraid. They say that because of the Soviet immigration, the Sephardis [Oriental Jews] will have to go back to their previously low status as second class Israeli citizens.[78]

This antipathy towards Soviet Jews was shared among all ages of the Oriental Jewish community. As more Soviet immigrants began to establish themselves in and around the development towns, a survey of Oriental children in the town of Kiryat Malachi revealed that 46 per cent would refuse aid to new *olim*: a further 33 per cent believed that such large-scale *aliyah* was detrimental to their own job prospects and questioned the need to absorb Soviet Jews into their particular towns. In short, immigration stretched the social cohesion of the recipient society.[79] Such sentiment had wider political and economic consequences. The Oriental community represented the historical bedrock of Likud Party support. If this support was to be maintained, Shamir had to cushion the financial upheaval created by Soviet immigration.

Already, one opinion poll conducted by the Dahaf research organization at the beginning of 1991 had indicated that 63 per cent of Israeli Jews were not prepared to accept lower standards of living for the sake of immigration. This raised important questions concerning the extent to which Israelis were prepared to see societal security undermined by the transnational flow of Soviet Jewish migrants.[80] Unable to restructure the industrial base of the Israeli economy, loan guarantees appeared the best means to meet two parallel demands: offsetting the financial burden of *aliyah* on Israelis in general and Orientals in particular, while continuing to fund Jewish settlement across the Green Line.

This reinforced dependence upon American largesse, a position that Washington exploited to the full. Although acquiescing in the $400 million loan guarantee, the United States imposed conditions upon Israeli access to the $10 billion request that effectively denied the financial cushion Shamir required for his domestic audience.[81] This preference for ideological orthodoxy over more pressing domestic concerns began to have a profound effect on the attitude of Israeli society towards the Soviet Jews. In 1990, with euphoria surrounding *aliyah* at its height, Israelis had volunteered in droves to host new immigrants at festivals marking Jewish holidays. Such benevolence had dissipated by the following year, once more giving rise to the bitter refrain that 'Israelis love immigration but not the immigrants'.[82]

This sentiment gave rise to cheap, often racist, jibes against the immigrants, which none the less underlined the perceived threat that mass *aliyah* presented to the existing social order. The controversy over the number of non-Jews among the immigrants became the subject of bitter debate and equally barbed comment. Failing to take account of the erosion of core Judaic values under the Soviet system, immigrants were commonly viewed as *goyim*, a disparaging term reserved for non-Jews, either because so many of the male immigrants were not circumcised or because knowledge of religious customs remained limited.[83]

The penchant for pork among the *olim* – a staple food of the Soviet diet – provided a focus for discontent among some sections of Oriental communities in development towns. While the majority did not subscribe to Orthodox religious norms, adherence to traditional Jewish values, including dietary laws, had regulated daily life in these areas. Thus the appearance of butchers shops, openly selling pork bought from local kibbutzim, was viewed as an affront to these values. While peaceful demonstrations were held outside one such establishment in Kiryat Shemonah, recourse to violence by Ultra-Orthodox Jews marked the opening of similar premises in the coastal town of Ashdod.[84] The comments of Peretz concerning the Halachic legitimacy of this *aliyah*, therefore, struck a responsive chord among many Israelis. His comments reflected deep concerns over social status and Jewish values that accompanied Soviet immigration, a position demonstrated by one Oriental who declared: 'They [the Soviet Jews] are more Ashkenazi than the Ashkenazim. Real Christians, it's frightening'. Another, in a moment laced with black humour, professed that with the number of non-Jewish *olim* arriving in Israel, they would soon be having to endure pogroms.[85]

Certainly, a clear correlation existed between immigration and the growth of national unemployment. While the proportion of jobless was greatest among the immigrants themselves, the inhabitants of development towns were particularly hard hit. The national rate of unemployment in December 1991 stood at 10.5 per cent with a further two per cent rise forecast for 1992. Yet in development towns, unemployment was expected to reach 20 per cent for that same year. The main cause of the rise was the drop in the number of construction projects, a problem exacerbated by a marked reluctance of some Soviet immigrants to take employment in the building industry. This stemmed in part from the high educational profile of the *olim*: many felt acceptance of manual labour would condemn them to undertake such work in perpetuity, negating any opportunity to pursue a career in their chosen profession.[86]

This attitude often provoked resentment, particularly in the development towns. Yitzhak Rager, mayor of Beersheba, a town that had accepted over 20,000 immigrants by 1992, admitted that the welfare benefits and tax breaks given to Soviet Jews had caused deep hostility among his largely Oriental constituents.[87] Aside from problems of cultural identity and employment, the distinct paucity of Zionist ideals amongst the *olim* reinforced among some Israelis a pervasive stereotype of Soviet immigrants as threatening to national identity. As a result, the immigrants were castigated as alcoholics, a people who beat their children, and as a community rife with drugs and prostitution. In short, Soviet Jews were blamed for importing social problems. Such censure was preferred over the more prosaic view that the actual scale of this *aliyah* exacerbated socio-economic disparities that already existed.[88]

Large sections of the population began to see themselves as victims of the immigrants, unwilling or unable to appreciate the painful adjustments and problems which the Soviet Jews had to endure. While the Oriental community were the most vocal in their protestations, the wisdom of mass *aliyah* began to permeate the debates among Ashkenazim Jews. Where large numbers of immigrants had managed to locate to urban areas, genuine fears were expressed over the erosion of the Israeli identity. In Haifa, the city with the most immigrants – some 38,000 – whole areas were transformed into Russian-speaking neighbourhoods. The density became such that the district around Hadar Ha'Carmel became known as 'Little Russia', with Hebrew relegated to the status of a second language.[89]

The erosion of linguistic hegemony forced many residents of Hadar Ha'Carmel to address the everyday implications of mass immigration. Tamara Amitai, an author of children's books and a staunch supporter of the Israeli left, lives in an apartment overlooking Pevsner Park in which can be found large numbers of unemployed immigrants, most playing cards or backgammon, but some intoxicated. In light of this, she has come to question the conventional rationale behind this *aliyah*. Her argument placed emphasis on the strict imposition of migration quotas in the United States, a policy that pushed Soviet Jews to Israel regardless of ideological attachment. This policy was ill-conceived since immigrants possessed little motivation to endure the privations that enveloped mass *aliyah*. For Tamara Amitai, Soviet Jews should come to Israel for ideological reasons, and not because they had precious little alternative.[90]

Although a minority view, such sentiment did reflect a need to impose a Zionist criterion on future immigration. This was perhaps unjust on those *olim* who had made *aliyah* under naive expectations fostered by the activities of the *schlichim*. None the less, concern at the influx of Soviet immigrants into urban areas often had unpleasent consequences. One immigrant, a former opera singer from Tashkent, was forced to move from Neve David, an Oriental suburb of Haifa, to the caravan park of Neve Carmel following the overt hostility exhibited towards his family.[91] Such direct antipathy was, however, a reaction to increased levels of homelessness that had afflicted Israeli society since the start of this *aliyah*. As with the problems that accompanied Soviet Jewish immigration in the 1970s, young Israelis, particularly those who had just completed their military service, found the cost of rented accommodation beyond their immediate ability to pay.[92]

The negative assumptions applied to Soviet Jewish *aliyah* served to reinforce the sense of isolation among the *olim*. Their own recourse to social stereotypes became a defence mechanism against attitudes that they felt denied legitimacy to their own aspirations and sense of identity. An adversarial approach was adopted towards their new environment that too often found expression in racial slurs. If Soviet Jews were deemed to configure a social and racial underclass, many immigrants were no less damning in their appreciation of Oriental Jews, a community synonymous with 'dirt, lack of culture and hygiene'.[93]

Such comments were habitual in caravan parks where Soviet immigrants shared facilities with Ethiopian *olim* who had made *aliyah*, under very trying circumstances, in 1991. At Neve Carmel, one of the largest caravan parks in Israel, both communities lived in self-imposed isolation from each other. While this was in part due to linguistic difficulties, the competition for work, however menial, engendered feelings of prejudice and hostility between the two groups. Co-existence was summed up by one Soviet immigrant in the phrase 'no contact and no problems', a remark that carried equal weight among the Ethiopian inhabitants of the park.[94] Indeed, the very layout of the Neve Carmel park provided ample physical testimony to the cultural and social divisions between the two communities. A main supply road, neatly bisecting the park, delineated the territorial limits of the two communities. Where Soviet Jews had managed to create small gardens around their particular caravans, the Ethiopians, in a vivid reminder of their former, barren, agrarian existence, grew maize.

Yet compounding the problem for many Soviet *olim* was the belief that an unofficial policy of discrimination in favour of the Ethiopians existed. Volunteer social workers, usually IDF soldiers engaged in social rehabilitation programmes, were accused by the Soviet Jews of spending a disproportionate amount of their time catering to the needs of the Ethiopians at their expense. This criticism, at one level was unfair: the Ethiopians were a product of a society where levels of socio-economic acculturation had remained particularly low. Yet the Soviet Jews believed that this perceived bias was also a product of the poor appreciation that had met their *aliyah* among many Israelis.[95]

This neatly encapsulated a self-fulfilling prophecy that defined the Soviet immigrant dilemma. The perception of the Soviet Jews as economic migrants, rather than Zionist émigrés, provoked antipathy towards them as an immigrant group once the economic and social cost to indigenous interests came to be realized. Questioning the citizenship, loyalty, and indeed, Judaic legitimacy of this *aliyah* was as much about the self-assertion of a communal identity in Israeli society as a critique of the nature of this immigrant wave. Often, such criticism of Soviet *olim* ignored the erosion of their cultural heritage under Communist rule, and belittled the problems that they faced in adapting to their new environment. Recourse to social stereotypes, therefore, proved to be a way to express defiance to the threats inherent within mass *aliyah*. However, this merely provoked a similar response from many *olim*, particularly those whose physical existence placed them outside mainstream Israeli society. To this extent, attachment to the symbols and culture of their past in the search for an identity reinforced communal barriers, and only served to justify the bias that so many Israelis held against Soviet Jewish immigrants.[96]

Conclusion

The social upheaval that accompanied Soviet Jewish *aliyah* was a product of the insufficient economic and political structures that accompanied the process of immigration. Not least, ideological dogma and bureaucratic disputes deprived Israeli society of the financial means to offset at least much inter-communal discord that accompanied this *aliyah*. Yet it was this milieu that shaped and determined the perceptions of Israelis and *olim* to the experience of absorption. While direct placement of immigrants into existing communities had been the preferred government policy, the utility of this option was rapidly undermined by the magnitude of immigration. Thus, at a very early stage, the key to achieving effective *mizug galuyot* was lost as the magnitude of this *aliyah* swamped the capacity of existing structures to cope.

Given the rather myopic expectations that accompanied Soviet Jewish immigration, the process of absorption was particularly hard psychologically. Israel had appeared to be a secure base in which to seek employment compatible with the needs and hopes of a highly trained and educated work-force. Instead, exposure to the vagaries of the free market undermined the material aspirations that had been a prime motive behind this *aliyah*. While demographic concerns encouraged the movement of immigrants to development towns, the paucity of employment opportunities at all levels resulted in ethnic and cultural tension; rather than widespread social co-operation, polarized relations between the disparate communities resulted.

This development was in no small part encouraged by the theocratic challenge to the legitimacy of this wave of Soviet Jewish immigration. If *olim* felt their secular identity and civil rights were subject to unjust Halachic strictures, the Ultra-Orthodox, with some sympathy from Oriental Jews, viewed the application of religious laws as justified. Not only was this an attempt to assert the pre-eminence of religious values in defining Jewish identity, but also a subtle endeavour to dilute the demographic impact of a mass, secular *aliyah* on the Oriental Jewish community.

This adversarial environment thus shaped the political development of Soviet Jewish *aliyah*. While many immigrants integrated with little effort, the levels of unemployment and under-employment among the Soviet *olim* shaped perceptions that displayed increased antipathy towards the governing élite. Furthermore, many within the Oriental community, the bastion of Likud Party support, came to question the cost of an allegiance that appeared to undermine their own economic and social status. If the process of economic absorption helped mould a political consciousness among the immigrants, Soviet Jewish *aliyah* led many Israelis to re-examine the basis of their own political convictions. Therefore, the cumulative effect of this process was to inflict the most profound upheaval upon Israel's political agenda.

NOTES

1. Edith Coron, *Le Dernier Exode* (Paris: François Bourin, 1993), p.70.
2. Ian Black, 'Israel Strains to Absorb the New Arrivals', *The Guardian*, 22 June 1990.
3. Interview with Professor A Harrell, Ichilov Hospital, Tel-Aviv, 24 Nov. 1992. Professor Harell was a board member of the Council for Soviet Russian Jewry. Of particular interest to him was the retraining and settlement of *olim* previously involved in the medical profession.
4. Bernard Sabella, 'Russian Jewish Immigration and the Future of the Israeli–Palestinian Conflict', *Middle East Report*, Vol. 23, No. 3 (May–June 1993), p.36.
5. Interview with Lesya-Shtance Smirnoff, absorption co-ordinator for Ratz (Meretz), Tel-Aviv, 18 Nov. 1992.
6. 'Ha Eum Shel Yom Ha Pogrom Negid Ha Yehudim Ha Russim Avar Be Shalom' (Pogrom Day Threatened Against Russian Jews Passed Peacefully), *Ha'aretz*, 6 May 1990; 'On the Immigration of Soviet Jews', *Israel and Palestine Political Report*, May 1990, p.4; Johnathan Steele, 'Soviet Jews Queue to Leave', *The Guardian*, 22 June 1990; David Mirkisk, 'Ha Israelim Ha Tomkhim be Pamyat' (The Israelis who Agree with Pamyat), *Ma'ariv*, 19 April 1990.
7. Yigal Amitai, 'Ha Hayim Ha Tovim be Eretz Betokha', (The Good Life in a Secure Country), *Ha'aretz*, 12 June 1992.
8. Interview with Soviet (Ukrainian) women, the Talcutchka Market, Haifa, 29 June 1993. See also Avishai Margalit, 'The Great White Hope', op. cit., p.20.
9. Joost R. Hiltermann, 'Settling for War: Soviet Immigration and Israel's Settlement Policy in East Jerusalem', *Journal of Palestine Studies*, Vol. XX, No. 2 (Winter 1991), p.72; Clare Longrigg, 'There We Were Jewish, Here We Are Russian', *The Independent*, 8 Jan. 1992.
10. Sabella, op. cit., p.37.
11. Moskovich, op. cit., p.14. Interview with Yigal Amitai, Haifa, 22 November 1991. Amitai was a freelance journalist covering the *aliyah* for *Ha'aretz* at the time of the interview.
12. Bernard Reich, Noah Dropkin, and Meyrav Wurmser, 'The Impact of the Soviet Jewish Vote on the Israeli Knesset Election', *Middle East Insight*, Vol. VIII, No. 4 (March–April 1992), p.50.
13. Amos Oz, quoted by Tad Szulc, 'The Great Soviet Exodus', *National Geographic*, Vol. 181, No. 2 (Feb. 1992), p.46.
14. Peter Freedman, 'Doc Land', *The Guardian Weekend*, 31 July 1993; Moskovich, op. cit., p.13.
15. Margalit, op. cit., p.20.
16. Interview with Hymie Bornstein, Mapam party headquaters, Tel-Aviv, 16 Nov. 1992. Hymie Bornstein, chairman of Mapam, was the campaign co-ordinator for Soviet immigrants during the 1992 national elections.
17. Herb Keinon, 'Newest Citizens are Secular', *The Jerusalem Post International*, 3 Nov. 1990.
18. Reich et al, op. cit., p.49; Coron, op. cit., pp.73-4.
19. Sabella, op. cit., p.37.
20. John King, 'Job Problems Face Soviet Immigrants', *Middle East International*, No. 374 (27 April 1990), p.19.
21. Interview with Professor A. Harrell, Ichilov Hospital, Tel-Aviv, 24 Nov. 1992. While pamphlets were produced that detailed employment opportunities in medicine, science, and the arts, these initially did not specify the problems that existed in Israel regarding vacancies in these fields. See, for example, 'Making it in Israel: Scientists and Researchers', *Ministry of Immigrant Absorption, Department of Aliyah and Absorption of the Jewish Agency*, Jerusalem, 1990. The leaflet only alludes to employment problems by stating that immigrants with research skills *may* have to retrain.

22. Ian Black, 'An Exodus on the Brink of Chaos', *The Guardian*, 20 Nov. 1990; Bill Hutman, 'Soviet Jewish Brainpower Sadly Going to Waste', *The Jerusalem Post International*, 9 March 1991; 'Soviet Scientists Face Nightmare of Non-Absorption, Warns Tel-Aviv University Scholar', *Tel-Aviv University News* (Autumn 1991), p.26.
23. *Ha'aretz*, 12 June 1992.
24. Joseph Finkelstone, 'Israeli Politics Goes Critical', *The Guardian*, 30 Dec. 1991; Herb Keinon, 'Immigrants Going Hungry', *The Jerusalem Post International*, 19 Jan. 1991.
25. Alan Cowell, 'The Ebbing Tide of Ex-Soviet Jews', *International Herald Tribune*, 31 Jan. 1992.
26. 'Most *Olim* Slam Services', *The Jerusalem Post*, 13 Dec. 1991.
27. *Ha'aretz*, 12 June 1992; Coron, op.cit., p.142.
28. Oleg Zuyenko, 'A Russian Party', *Asia and Africa Today* (Moscow), No. 6, 1991, p.29; 'Immigrants Exploited', *The Jerusalem Post International*, 26 Oct. 1991.
29. Interview with Svetlana Raviv, Histadrut headquarters, Holon, 27 June 1993. Svetlana Raviv was absorption director of the Holon Histadrut workers council with special responsibility for immigrant employment welfare.
30. Asher Wallfish, 'Peretz, Namir Deplore Growing Prostitution among Immigrants', *The Jerusalem Post International*, 3 Nov. 1991; Amos Kenan, 'Ekh Y'Israel Oresset et Ha Olim Shelah' (How Israel Ruins its Immigrants), *Ma'ariv*, 26 Oct. 1990.
31. Sima Kadmon, 'Olot be Ashdod: Al Ha Kvishim Ve Al Ha Kav Ha Onni' (Immigrant Women in Ashdod: On the Streets and on the Breadline), *Ma'ariv*, 19 Oct. 1990.
32. Interview with Mark Mirskin, Neve Carmel, Haifa, 22 Nov. 1992. The subject of the interview, a welder originally from Minsk, made *aliyah* at the beginning of 1992.
33. Coron, op. cit., pp.73–4; International Centre for Peace in the Middle East (ICPME), *Newsletter*, Vol. 22, No.2 (June 1993) p.10.
34. Roberta Cohen, 'Israel's Problematic Absorption of Soviet Jews', *Innovation*, Vol.4, No.3/4 (1991), pp.73–4.
35. Ibid., p.66.
36. Herb Keinon, 'Immigrant Squalid Hotels Stun MK's', *The Jerusalem Post International*, 16 April 1991.
37. 'Russim Mitrachchim Mein Ha Kibbutzim' (Russian Jews shun Kibbutzim), *Ha'aretz*, 30 April 1990; Joel Magid, 'Russian Kids Like Life on a Kibbutz', *The Jerusalem Post International*, 3 Nov. 1990.
38. *Ha'aretz*, 2 Feb. 1990.
39. Joseph Alpher, 'A Strategy for *Aliyah*,' *The Jerusalem Post*, 15 March 1990.
40. *The Independent*, 8 Jan. 1992; Coron, op. cit., p.142.
41. Joel Rebibo, 'Upper Nazareth: A Phoenix Struggles for Rebirth', *The Jerusalem Post International*, 14 March 1992.
42. Figures cited from Sabella, op. cit., p.37.
43. Interview with Yigal Amitai, Haifa, Israel, 22 Nov. 1992.
44. Ibid.
45. 'Israel: Shamir's Address to Knesset Presenting New Government', *BBC-SWB*, ME/0789 A/5, 13 June 1990.
46. Asher Arian, *Politics in Israel* (New Jersey: Chatham House Publishers, 1989), p.236.
47. Arian, op. cit., pp.95–100. For an argument presenting Shas as a party committed to the basic tenants of Zionism see Aaron Willis, 'Redefining Religious Zionism: Shas' Ethno-Politics', *Israel Studies Bulletin*, Vol.18, No.2 (Fall 1992), pp.3–8.
48. Margalit, op. cit., p.21.
49. Arian, op. cit., p.239.
50. Interview with Marina Heifetz, a Soviet immigrant lawyer working with the *olim* for Ratz (Meretz), Tel-Aviv, 24 June 1993.
51. Moskovich, op. cit., pp.10–11.
52. Walter Ruby, Herb Keinon and Judy Siegal, 'Peretz: Limit Number of Non-Jewish

Olim', *The Jerusalem Post International*, 24 Nov. 1990.
53. *The Jerusalem Post*, 18 Dec. 1990.
54. Arian, op. cit., p.179.
55. Robert O. Freedman, 'Soviet Jewish Immigrants and Israel's next Election'. Paper presented as part of a briefing session for the future United States Ambassador to Israel, Mr Harrop, Washington, D.C, 30 July 1990.
56. Interview with Yigal Amitai, Haifa, 29 June 1993. For an example of a leaflet contradicting the religious interpretation of the founding of the state, see '44-aya: Godovshchina Provozglashyeniya Nyezavisimosti Izrailya', (The 44th Anniversary of Israel's Declaration of Independence) ICPME, 9 April 1992. Among the contributors to this pamphlet were Israeli author Amos Oz and leader of the Meretz alignment, Shulamit Aloni.
57. Roberta Cohen, op. cit., p.73; Herb Keinon, Bill Hutman, and Allison Kaplan, 'Ministers Clash Over Tents for Immigrants', *The Jerusalem Post International*, 12 Jan. 1991; Abraham Rabinovich, 'Russian Jews find Kibbutz Life Delightful', *The Jerusalem Post International*, 9 Feb. 1991; Yosef Goell, 'Will Soviet Jews Rekindle Kibbutz Fire?', *The Jerusalem Post International*, 17 Nov. 1990.
58. Margalit, op. cit., p.22.
59. Interview with Yigal Amitai, Haifa, 29 June 1993.
60. *Ha'aretz*, 12 June 1992.
61. Interview with Marina Yeroshevsky, an 18-year-old immigrant from Neve Carmel, Haifa, Israel, 22 Nov. 1992. The subject of social and cultural isolation was visibly explored in the Israeli documentary, *St Jean*, produced by Amit Brener and directed by Julie Shless. It won critical acclaim following its release at the 1993 Jerusalem film festival.
62. Interview with Marina Heifetz, Tel-Aviv, 24 June 1993.
63. Arian op. cit., p.239.
64. Interview with Lesya Shtance-Smirnoff, Tel-Aviv, 23 June 1993.
65. Interview with Avraham Burg MK, the Knesset, Jerusalem, 23 Nov. 1992.
66. Derek Brown, 'The Vexed Question of Jewishness Revives in Homeland', *The Guardian*, 28 Aug. 1993.
67. Coron, op. cit., p.142.
68. Yair Sheleg, 'Ha Bank Ha Hashye Ha Kosher Et Ha Olim Le Israel' (The Secret Bank that Ties Immigrants to Israel), *Ha'aretz*, 23 Feb. 1990.
69. Herb Keinon, 'Numbers of *Yordim* Much Exaggerated', *The Jerusalem Post*, 19 Dec. 1991.
70. Yosef Yaakov, 'Soviets Assure Israel that *Aliyah* Will Be Allowed to Continue', *The Jerusalem Post International*, 19 Jan. 1991; Herb Keinon, '30 Per Cent of Soviet *Olim* Want Out', *the Jerusalem Post International*, 16 Nov. 1991; Herb Keinon, '5,000 Immigrants Seeking Israeli Passports', *The Jerusalem Post International*, 24 Aug. 1991.
71. Jacob Wirtschafter, 'Soviet Returnees Still Unsure of Who and Where They Are', *The Jerusalem Post*, 18 Dec. 1991.
72. 'Israelim Pochadim me Hagbalot me Artzot Ha'Brit' (Israelis Fear Easing of US Restrictions), *Yediot Aharanot*, 23 Nov. 1990.
73. Susanne Spulbeck, 'Integration and Identity: The Immigration of Jews from the Former USSR in Germany', *Analysis: Institute of Jewish Affairs*, No.3 (March 1993), pp.1-3.
74. Ibid., p.5.
75. Yossi Klein-Halevi and Tom Sawicki, 'Its Better Here Than There', *The Jerusalem Report*, Vol.IV, No.13 (4 Nov. 1993), p.18.
76. Report from Moscow by Jeremy Vine for *BBC Radio 4 Today Programme*, 8 May 1992.
77. 'Etnagdot Sephardim Pogesh et Ha Gal Shel Olim' (Oriental Jewish Protest Meets Immigration Wave), *Yediot Aharanot*, 8 Dec. 1989. See also Lili Galili, 'Hamehaneh

Integration and Dislocation 153

Hameshutaf Nikra Mahasor' (A Common Denominator Called Deprival), *Ha'aretz*, 15 March 1990; Cohen, op. cit., pp.76–77.
78. Quoted from the Israeli newspaper *Hadashot* in Margalit, op. cit., p.23.
79. 'Talmedim Sephardim Michulachim al Ha Olim' (Oriental Jewish Pupils Divided over Immigrants), *Yediot Aharanot*, 21 March 1990.
80. Margalit, op. cit., p.21.
81. Ian Black, 'The Squabbling Tribes of Israel', *The Guardian*, 1 April 1992.
82. Ian Black, 'Sweet Wine Leaves a Bitter Aftertaste', *The Guardian*, 29 March 1991.
83. *The Guardian*, 20 Nov. 1990.
84. Jerrold Kessel, 'Pork Disturbs Hopes of the New Migrants', *The Guardian*, 31 Oct. 1992; Sarah Helm, '"Pork Police" Attack Shops in the Name of Judaism', *The Independent*, 23 Aug. 1993.
85. *The Guardian*, 20 Nov. 1990.
86. Herb Keinon, Dan Izenberg and Alisa Odenheimer, 'Unemployment in Some Towns Will Top 20 per cent in 1992', *The Jerusalem Post International*, 7 Dec. 1991.
87. Philip Jacobson, 'The Dream Turns Sour', *The Sunday Times Magazine*, 25 Oct. 1992.
88. *Ha'aretz*, 12 June 1992.
89. *Ha'aretz*, 10 April 1992.
90. Interview with Tamara Amitai, Haifa, 22 Nov. 1992.
91. Interview with Soviet immigrants, Neve Carmel, 22 Nov. 1992. See also the comments of Natalie Eisenberg in ICPME *Newsletter*, No. 1 (April 1993) p.10.
92. *The Guardian*, 22 June 1990. Some Israelis, in a visible demonstration over the growth in the number of homeless, were forced to live in tents. See Hiltermann, op. cit., p.75; 'Soviet Jews in Tent Protest', *New York Times*, 22 June 1990.
93. Margalit, op. cit., p.23.
94. Interviews with Russian, Ukrainian and Ethiopian Immigrants, Neve Carmel, Haifa, 29 June 1993.
95. Ibid.
96. Interview with Shai Grishpon, Mapam Party headquarters, Tel-Aviv, June 23 1993. A former immigrant himself, Shai helped co-ordinate youth activities among the *olim* throughout Israel.

6 Arab Responses to Soviet Jewish Aliyah

On 8 March 1990, during a speech to mark the opening of the fifth congress of the Syrian Revolution Youth Federation in Damascus, President Hafiz al-Asad declared:

> Brothers, let us see now how Israel has become the main beneficiary among all world nations from the international changes which have taken place. It has restored its relations with some countries and increased its influence in others. While Zionism was unwelcome and unable to engage in any activity in the socialist bloc countries, on the basis that Zionism is a racist movement, we find that what is taking place today is contrary to all that.[1]

While Israel welcomed the development of diplomatic ties with states throughout eastern Europe, the main benefit accruing to the Jewish State was the sudden and overwhelming influx of Jews from the Soviet Union. Moscow's withdrawal of draconian emigration restrictions, coupled with the imposition of strict immigration quotas by Washington in October 1989, resulted in Israel becoming the only viable destination for increasing numbers of Jews, propelled by the uncertainty engendered by Gorbachev's reforms to seek a new life elsewhere.

The prospect of the mass migration of Soviet Jewry elicited immediate and widespread protests from around the Arab world, concerned that the demographic effects of large-scale Jewish *aliyah* would enforce the moral, political, and strategic claims of the ruling Likud coalition to continued Israeli rule over the West Bank and Gaza Strip. Yet despite strong representations to the Soviet Union, the convening of a pan-Arab conference in Baghdad and the imposition of punitive economic measures, Soviet Jewish emigration to Israel stood at 328,187 by the end of 1991.[2] Divisions within the Arab world, particularly in the aftermath of the Gulf Crisis, appeared to preclude any effective strategy designed at least to dilute the mass Jewish exodus.

However, while failing to forestall Soviet Jewish *aliyah*, Arab protests did force Washington to seek assurances from Israeli premier, Yitzhak Shamir, concerning the settlement of Soviet Jews in the West Bank, East Jerusalem, and the Gaza Strip. Such pressure prevented Shamir from undertaking any concerted effort to settle large concentrations of Soviet Jews openly throughout the Occupied Territories. The subsequent concentration of the new Soviet *olim* in the main conurbations along Israel's coastal plain resulted in severe social dislocation, particularly in employment and housing. This in turn fuelled resentment among large sections of Israeli society towards the ruling state élite, not least among Israeli Arabs as well as Palestinians in the Occupied Territories.

For the Palestinians, Jewish immigration, taken in conjunction with the settlement policy of the Likud coalition government, threatened to usurp Palestinian claims to statehood. In addition, the arrival of the Soviet *olim* lessened the dependence of the Israeli economy on Palestinian labour. Although largely employed in the low-skilled, low-waged sector of the Israeli labour market, many Palestinians remained dependent upon such work, offsetting as it did the chronic lack of employment opportunities within the territories. This dependency had been exacerbated by the outbreak of a widespread insurrection in the Gaza Strip and on the West Bank in December 1987: the *intifada*. The consequent economic hardship endured by Palestinians only served to increase resentment towards Israeli rule.[3]

Although expressing sympathy for their Palestinian brethren, Israeli Arabs adopted a more pragmatic approach towards the issue of Soviet Jewish immigration. Despite being full Israeli citizens, Arabs had suffered from official discrimination, particularly in the allocation of government funds required to finance and update the infrastructure of many towns and villages.[4] Consequently, the mass *aliyah* appeared to threaten existing resource allocation, a fear shared with Israel's Oriental community.

Nevertheless, other ethnic groups, particularly the Druze, welcomed the influx of Soviet *olim* and openly endorsed their settlement amongst their villages and small towns in northern Israel. Traditionally the most loyal of the Jewish State's ethnic minorities, the Druze saw the concomitant economic benefits that could accrue from the settlement of Soviet Jews in contiguous areas. In addition, members of Israel's peace movements became active in facilitating the process of communal acculturation. They established workshops through which the cultural, linguistic, and political barriers separating Israeli Arabs and Soviet *olim* could be breached.

Given the scale of *aliyah* between 1989 and 1992, it would be easy to dismiss Arab attempts to restrict immigration as ineffective. Yet adverse reaction to the possibility of mass settlement in the Occupied Territories forced Washington to take account of Arab sensibilities. In turn, the United States sought strict compliance from Tel-Aviv regarding the settlement of Soviet Jews within Israel's pre-1967 borders. With the need to harness American financial support for the absorption process, Shamir had to defer the direct placement of immigrants in the Occupied Territories. However, the failure to attract sufficient numbers of Israelis to the West Bank and Gaza Strip Territories exacerbated social tensions in all sectors of the Jewish state, not least among the *olim* and Israel's Arabs. The votes of both groups proved decisive in ousting the Likud government from office in June 1992, and in the election of a Labour-led coalition under Yitzhak Rabin, a government prepared to accept the principle of land for peace.

The Arab Regional Response to Soviet Jewish Immigration
The decision by the Bush Administration to enforce strict immigration quotas in October 1989 meant that those Jews who wished to leave the USSR had only Israel to go to as a viable alternative. The realization that a demographic *mahapach* or upheaval could occur, fortifying Israeli claims to the territories captured following the June 1967 war, soon met with strong condemnation throughout the whole of the Arab world. The Libyan leader, Mu'ammar al-Qaddafi, quick to condemn the United States, stated that: 'America is pushing them [the Soviet Jews] into Palestine pretending to be sympathetic towards them. I stress that this is a big international conspiracy against the Jews.'[5]

While easy to dismiss Qaddafi's statement as political rhetoric designed to bolster Libya's continued opposition to Washington's regional interests, his view appeared to be vindicated in Arab eyes following remarks made by Israeli Prime Minister Yitzhak Shamir.

On 14 January 1990, Shamir declared that retention of the territories was necessary for the successful absorption of Soviet Jewish immigrants.[6] This brash statement struck at the heart of Arab sensibilities, resulting not just in severe pan-Arab condemnation, but plans to exercise Arab diplomatic influence to offset the mass *aliyah*.

Initial Arab condemnation of Soviet Jewish emigration focused upon the perceived superpower collaboration in originally directing Soviet Jewish migrants towards Israel. The threat that mass migration posed had been recognized by constituent elements within the PLO as early as August 1989. The Fifth General Congress of Yasser Arafat's Fatah movement had already set up a committee to co-ordinate opposition to Soviet *aliyah* given the importance of 'the demographic factor in our conflict with the Zionist enemy'. Most vehement in its criticism in this perceived collusion was the Palestine National Council (Al-Majlis al-Watani al-Filastini: PNC), the Palestinian parliament-in-exile, which charged that immigration was a 'vulgar transaction endorsed through the complicity of Washington and Moscow'.[7] This view was put more succinctly by the Egyptian writer Mohamed Sid-Ahmed, who wrote:

> In the view of many Arab parties, Moscow's new policy towards the Middle East subordinates its previous stand on the Arab-Israeli conflict to the relations it is now keen to develop with Washington. Moving from 'confrontation to co-operation and mutual involvement' with the US appears incompatible with the longstanding policy of holding relations with Israel hostage to that country's withdrawal from the Occupied Territories. As for the wave of Soviet Jewish emigration to Israel, respect for the right of Soviet Jews to emigrate in the name of the Helsinki accords on human rights is one thing; using the emigration issue as a trump card in a deal at the expense of the Arabs is quite another.[8]

Recourse to the Helsinki Accords, in order to challenge the legality of Washington's imposition of strict immigrant quotas, was the immediate response of the Arab League based in Tunis. As a signatory to the Accords, or the Helsinki Final Act of the Conference on Security and Co-operation in Europe (CSCE), the United States had agreed to work towards increased freedom of movement of groups and individuals. However, this was purely a statement of intent and not a policy that was legally binding. In short, no clause stipulating the right of free movement was endorsed.[9]

Yet while the legal use of the Helsinki accords was questionable, the moral case against Washington's restrictions appeared substantial, given the apparent ease with which the Soviet migrants of the 1970s had been permitted to enter the United States. Chedli Klibi, Secretary General of the Arab League, denounced the mass migration to Israel, stating that the exclusion of any alternative destination for Soviet Jewry was a clear contravention of their human rights, and those of the Palestinians. In support of Klibi, Faruq Qaddumi, head of the Political Department of the PLO, urged at the end of January 1990 that collective measures be agreed by the Arab League forthwith.[10]

Initial attempts at co-ordinating a united Arab position on the issue of Jewish immigration proved difficult, despite the depth of feeling. Jordan had already expressed concern that the settlement of Soviet Jews upon the West Bank 'could only disturb' an already faltering peace process. Jordanian Foreign Minister Marwan al-Qassim had already cited the reported settlement of Soviet Jews in Gilo and Ma'ale Adunim – two settlements regarded by Israel as suburbs of Jerusalem – as illustrating the urgent need for effective action. Indeed, the extent of Jordanian concerns over the geopolitical ramifications of large-scale settlement in the Occupied Territories led the Hashemite king to issue veiled military threats against Israel. Remarking on the establishment of a joint Jordanian–Iraqi airforce squadron, the Jordanian monarch declared that:

> Calling on the world to stop Jewish immigration to Israel is useless. Arab unity is the real response to this immigration. There is no doubt that forming a united pan-Arab Jordanian–Iraqi squadron is a first step down the path of forming a unified Arab corps.[11]

Yet King Hussein's call for an immediate summit to discuss immigration to Israel in February 1990 met with a cool response from both Saudi Arabia and Egypt. Both King Fahd and President Mubarak felt that such a conference would jeopardize Egyptian negotiations with Washington and Tel-Aviv for the holding of free elections for Palestinians in the Occupied Territories. More importantly, it was felt that any open display of Arab disunity over the issue would further erode Arab credibility, already struggling to recover in the aftermath of the Iran–Iraq war.[12]

Some collective action had, however, already been sanctioned. At the beginning of February it was announced that a delegation of foreign ministers from Algeria, Iraq, Syria, Jordan, and Saudi Arabia would visit Washington, Moscow and Dublin – Ireland then held the Presidency of the European Community – to register a collective protest over Soviet Jewish emigration to Israel. In addition, an appeal lodged with the United Nations Security Council stated that the mass migration of Soviet Jewry 'could pose a threat to international peace and security'.[13]

Although the Jordanians failed to convene an official conference, a mini-summit, designed to address the issue of Soviet Jewish *aliyah*, was held in Amman on 24 February 1990 between the King and his Iraqi counterpart, Saddam Hussein. Taking an aggressively anti-American stance, Saddam called for an Arab economic boycott of Washington, arguing that billions of dollars of investment in the United States should be directed towards the rebuilding of the economies of eastern Europe. In what was perhaps a portent of things to come, the Iraqi leader attacked the pro-Western stance of Gulf states, stating that they had been reduced to an 'ineffective rejection or silence' by Washington's actions in the region. The United States, he maintained, was primarily responsible for the Jewish influx that was 'an open aggression against the rights of the Palestinian people and a threat to the Arab order'.[14] Indeed, possibly in an effort to neutralize Iranian opposition over his planned invasion of Kuwait, Saddam Hussein sought to manipulate the issue of Soviet Jewish immigration as a pretext for holding an urgent meeting with Tehran.[15]

However, most Israelis across the Zionist political spectrum believed that Arab opposition to Soviet *aliyah* was based not just upon fears of demographic annexation of the territories, but on the settlement of Jews anywhere in Israel *per se*. It was all too easy for reference to be made to the January speech of Mu'ammar al-Qaddafi, promising that the liberation of the whole of Palestine was only a matter of time.[16] Given that *aliyah* had historically been the bedrock of the Jewish State, the Israeli journalist Arieh Palgi viewed Arab, and in particular PLO, opposition to immigration as tantamount to a rejection of Israel's right to exist:

> If the leaders of the PLO have not yet learned that *aliyah* and

the State of Israel are like oxygen and a lung, a blood system and a human life, then they have not yet learned a thing about us. If they have heard something of all of this but are still fighting so nobly for Jews' freedom to emigrate anywhere at all in the world, then contrary to their statements, they have still not accepted us.[17]

But while the PLO position on *aliyah* may have appeared ambiguous, the Arab League, meeting in Tunis on 13 March 1990, did issue a statement that only condemned the settlement of Soviet Jews in the Occupied Territories but not those within Israel's pre-1967 borders.[18] Yet because of serious cleavages within the Arab world, no clear policy concerning the moral legitimacy of Jewish *aliyah* was ever defined.

While continuing to condemn Washington's volte-face on immigration policy, various Arab states and organizations applied diplomatic pressure on Moscow to reconsider its approval of mass Jewish emigration. Already, the Soviet Union had decided to suspend an agreement on direct flights, reached in principle between Aeroflot and El Al, that would have greatly facilitated the Jewish exodus from the USSR. This was in response to Shamir's speech of 14 January, even though an Israeli government spokesman, Yossi Ben-Aharon, had later stated that 'There is no policy of directing immigrants to Judea, Samaria, and Gaza. We are a free country and anyone who comes to Israel can go and live wherever he chooses.'[19]

In an effort to assuage Arab concerns, Gennady Tarasov, advisor on Middle Eastern affairs to the Soviet Foreign Ministry, was dispatched by Moscow to meet Palestinian leaders. However, despite stating that Soviet *aliyah* should not be used to displace Arabs in the Occupied Territories, Tarasov refused to recommend the suspension of Jewish emigration from the USSR. To have done so could have proved devastating to Gorbachev's attempts to restructure the Soviet economy, dependent as they were upon attracting substantial United States aid and investment.[20]

Many Arabs continued to question Soviet awareness as to the true political significance of the mass exodus, with King Hassan of Morocco calling the migration a nightmare that was 'haunting the Arab nation'.[21] Moscow, anxious to mitigate such concern in Arab capitals, remained keen to exert at least some form of international pressure upon Israel regarding the settlement of its erstwhile citizens. This explains the Soviet rejection of Washington's appeal for the implementation of the moribund agreement on direct flights.[22] Indeed, while continuing to condemn any Israeli settlement of the West Bank, the Soviet Ambassador to the United Nations, Alexandr Belonogov, argued that the United States should revoke its restrictions on immigration.[23]

Still, Moscow continued to reject any overt linkage made in the Arab world between emigration policy and superpower relations. Following a meeting with President Asad on 28 April 1990, Gorbachev denounced accusations of collusion with Washington over the issue, stating that emigration policy was driven purely by 'internal processes in the Soviet Union and by certain undesirable phenomena in inter-ethnic relations'. Yet he went on to add that the 'United States, while provoking emigration from the USSR, has simultaneously closed its doors to emigrants', by itself a tacit recognition of superpower linkage that the Soviets remained so keen to deny.[24]

Despite Moscow's liberal emigration regime, the issue of Soviet Jewry still remained an important function of superpower politics. On 18 May 1990, on the eve of the Washington summit between Presidents Bush and Gorbachev, the Soviet leader conceded to Secretary of State James Baker that he was under considerable pressure from the Arab states to slow substantially, though not halt, the exit of Jews to Israel. Six days later, Gorbachev withdrew legislation enshrining the right of emigration from the Supreme Soviet, a move that caused some disquiet in Washington. When coupled with the imposition of Soviet sanctions against Lithuania, Gorbachev appeared to prejudice a key Soviet objective at the forthcoming summit: the implementation of a trade agreement, including access to Most Favoured Nation status with the United States.[25]

During the course of the summit, held between 30 May and 2 June 1990, Gorbachev elaborated on domestic and international pressure that had forced a postponement of the emigration bill. Opposition within his own politburo had questioned the sagacity of a bill that would allow the unfettered migration of emigrants, both Jews and non-Jews, with skills deemed vital to the economic success of the Soviet leader's own reform programme. Moreover, in a clear attempt to dilute Arab pressure, a press conference held during the course of the summit allowed Gorbachev the opportunity to pour scorn on Israeli settlement policy in the Occupied Territories. Referring to the migration of Soviet Jews to Israel he declared:

> The Soviet Union is now being bombarded by a lot of criticism from Arab countries. Lately I have had meetings with President Asad of Syria and President Mubarak of Egypt. Those were very important talks with them. Nevertheless, this question [Soviet Jewish emigration] was the question that was also raised by them in acute terms.[26]

None the less, Moscow's dependence on gaining access to Western aid negated any serious attempt to impede the exit of Soviet Jewry. Bush did conclude a trade agreement with Gorbachev but made its ratification by Congress dependent upon the passage of the emigration bill through the Supreme Soviet. While this was completed in May 1991, Soviet Foreign Minister Eduard Shevardnadze assured Baker in the aftermath of the summit that nothing would be done to 'jeopardize' the exodus of Soviet Jews.[27] Yet disunity continued to bedevil Arab attempts to co-ordinate an overall strategy designed to thwart the growing exodus of Soviet Jews to Israel. By the end of May 1990, some 38,560 Jews had emigrated to the Jewish State, with the numbers seemingly set to increase. Inter-Arab dissension clearly degraded the effectiveness of the Arab League Summit of 28 May, convened by Saddam Hussein in Baghdad. The summit was primarily concerned with negotiating new oil quotas beneficial to the restructuring of the Iraqi economy in the wake of its long and bloody war with Iran. But at the behest of PLO Chairman Yasser Arafat, the formulation and implementation of a pan-Arab strategy designed to thwart the mass exodus of Soviet Jewry to Israel were placed high on the summit agenda.[28]

Reflecting the continuing ideological and national cleavages that marked Syrian–Iraqi relations, Damascus announced its intention to boycott the meeting. Given that Syria was the most important state belligerent in the Arab–Israeli conflict, al-Asad's decision was a severe body blow to any unified action.[29] Growing unease at the increasingly bellicose stance of Saddam Hussein also resulted in the dispatch of low-ranking Moroccan, Algerian and Omani officials to the summit.

In an effort to invoke broad-based support for Arab opposition to Jewish migration, President Mubarak of Egypt issued a stern warning on the eve of the Baghdad summit: the settlement of Soviet Jews in the territories, he said, would inevitably lead to 'bloody confrontation' in the Middle East.[30] Mubarak's comments came in the aftermath of conflicting statistics regarding the number of Soviet Jews who had settled in the West Bank and Gaza. A report by the United States Central Intelligence Agency stated that ten per cent of the Soviet *olim* had settled in the West Bank and East Jerusalem, annexed by Israel following the June 1967 war. These figures were immediately disputed by Tel-Aviv, which claimed the figure was three per cent for Jerusalem, and half of one per cent for the Occupied Territories as a whole. One Israeli source gave the total number of Soviet immigrants settled on the West Bank between April 1989 and June 1990 as 285, although these figures failed to include those housed in East Jerusalem and its environs.[31]

Israel had captured and annexed East Jerusalem in 1967 but failed to elicit recognition of its sovereignty over it from all Arab and almost all Western states. To the Palestinians of East Jerusalem it seemed obvious that the Israeli government would use the new *olim* to achieve sovereignty through numbers by employing salami-style tactics: settlements such as Gilo and Ma'aleh Adunim would be established claiming jurisdiction under the municipality of the city, which gradually expanded onto the West Bank proper. Indeed, the United States Vice President, Dan Quayle, had already given tacit endorsement to the settling of Soviet Jews in Arab East Jerusalem, but added that this should not encompass the West Bank. The differentiation between East Jerusalem and the West Bank was not expanded upon.[32]

However, Arab hopes of formulating an effective strategy at the Baghdad summit failed to be realized. While all could agree that Soviet Jewish settlement of the Occupied Territories was antithetical to Arab interests, consensus failed to be reached on the legality of any form of *aliyah*, and the culpability of the United States in its implementation. During his opening address to the summit, Saddam Hussein declared:

> There will be no concession on the liberation of Palestine. The United States has demonstrated that it is primarily responsible for the aggressive and expansionist policies of the Zionist entity against the Palestinian Arab people and the Arab nation – never mind the occasional disagreement it

professes with this or that stance or behaviour of the Zionist entity.³³

The Iraqi leader's comments stimulated strong support from both King Hussein and Yasser Arafat, united in the belief that it was incumbent upon the Arab nation to resist Soviet Jewish immigration. Of particular concern to the King was the threat that indigenous Arabs would be uprooted from the West Bank and forced to seek social and economic assistance from the Jordanian government. With the support of Washington and Moscow, Israel, declared Hussein, 'must have selected Jordan out of the broad Arab front as the point through which to penetrate in its premeditated aggression against the Arab nation'.³⁴

The argument that immigration constituted a flagrant act of aggression against the Arab nation was much in evidence during Arafat's address. The mass *aliyah* had placed the PLO chairman in a difficult position. With little of tangible political benefit to show his Palestinian constituency after nearly three years of the *intifada*, Arafat needed firm political action from the wider Arab world if his credibility, seriously challenged by Islamic fundamentalist groups in the Occupied Territories, was not to be seriously eroded. Already, Hamas, in an effort to cultivate support among Palestinians in the Occupied Territories, had presented mass migration as visible proof of Israel's 'unbounded [territorial] ambitions'.³⁵

In an emotive speech, the PLO leader poured scorn upon the United States, claiming that Washington was directly responsible for the 'Judaization' of Palestinian land. Stating that the realization of Jewish national rights was realized at the expense of Palestinian human rights, Arafat proposed a plan for unified Arab action that included 'sanctions, economic boycotts and political and moral pressure on countries, institutions and companies which take part in the process of aggression on Arab land and help in this regard by transferring the Jews'.³⁶

But the conciliatory address delivered by President Mubarak to the conference highlighted the importance of national interest over any moves towards collective Arab action. With his economy heavily dependent upon United States financial aid, the Egyptian leader boldly stated that Washington understood that Arab opposition to the Soviet *aliyah* was based upon a concern for Palestinian human rights, and not on 'fanaticism or racism'. No condemnation of United States immigration policy was ever issued. In seeking to dilute criticism of the Bush Administration, Cairo effectively distanced itself from the hardline attitude of the PLO, Jordan, and Iraq, and merely stated that measures to curb the negative effects of Soviet Jewish immigration would soon emerge. The substance of these measures was not disclosed.[37]

The final communiqué issued by the Arab leaders highlighted the overall failure to conclude any effective strategy. While the obligatory references were made to Israeli aggression and terrorism, it was the United Nations which was charged with creating a supervisory body to prevent the settlement of Jews in 'Palestine and the other Occupied Arab Territories'.[38] The call for United Nations involvement appeared to be a convenient political mechanism, alleviating the Arab League of the responsibility to implement diplomatic sanctions that would never enjoy pan-Arab support. Indeed, it was not until a meeting of Arab foreign ministers held in Tunis in July 1990 that any form of collective action was agreed upon. This involved an Arab boycott of commercial companies and non-governmental institutions – though not states – that helped facilitate the migration of Soviet Jewry.[39]

Washington and the Arabs
With Jewish Agency Chairman, Simcha Dinitz, announcing that some 50,000 Soviet Jews had migrated to the Jewish State since April 1989, Arab attempts to influence, let alone stem, the mass *aliyah* to Israel appeared to be marked by failure.[40] But even before the Gulf Crisis of August 1990, individual Arab representations to Washington, coupled with international protest at Yitzhak Shamir's speech of 14 January, placed increasing pressure on the Bush Administration to seek guarantees on the settlement of the new Soviet *olim* firmly within Israel.

President Bush had announced in October 1989 that he would favourably consider any request for financial aid from Tel-Aviv in the resettlement of Soviet Jews, providing this excluded settlement in the West Bank.[41] Nevertheless, Arab concern at Israeli intent following Shamir's speech was forcefully expressed to the White House by the Egyptian Ambassador to Washington.[42]

Direct US aid to Israel at the beginning of 1990 stood at some $3bn per annum, sanctioned by Congress. Israel was also the recipient of indirect aid or grants that were not based on laws by

Congress. These grants included money already earmarked for the absorption of Soviet *aliyah* as well as $180m in strategic co-operation for the development of advanced military technologies. In March 1990, Israel's debt to the United States totalled $11bn, yet Tel-Aviv now sought a further $400m for the absorption of Soviet Jews, a clear indication that the Jewish State had insufficient societal resources to cope with the demands of an ever growing *aliyah*.[43]

Yet despite Shamir's dependence upon Washington's largesse, a study by the Jerusalem-based West Bank Data Project showed that the Israeli government was providing substantial financial inducements for its citizens to settle in the Occupied Territories. These inducements included large cash subsidies, low interest mortgages, and free land, often expropriated from the indigenous population. Depending on size of family, up to $21,600 was available in housing benefits for those choosing to move to West Bank settlements, compared with $20,200 for those who chose to opt for a development town within Israel's pre-1967 borders.[44]

By March 1990, Washington had become increasingly concerned over Israel's continuing settlement of the West Bank. This was proving the main impediment to renewed efforts by Secretary of State James Baker to revitalize the moribund Middle East peace process. Now, stung by Arab criticism, particularly that from the Gulf states, of complicity in the absorption of Soviet Jews into the Occupied Territories, President Bush linked the granting of $400m requested by Tel-Aviv in housing guarantees to a total cessation of construction activity in the West Bank and Gaza Strip.[45]

Failure by the Likud government to acquiesce in Washington's conditions resulted in American co-operation with a number of Arab countries in the drafting of a UN resolution condemning any settlement of Soviet Jews in the territories. While the State Department was unable to agree to the wording of the final text, the fact that the United States – which had customarily vetoed Arab resolutions hostile to the Jewish State – had been involved in the process at all caused acute anger and dismay in Israel.[46]

However, with Soviet *aliyah* reaching 101,736 by the end of September 1990, Israel's need for financial aid became ever more urgent if severe dislocation to the social and economic fabric of the country was to be avoided.[47] With the outbreak of the Gulf Crisis, Washington did eventually agree to the implementation of the $400m loan guarantee in November 1990. While in part a political move, designed to dilute Israeli fears regarding the US–Arab coalition against Iraq, Foreign Minister David Levy was still required to give assurances that the money would not be used to settle Soviet immigrants in either East Jerusalem or the Occupied Territories.[48] The clear inclusion of Arab East Jerusalem was deliberate, erasing the ambiguities in American policy following Vice-President Quayle's remarks, and closely aligning the United States with Egypt, its most moderate Arab coalition partner, in its policy towards Soviet Jewish immigration.

Despite obtaining the $400m loan, Israel's need for even greater financial support in the absorption of Soviet Jewry became all too apparent. On 26 January 1991, during a visit to Washington, Israeli Finance Minister Yitzhak Mo'dai made a request for $10bn in loan guarantees from the United States government. The loan guarantee would not involve actual direct aid to Israel, but would enable it to borrow money from US commercial banks at a preferential rate of interest. Israel was hopeful of a sympathetic hearing, given Tel-Aviv's restraint in the face of Iraq's missile attacks on Israel's main cities.[49]

Yet access to the loans and continued construction and settlement in the Occupied Territories ran counter to the revitalized peace process in the region in the aftermath of the Gulf War. While Israel had accrued international sympathy in the face of Scud missile attacks, the debt incurred by Washington to its Arab coalition partners throughout the conflict far outweighed any political credits that the Likud government had with the Bush Administration. With Washington refusing to grant the loans in the absence of any settlement freeze, the absorption of Soviet Jews severely stretched the social fabric of Israeli society, resulting in growing discontent against the government of Yitzhak Shamir throughout Israel. The position of the Bush Administration was lauded by Saudi Arabia, anxious perhaps to use the issue of Soviet Jewish immigration as a counterbalance to the regional dissonance that still permeated inter-Arab relations. By contrast, Israeli Defence Minister Moshe Arens accused the United States of succumbing to Arab blackmail, referring to statements made by delegations to the Madrid peace process that they would cancel their participation if Washington gave in to Israeli pressure over the loan guarantees.[50]

The Palestinians and Israeli Arabs

The mass *aliyah* of Soviet Jews was met with outright opposition from Palestinians in the West Bank and Gaza Strip, while encountering a mixed reaction from Israel's Arab community. The support of the PLO for Saddam Hussein during the Gulf Crisis, coupled with a benign attitude to the attempted Moscow coup d'état of August 1991 against Gorbachev, discredited the political standing of Yasser Arafat in Moscow. Thus, while Gorbachev restated his opposition to the settlement of Soviet migrants in the Occupied Territories during an interview with the Cairo newspaper *Al-Ahram*, three days later on 30 September, the first direct flight transporting Soviet Jews left Moscow for Tel-Aviv.[51]

This was a bitter blow to the Palestinians in the territories, whose spokesman in East Jerusalem, Feisal Husseini, had always maintained that immigrants were being used to annex Arab land. In February 1990, he espoused the moderate Palestinian position, stating:

> We are not opposed to the immigration of Soviet Jews to Israel. But we are opposed to their being settled on our lands. In other words, we are opposed to a situation in which the rights of some are upheld at the expense of the rights of others. We believe that every person should have the right to leave his country. But he should have the right to choose where he will settle. Soviet Jews have been given the right to leave, but the United States and Israel are depriving them of the right to choose.[52]

With Soviet Jewish *aliyah* totalling some 8,000 for the first six weeks of 1990, Palestinians in the West Bank, Gaza Strip, and East Jerusalem declared a one-day strike in protest. On 19 February 1990, all shops, offices, schools, and factories shut down in protest at the feared influx of Soviet Jewry. Despite evidence to the contrary, many Palestinians declared that hundreds of Soviet *olim* had already settled in the territories, attracted by cheap, subsidized housing provided by the Likud government.[53] The following month, Palestinian deportees in Algiers occupied the US and Soviet embassies in protest at superpower involvement in the migration of Soviet Jews.

Yet while useful in highlighting the real fears of the Palestinians, such actions appeared to achieve little tangible benefit in the absence of a concerted, unified Arab response. In the spring of

1990, a Palestinian delegation, comprising figures from the Occupied Territories, travelled to Moscow in an effort to alert both Jewish leaders and Soviet authorities to Arab concerns underlying mass migration. However, other than conceding to pan-Arab pressure over the issue of direct flights, Moscow was unwilling to link Jewish emigration to Palestinian rights, or the cessation of Israeli settlement activity.[54] A suggestion by the Egyptian Foreign Minister, Esmat Abd al-Meguid, that Soviet Jews be allowed to retain their passports on leaving the USSR was met only by an ephemeral interest in Moscow. Therefore, anger, coupled with severe frustration at their political impotence, characterized the mood of the Palestinians. According to Yahya Abu Sharif of the East Jerusalem newspaper *Al-Ittihad* (Union), many now felt that Shamir was 'going for broke, exploiting the present situation to the fullest and actively settling newcomers to Israel in the Palestinian territories'.[55]

With Jewish *aliyah* continuing to increase, and in the absence of any effective political counter-strategy, the threat of terrorist action was made against those involved in the migration of Soviet Jewry, particularly national airlines. On 21 March 1990, the Hungarian carrier, Malev, briefly suspended its regular and charter flights to Tel-Aviv, following warnings it received from Islamic Jihad.[56] Similarly, on 2 April, the *Jordan Times* reported that the Islamic Army for the Liberation of Palestine had vowed to attack Polish airports used in the transfer of migrating Jews. However, the only serious attack, claimed by the previously unknown Movement for the Protection of Jerusalem, occurred in Budapest on 25 December 1991. A bomb exploded on a bus carrying Soviet Jews to the airport for their flight to Israel. Six people were wounded.[57] Yet these threats failed totally to have any effect upon the scope and pace of the mass *aliyah*.

Further adding to the hardships endured by the Palestinians was the economic consequences of Jewish immigration. In an effort to create employment opportunities for the new *olim*, the Israeli government announced that it planned to halve the number of Palestinian labourers working in Israel to 60,000.[58] Already, the mayor of Rishon Le Zion, a suburb of Tel-Aviv dependent upon Palestinians to run the municipal services, had openly called for the Judaization of labour.[59]

Yet even though unemployment stood at eight per cent among Israelis in January 1990, few had been prepared to undertake menial employment, arguing that such tasks had become the preserve of cheap Arab labour since 1967. But such work was often all that was available to the new immigrants, unable to find employment in many of their chosen professions. Indeed, this *aliyah* contained engineers, scientists, and doctors in abundance. This created tensions for both sides: the immigrant felt frustrated in a menial job, and the Palestinian faced economic hardship that only fuelled his resentment towards Israeli rule.[60]

In addition, many Palestinian families had to endure the loss of remittances from relatives working in Kuwait following the Gulf Crisis and their subsequent expulsion from the region.[61] However, despite increasing levels of poverty throughout the West Bank, the withdrawal of skilled Palestinian labourers from building sites throughout Israel exacerbated the already critical shortage of adequate housing stock, adding to a growing sense of disillusion amongst Israelis.[62] Given the social costs incurred in the absorption of the new *olim*, this proved to be the most effective measure the West Bank Palestinians could implement against the Likud government.

Initially, Israeli Arabs had much to fear from the Soviet *aliyah*. Concentrated primarily in and around the Galilee, an area of high absorption for Soviet Jews, this community already suffered an unemployment rate 50 per cent above the national average. Despite being full Israeli citizens, such levels were indicative of the failure of successive Israeli governments to provide sufficient societal security for their Arab subjects even before the full impact of this immigrant wave came to be realized. Moreover, the high educational profile of this immigrant wave appeared set to undermine employment opportunities among Israeli Arab graduates still further: 40 per cent were already unemployed or underemployed. The magnitude of *aliyah* also seemed to presage the large-scale expropriation of land around existing Arab communities, a portent that these areas would become subject to Judaization in a very real, physical sense. In turn, this posed a very real threat to social cohesion of the Israeli Arab community.[63]

Discrimination in the allocation of resources at the hands of the Jewish-dominated Israeli Knesset had resulted already in growing support for Islamists in Arab towns such as Umm al-Fahem, following national municipal elections in February 1989.[64] Thus, with the arrival of the first Soviet migrants, it became necessary for established figures within Israeli Arab politics to express strong reservations about this *aliyah* if their grass roots support was not to be further eroded. Attempts to alert successive Israeli governments to the discrepancy in the allocation of resources to Arab towns and villages were ignored. A threat to suspend all municipal services by the National Association of Arab Councils, and a protest in February 1990 by 4,000 Israeli Arabs in Haifa against inadequate aid to offset increasing municipal debt, failed to elicit any positive government response.[65]

A more active position was taken by Abna al-Balad (Sons of the Land), the only Israeli Arab movement to confront Soviet Jewish *aliyah* openly. Abna al-Balad, formed in 1972, was the product of a split within the binational Israeli Communist Party, Rakah. It set out to challenge the leadership of Rakah, which, despite its non-Zionist stance, was deemed too moderate and too pro-Israeli, particularly in the aftermath of the June 1967 war. Popular among students, Abna al-Balad aligned itself with the aims of the PLO, though it had refused to condone acts of terror in pursuit of those aims. Moreover, it refrained from openly declaring itself as a national political organization among Israeli Arabs, fearing that to do so would only invite repressive measures from the Israeli authorities. Rather, it had confined its activities to cultural and social events, while allowing members as individuals to stand for seats in municipal elections.[66]

Now, openly explaining that the cost of Jewish immigration had always been borne by the Palestinian people, the Secretary General of Abna al-Balad, Raja Ighbarieh, concluded in an interview with *Ha'aretz* that, 'Adding one million Jews to Israel [the expected total of this immigration wave] forms an actual danger to the very fact of our existence. Transfer of the remaining Palestinians comes closer to realization than it had been before'.[67] A secular, nationalist movement, Abna al-Balad none the less disavowed violent confrontation with the Israeli authorities and concentrated on mobilizing support within the parameters of lawful opposition. It issued a number of pamphlets that re-emphasized the historical continuity that this *aliyah* represented, both in reinforcing a Jewish physical presence and, by extension, in eroding that of the Palestinians. However, the movement also used the economic upheaval in Israeli society to broaden its appeal beyond the remit of its own community. In a pamphlet produced in August 1990, Abna al-Balad called for a co-ordinated position to be established with what were termed 'oppressed Jews', a euphemism for Israel's Oriental Jews. While contacts were established, these never developed into substantive positions that seriously challenged government policies. Rather, the movement concentrated on organizing peaceful demonstrations among Israel's disparate Arab localities, and organizing a mass petition to Moscow urging it to reconsider its policy on emigration.[68]

The activity of Abna al-Balad revealed more discord than consensus in the Israeli Arab position. Several leading community figures, including the Arab Knesset Member, Hussein Faris, criticized the movement for its wholesale opposition to immigration, rather than the threat of settlement over the Green Line. Consequently, opposition to this *aliyah* in the Arab community was centred on economic issues, since the financial burden it imposed remained the only issue over which a broad consensus existed. Thus the Arab mayor of Umm al-Fahem, Sheikh Riyad Zalah, pointed to the 'billions of shekels' set aside to absorb Soviet Jews, at the same time that a 'hundred million shekels' could not be found for Arab councils. The underlying suspicion remained that the new immigrants were part of a broader strategy directed towards the Judaization of the Galilee. As the Israeli Arab journalist Attallah Mansour stated: 'It [Soviet Jewish immigration] threatens the Arab majority, and the prospects of an Arab political, economic, cultural and religious hegemony here. It also reflects a realistic fear of job competition from the new immigrants.'[69]

The fears expressed by Israel's Arabs did find sympathy, albeit limited, among some sections of Israel's Oriental community. Like the Arabs, they had suffered discrimination in jobs and housing; the new *aliyah* seemed to offer more of the same. Despite advances into the professional sectors of the Israeli economy, Oriental Jews were still under-represented in white collar professional occupations – the preserve of the Ashkenazim – while over-represented in occupations of low income and amongst the unemployed. Many lived and continue to live in slum housing, particularly around the southern suburbs of Tel-Aviv. Indeed, a report in *Ha'aretz* on 15 March 1990 disclosed that the start of this immigrant wave coincided with a report by the Israeli National Insurance Institute which revealed that 600,000 Israelis, a disproportionate number of them of Oriental origin, were living below the official poverty line.

Thus, when Arab MK Toufiq Toubi of the Democratic Front for Peace and Equality called on Gorbachev to solve the Soviet Jewish problem within the borders of the USSR, his remarks were endorsed by notable figures among Israel's Oriental Jewish community.[70] Yemin Svissa, leader of Jerusalem's Oriental community, spoke for many, when, in an open letter to the Soviet leader, he called for a delay in the departure of Soviet Jews, and stated that Israel was not prepared, either socially or economically, to absorb such numbers.[71] Co-ordination of the positions of the two communities over the question of *aliyah* was conducted via telephone. Further contacts and meetings were held in the Israeli Arab village of Arara with the active participation of Feisal Husseini. Yet as Dror Ben-Yemini, editor of *Ha'patish*, a journal distributed throughout the poorer areas of Tel-Aviv readily conceded, the search for common ground between Oriental Jews and Israeli Arabs remained confined to the leaderships of both communities. He concluded that mass, popular, co-operation between the two communities in the foreseeable future would continue to remain 'wishful thinking'.[72]

However, even the apparent confluence of interests with Israel's largest Jewish community failed to realize Arab economic and social aspirations. Therefore, when large-scale rioting broke out in Nazareth and other Arab urban areas, following the murder in May 1990 of seven Palestinians from Gaza, many felt that the Palestinian *intifada* would increasingly become a feature of Israeli Arab political life. While an effective demonstration of support for their Palestinian brethren in the Occupied Territories, these overt displays of violence were also recognized as Israeli Arab protest at their economic and social position. As one commentator stated:

> Significantly, both cited grievances over social and economic inequality between Jews and the Arab minority in Israel as being equally important in fuelling resentment as the issue of Palestinian national rights. They listed lack of education, housing and employment opportunities, among Arab grievances. A tour of Lod's Arab slums, which are every bit as squalid as the notorious refugee camps of Gaza, made the point.[73]

The failure of the Likud government to gain the $10bn it had requested in loan guarantees from Washington intensified the hardship and increased resentment towards the Likud government throughout Israeli society. Furthermore, increasing numbers of *olim* became embittered with Likud's handling of the whole absorption process. Emphasis continued to be placed on the construction of settlements in the Occupied Territories, while reliance on the free market to satisfy employment and housing needs within Israel had failed to meet increased demand.

The growing pool of discontent proved fertile ground for political organizations on the centre-left. The International Centre for Peace in the Middle East began to organize workshops, enabling new Soviet *olim* to interact with both Israeli and Palestinian Arabs. The ICPME acknowledged that, at first, extreme caution characterized initial contacts, 'due to the large degree of foreigness separating the two populations, coupled with a growing awareness that both are currently competing for the same jobs'.[74] However, workshops with Palestinian academics trained in the Russian language, combined with visits to Arab Israeli villages, did much to undermine many preconceived views held by the *olim* concerning the Arab world that had been harboured while still resident in the USSR. However, given the financial strictures placed upon the programme, its impact on community relations remained somewhat circumscribed.

Although widespread antipathy appeared dominant in Israeli Arab attitudes towards the Soviet *aliyah*, some welcomed the new arrivals. A case in point was the Druze community, generally considered to be the most benign in its attitude towards the Jewish State. In the village of Jasr el Zarka, the head of the local council, Az al-Din Amash, expressed the hope his village would be able to absorb Soviet Jews, because he believed that this would attract substantial inward investment from the government.[75]

The collapse of the Likud coalition government in January 1992 allowed Israel's Arabs to contribute decisively to the election victory of the Labour alignment under Yitzhak Rabin. The clear commitment by the Labour Party to equal rights and benefits for all Israel's citizens, combined with pledges to halt the construction of political settlements in the Occupied Territories, resulted in more Arabs voting for mainstream Zionist parties than Arab-based parties.[76] Indeed, it was noticeable that the smaller the voting community, for example, single villages, the greater the tendency to vote for either Labour or its coalition partner Meretz.[77] While this was undoubtedly a reflection of political pragmatism rather than an endorsement of mainstream Zionist politics, the five seats won by Hadash and the Democratic Front for Peace and Equality under MK Abd el-Wahab Darousha proved vital in enabling Rabin to form a new government by the narrow margin of just four Knesset seats.

Conclusion
Just as it would be wrong to describe Arab pressure as being paramount in the election of the Labour alignment to power on 23 June 1992, so it would be wrong to dismiss its worth in helping to change the Israeli political landscape. By a process of cause and effect, Arab political pressure did bear fruit, though perhaps not in the way initially intended. As a transnational flow, Soviet Jewish migration was, ironically enough, perceived by both the Arab world and the Likud coalition government as strengthening the strategic capabilities of the Jewish State and its hold upon the Occupied Territories. But in spite of this, the Arab states failed in their attempts to thwart Soviet emigration, not least because internal political division over the legality of *aliyah* to any part of Israel negated effective action.

Nevertheless, Arab protest, particularly its accusations of collusion between the United States and Israel, touched a raw nerve with the Bush Administration, already angered at reports that Soviet Jews were being directed to the Occupied Territories. By originally linking absorption aid to the settlement of Soviet Jews within Israel's pre-1967 borders, and later to the total cessation of all construction activity in the territories, Washington, under Arab pressure, exacerbated tensions already evident in the absorption process.

The ensuing strain on the fabric of Israeli society, not least in the fierce competition for housing and jobs, resulted in widespread anger and disillusion among the new *olim*, sections of the Oriental community, as well as Israel's Arabs. This resentment at the apparent costs involved in absorption, not least in terms of societal security, found its very real expression in the election result of June 1992. In this sense, Arab pressure on the issue of Soviet Jewish *aliyah*, albeit at times convoluted, demonstrated the influence that individual states, Palestinians in the Occupied Territories, and Israeli Arabs could wield in their efforts to oppose the regional agenda of Israel's state élite. These interconnected levels of influence were significant in bringing the Jewish State to a new juncture and one with implications for Israeli-Palestinian peace.

NOTES

1. 'Syria: Asad says Israel "Main Beneficiary" of International Changes, calls for *Jihad* "As long as Time"', *BBC-SWB*, ME/0709 A/3-4, 10 March 1990.
2. *Jerusalem Post International*, 4 Jan. 1992.
3. Andrew Rigby, *Living the Intifada* (London: Zed Press,1991), p.133.
4. Adam Keller, op. cit., pp.89-102.
5. 'Libyan Leader on Arab-Israeli Dispute and other Regional and International Issues', *BBC-SWB*, ME/0656 A/6-7, 8 Jan. 1990.
6. 'Les "Russes" Arrivent, Mais Ou Les Mettre?' (The Russians Are Ariving but Where Will They Go?), *Le Monde*, 25 Jan. 1990.
7. 'M. Arafat Semble Sans Illusion' (Arafat Seems to be without any Illusions), *Le Monde*, 3 Feb. 1990; *Filastin al-Thawra*, 13 Aug. 1989, quoted by Joshua Teitelbaum, *The Arabs and the New Wave of Jewish Immigration to Israel: Back to the Old Ideology?* (Tel-Aviv: The Dayan Center for Middle Eastern and African Studies, Tel-Aviv University, May 1990), p.3.
8. Mohammed Sid-Ahmed, 'Consequences of Perestroika', *Middle East Report*, Vol.20, Nos.3/4 (May–Aug. 1990), p.58.
9. Laurie P. Salitan, op. cit., pp.57-8.
10. 'PLO's Faruq Qaddumi Reviews Coming Arab Moves to Counter Soviet Jewish Emigration to Israel', *BBC-SWB*, ME/0676 A/1, 31 Jan. 1990.
11. *Financial Times*, 25 Jan. 1990; *Al-Dustur* (Amman), 18 Feb. 1990, quoted in Teitelbaum, op. cit., p.7.
12. *New York Times*, 18 Feb. 1990.
13. *New York Times*, 8 Feb. 1990.
14. *Financial Times*, 26 Feb. 1990.
15. R.K. Ramazani, 'Iran's Foreign Policy: Both North and South', *Middle East Journal*, Vol 46, No. 3 (1992), pp.397-8.
16. 'Libyan Leader on Arab-Israeli Dispute and other Regional Issues', *BBC-SWB*, ME/0657 A/6, 8 Jan. 1990.
17. Arieh Palgi, 'Sheor Be Tzionit le Arafat' (A Lesson in Zionism for Arafat), *Al Hamishmar*, 27 March 1990.
18. 'Statement by the League of Arab States on the Settlement of Soviet Jewish Emigrants in the Occupied Territories and South Lebanon, Tunis, 13 March, 1990', in Yehuda Lukacs (ed.), *The Israeli–Palestinian Conflict: A Documentary Record, 1967–1990* (Cambridge: Cambridge University Press/ICPME, 1992), pp.539-40.
19. Ian Black, 'Israel Denounces Kremlin Warning', *The Guardian*, 31 Jan. 1990.
20. Galia Golan, *Soviet Policy in the Middle East: From World War II to Gorbachev* (Cambridge: Cambridge University Press, 1990), pp.267-8; *Izvestia*, 30 Jan. 1990.
21. Simon Tisdall, 'US Calls for Direct Flights to Israel', *The Guardian*, 22 Feb. 1990; *BBC-SWB*, ME/0680 A/4, 5 Feb. 1990.
22. *New York Times*, 20 Feb. 1990.
23. *Washington Post*, 16 March 1990.
24. *Pravda*, 29 April 1990.
25. Michael R. Beschloss and Strobe Talbott, *At the Highest Levels: The Inside Story of the End of the Cold War* (London: Warner Books, 1994), pp.211-17.
26. Gorbachev's remarks are taken from Robert O. Freedman, 'Jewish Emigration as a Factor in Soviet Foreign Policy toward the United States and Israel', Unpublished Paper, 1992, p.29.
27. Beschloss and Talbott, op. cit., p.230.
28. Efraim Karsh and Inari Rautsi, 'Why Saddam Hussein Invaded Kuwait', *Survival*, Vol.XXXIII, No.1 (1991), pp.22-3.
29. *Financial Times*, 11 May 1990.
30. 'Egyptian President Comments on Emigration of Soviet Jews, Iraqi Intentions',

BBC-SWB, ME/0772 A/6, 24 May 1990; *Financial Times*, 23 May 1990.
31. Wolf Moskovich, op. cit., p.42. Figures released by the CIA cited by Hugh Carnegy and Peter Riddell, 'Israel Says US is Backing Arabs on Migrants', *Financial Times*, 11 May 1990; *Ha'aretz*, 22 March 1991.
32. 'Quayle: Artzot Ha'Brit Eno Mitnaged Le Yehudim Russim be Mizrach Yerushalayim' (Quayle: US Not Opposed to Russian Jews in East Jerusalem), *Ha'aretz*, 7 March 1990.
33. 'Arab summit: Opening Speech by President Saddam Hussein', *BBC-SWB*, ME/0777 A/1-2, 30 May 1990.
34. 'Speech by King Hussein of Jordan', *BBC-SWB*, ME/0777 A/4-5, 30 May 1990.
35. James Piscatori, 'Islamic Fundamentalism in the Wake of the Six Day War: Religious Self-Assertion in Political Conflict', in Silberstein (ed.), op. cit., p.87; Legrain, op. cit., pp.70–87.
36. 'Speech by PLO Leader Yasser Arafat', *BBC-SWB*, ME/0777 A/11, 30 May 1990.
37. 'Egyptian President Addresses Arab Summit', *BBC-SWB*, ME/0778 A/3, 31 May 1990.
38. 'Arab Summit League Final Statement, Baghdad, 30 May 1990' in Lukacs (ed.), op. cit., pp.540–1; *Washington Post*, 31 May 1990; *Izvestia*, 31 May 1990.
39. *Financial Times*, 17 July 1990.
40. 'Israel: Jewish Agency Head Gives figures for Arrivals of Soviet Jews', *BBC-SWB*, ME/0801 A/3, 27 June 1990.
41. *New York Times*, 10 Oct. 1989.
42. 'Soviet Message to PLO on Emigration of Soviet Jews to Israel', *BBC-SWB*, ME/0678 i, 2 Feb. 1990.
43. Amnon Abramovitz, 'Ekh Le Hav'e Et Ha Zam Ha America' (How to Incur America's Displeasure), *Ma'ariv*, 16 March 1990.
44. *New York Times*, 4 March 1990; *Ha'aretz*, 14 June 1990.
45. Peter Riddell, 'US Irritation with Israeli PM Grows', *Financial Times*, 13 March 1990. For protest from the Gulf States see for example Hani al-Rahib, 'Lebensraum for Israel', *al-Watan*, 27 Jan. 1990. Cited in *Middle East International*, No.368 (2 Feb. 1990), pp.20–1.
46. *Financial Times*, 11 May 1990.
47. *Washington Post*, 29 Sept. 1990.
48. 'Shamir Stands by Levy Letter to Receive $400m Guarantee', *Jerusalem Post International*, 10 Nov. 1990.
49. Jeffrey Blankfort, 'Bush Locks Horns with Shamir', *Middle East Report*, Vol.21, No.6 (Nov.–Dec. 1991), p.38.
50. 'Saudi Arabian Commentary Praises USA's Decision on Loan Guarantees to Israel', *BBC-SWB*, ME/1317 A/3, 29 Feb. 1992; 'Arens says Israel "Disappointed" at US Stance on Loan Guarantees', *BBC-SWB*, ME/1293 A/4, 1 Feb. 1992.
51. Vladimir Belyakov, 'Where's a poor Arab to turn?', *Pravda*, 10 Oct. 1991. Cited in *The Current Digest of the Soviet Press*, Vol.XLII, No.41 (13 Nov. 1991), p.24.
52. P. Davidov and N. Sologubuvsky, 'How unwanted guests are received', *Pravda*, 5 Feb. 1990. Cited in *The Current Digest of the Soviet Press*, Vol.XLII, No.5 (7 March 1990), p.21.
53. 'Palestinians Fear Soviet Influx', *Financial Times*, 20 Feb. 1990.
54. Galia Golan, *Moscow and the Middle East: New Thinking on Regional Conflict* (London: Pinter/RIIA,1992), pp.40–1.
55. D Veliky, 'Black Flags over Jerusalem', *Izvestia*, 5 May 1990. Cited in *The Current Digest of the Soviet Press*, Vol. XLII, No. 18 (6 June 1990), pp.21–2.
56. *New York Times*, 22 March 1990.
57. Herb Keinon, 'Budapest Car Bomb Misses Busload of Olim', *The Jerusalem Post International*, 4 Jan. 1992.
58. *Financial Times*, 15 Nov. 1990.
59. 'Rosh Ha' Yair Mekavey She Olim Yikko Et a Mekhomot Ha Avoda Shel Ha Aravim'

(Mayor Hopes that New Immigrants will take Arab Jobs), *Ha'aretz*, 12 Jan. 1990.
60. Ian Black, 'An Exodus on the Brink of Chaos', *The Guardian*, 20 Nov. 1990.
61. Richard Owen, 'Migration Dismays Palestinians', *The Times*, 19 Sept. 1990.
62. Peretz Kidron, 'Knives make Repression Harsher', *Middle East International*, No 397 (5 April 1991), p.9.
63. Sammy Smooha, 'Part of the Problem or Part of the Solution: National Security and the Arab Minority', in Yaniv (ed.), op. cit., pp.118–19. See also Joel Migdal, *Strong Societies and Weak States* (Princeton: Princeton University Press, 1988), p.173. Migdal makes the point that although Israeli Arabs have participated in Israeli social programmes, for example, health and education, the symbols of the Israeli state have continued to remain alien to their wider communal identity.
64. *New York Times*, 11 Feb. 1989.
65. *New York Times*, 27 Feb. 1990.
66. For a detailed discussion of the origins of Abna al-Balad see Elie Rekhess, 'The Arab Nationalist Challenge to the Israeli Communist Party (1970-1985)', *Studies in Comparative Communism*, Vol.XXII, No.4 (1989), pp.337–50. See also Helena Cobban, *The Palestine Liberation Organization* (Cambridge: Cambridge University Press, 1990), p.189.
67. *Ha'aretz*, 4 March 1990, quoted by Majid Al-Haj, 'Soviet Immigration as Viewed by Jews and Arabs: Divided Attitudes in a Divided Country', in Calvin Goldscheider (ed.), *Population and Change in Israel* (Boulder, CO: Westview Press, 1992), pp.98–9.
68. Ibid., p.98.
69. Attallah Mansour, 'Lama Aravim Israelim Metnagdim Le Aliyah' (Why Israel's Arabs Resent Immigration), *Ha'aretz*, 6 March 1990.
70. *Yediot Aharanot*, 21 March 1990; Lili Galili, 'Hashashot Ha Koshrim Sephardim ve Aravim Israelim' (The Fears that Unite Oriental Jews and Israeli Arabs'), *Ha'aretz*, 15 March 1990.
71. *Ha'aretz*, 15 March 1990.
72. Moskovich, op. cit., p.41; *Ha'aretz*, 15 March 1990.
73. Hugh Carnegy,'Israelis uneasy as *Intifada* spreads', *Financial Times*, 23 May 1990.
74. *Interim Report: Public Education Project for New Russian Immigrants* (Tel-Aviv: ICPME, Nov. 1991).
75. Moskovich, op. cit., p.42.
76. Elie Rekhess, 'New Approach, New Power', *Jerusalem Post Magazine*, 12 Feb. 1993.
77. David Capitanchik, 'The Stalemate is Broken: The 1992 Israeli General Election', *Research Report No.4* (London: Institute of Jewish Affairs, 1992), p.11.

7 The June 1992 Israeli General Election: The Impact and Influence of Soviet Jewish Immigration

On 19 January 1992, the Likud coalition government of Yitzhak Shamir collapsed with the resignations of Rehavam Ze'evi and Yuval Ne'eman, leaders respectively of the far-right Moledet and Tehiya parties. Their action was in protest over Israel's presentation of a draft document to the Jordanian–Palestinian delegation during peace talks in Washington that sketched out proposals for the implementation of Palestinian autonomy in the Occupied Territories. Despite assurances to both men 'that the discussion of autonomy is still far away', Shamir was unable to alleviate their concerns that talks on autonomy merely foreshadowed the creation of a Palestinian state.[1] With his government unable to secure the allegiance of a majority in the Knesset, Shamir, after consultation with the opposition Labour alignment, chose 23 June 1992 as election day for parties to the thirteenth Knesset.

Realizing the challenge that had resulted from his own adherence to the concept of *Eretz Y'Israel*, Shamir quickly signalled his intent to continue settlement activity apace in the Occupied Territories, in spite of 'land for peace' as the central issue of the new peace process. Speaking at Betar, a settlement south-east of Jerusalem, just two days after the cabinet crisis, he loudly proclaimed, 'We see the building here and all over Judea and Samaria. This building will continue and no force on earth will halt it.'[2] This constituted a clear and continued rejection of the correlation that Washington had established between the loan guarantees and the settlement policy of the Israeli government. Indeed, despite Israeli government claims that the loan guarantees were a humanitarian issue and not a political one, US policy remained steadfast. Washington had come to realize that the loan guarantees had the capacity to release capital, as had the $400m aid package, for use beyond the Green Line.

Shamir remained optimistic none the less that the loan guarantees would be forthcoming. Many felt that Washington's endorsement of Soviet Jewish emigration, dating back to the period of *détente*, placed a moral duty on the United States to meet the financial demands that mass *aliyah* had placed upon Israel. Moreover, Shamir also remained confident that he would receive the necessary mandate from the Israeli electorate, and one that remained premised upon the 'the three no's': no independent Palestinian state; no return of land captured in the June 1967 war; and no negotiation with, or recognition of, the PLO.[3] Such confidence was born from several factors, most notably the apparent disarray among the leadership of the Labour alignment, and the supposition that Oriental support for the Likud remained a political given. This propensity to regard political allegiance through the prism of historical determinism also reflected Likud's approach to the Soviet Jews who were entitled to participate in the forthcoming election.

Of some 400,000 immigrants who had arrived in Israel since 1989, 260,000 were entitled to vote. Therefore, while Soviet immigrants now superseded Oriental Jews – particularly those of Moroccan origin – as the largest ethnic community in the Jewish State, it also empowered them with the demographic potential to command the destiny of up to ten seats in the new Knesset. Such votes were crucial to the formation of the new Israeli government and, by extension, the scope and pace of negotiations to resolve the Arab–Israeli conflict.[4]

Likud appeared confident that it would be the net beneficiary of Israel's newest constituency, not least because it had been responsible for facilitating the passage of the Soviet Jews to the Jewish State. Furthermore, the voting patterns of previous waves of Soviet immigrants, most notably those who made *aliyah* throughout the 1970s, were taken as the benchmark for determining the political allegiance of the Soviet *olim*. This thinking placed normative assumptions on the Soviet Jews, particularly the belief that most of them remained hostile to any institution that contained even a vestige of socialist ideology.[5]

The assumption of what the Soviet immigrants should believe and do ignored empirical data on what they were actually becoming. While initial immigrant reaction to the Likud government had been positive, the problems of housing and employment had begun to erode support for Shamir among both

Israelis and *olim* alike. Further to these grievances and particular to the Soviet Jews remained the distress over social status and civil rights, an issue over which Likud had paid deference to an Orthodox agenda. Such existential problems associated with absorption dominated immigrant concerns, rather than the more vexed debates surrounding territorial consolidation or compromise.

This was clearly reflected in the nascent development of a political culture within the immigrant community. The list of parties running for election included several formed by Soviet *olim*, most notably Da (Democracy and *Aliyah*). Yet despite attracting widespread sympathy among the immigrants, financial paucity, coupled with a naive approach towards Israeli politics, negated any meaningful support for a party whose success was premised upon a narrow socio-economic agenda. Many Soviet immigrants were, however, attracted to the party platforms of Israel's centre-left Zionist parties. Having resolved the struggle for its leadership, Labour began to mount an impressive campaign that placed socio-economic issues within the broader context of Israel's security and ideological debates.

Furthermore, the formation of Meretz, a coalition of the civil rights party Ratz, the socialist Mapam, and liberal Shinui parties, created a political bloc whose avowedly anti-religious platform found a particular resonance among both immigrants and young or first-time Israeli voters. With widespread disenchantment with Likud among both immigrants and Israelis, the centre-left parties proved much more effective in promoting their respective party platforms than the right. That they were able to do so produced what Leon T. Hadar has termed a *mahapach*, a mini-revolution, the consequences of which impacted directly upon the configuration of the Arab–Israeli conflict.[6]

Immigration and the Political Right in Israel
Despite the socio-economic malaise that accompanied Likud's handling of Soviet *aliyah*, Yitzhak Shamir remained confident that his party would attract the majority of immigrants' votes in the forthcoming election. Such confidence was born of several factors that appeared to work in favour of the Likud and parties to the right. The Likud believed the rejection of communist ideology, apparent in the very act of Soviet Jewish emigration, would supersede any frustration over the absorption process, and negate any substantial support for the centre-left parties in Israel.[7]

The belief in an inherent right-wing homogeneity among the *olim* extended to the realm of geopolitical certainty. Likud strategists believed that immigrants' experience of anti-Semitism throughout the USSR had conditioned them to accept a right-wing territorial agenda. This argument was most forcefully put by Alec Glassman, Likud campaign co-ordinator among Soviet Jews and himself a former immigrant from Latvia. Glassman declared that, 'They [Soviet immigrants] come here traumatized by wars and revolutions. They are open to the idea that the further away from the border, the better.'[8] Others inferred that the sum total of Jewish experience throughout the USSR had imparted collective support for the more extreme forms of territorial aggrandizement among *olim*.

> The immigrants come from the wide expanses of Russia to this tiny country, and then Israel's left-wing politicians tell claustrophobic Russians that even this country, for all its tiny size, must be divided. This seems a lunatic notion to them. And since they come from a country where entire nations have been transferred from place to place, the idea of transfer doesn't seem terrible to them.[9]

Such social and historical determinism placed immigrants firmly within the orbit of the more extreme forms of right-wing Zionist ideology. Certainly, Tsomet, Tehiya, and Moledet, a party whose manifesto called for the mass expulsion of the Palestinian populace from the Occupied Territories, were particularly active among immigrant communities throughout the country. While refusing to condone such policies, the Likud campaign amongst immigrants clearly placed emphasis upon the strategic benefits that Israel had accrued in continuing to hold territory captured in the June 1967 war. In well-rehearsed coach trips around the Jewish State – a method of canvassing used by all parties in an attempt to harness immigrant votes – Likud Party workers placed particular emphasis upon the vulnerability of the coastal conurbations to Arab attack if Israel were to relinquish control of 'Judea and Samaria'. Subordinate to the needs of security, informed discussion of Likud's ideological claim to the territories remained the exception rather than the rule. Moreover, Likud's immigrant campaign negated any meaningful debate over the ethics and efficacy of Israel's continuing rule over some two million Palestinian Arabs.[10]

Early opinion polls conducted among Soviet Jews demonstrated their identification of territorial interest with the political right. In October 1990, 55 per cent of immigrants preferred retention of the West Bank and Gaza over any formal peace treaty, with 85 per cent expressing some support for the idea of population transfer. A similar poll taken among immigrants in January 1992 seemed to confirm immigrant support for territorial consolidation: 60 per cent of those asked opposed territorial concessions. Yet when the question was restructured to include the return of land if this promoted employment opportunities throughout Israel, 72 per cent replied in the affirmative.[11]

This survey revealed a broader conceptual base behind the immigrant concept of security than Likud and the political right were prepared to appreciate. While concerns over Arab military potential attracted immigrant support for the idea of strategic depth, threats to their social well-being were more immediate to their experience of life in Israel. The atrophy in bilateral relations with Washington, coupled with the poor performance of Israel's absorption bureaucracy, only reinforced the immigrants' need for social protection within the milieu of the free market. While this *aliyah* had in part been premised upon material fufilment, social security previously enjoyed in the USSR however basic, had at least afforded employment opportunities commensurate with a person's skills. This social inheritance, deeply embedded within the collective psyche of the immigrant community, proved inimical to Likud's economic, political, and ideological agenda beyond the Green Line.[12]

Yet adherence to ideological orthodoxy precluded meaningful investment in this dimension of security. Rather, as a caretaker government in the run-up to the June elections, Shamir endorsed an increase in the number of housing starts throughout the Occupied Territories. Therefore, despite a Finance Ministry report predicting an unemployment rate of 16 per cent if the loan guarantees were not forthcoming, Shamir dismissed any causal link between access to the loan guarantees and 'the absorption of hundreds of thousands of immigrants and the continued development of Judea, Samaria, and the Gaza district'. Such statements reaffirmed his personel commitment to *Eretz Y'Israel*, while representing an attempt to enforce party discipline under the banner of ideological conformity.[13]

Unity within the Likud Party leadership had, by March 1992,

become a scarce commodity. The selection of candidates for the party list, a particularly convoluted process, had exposed cleavages within the party hierarchy that at one time threatened to split the party. Election to the party leadership, determined by 3,150 members of the Likud central committee, resulted in Shamir receiving 46 per cent of votes cast, the largest of all competing candidates. The runner up, David Levy, received 32 per cent of the vote, support that convinced the Foreign Minister that he had secured a position of influence second only to that of Shamir himself. Yet in the second round of voting called to determine the party list of 50 Likud candidates for the Knesset, Levy achieved only eighteenth place. Furthermore, and much to the chagrin of David Levy, only eight of his supporters within the Likud party structure received the necessary votes to be placed on the party list. Four of these were in such lowly positions that they were unlikely to receive a sufficient quota of votes necessary to support entry to the Knesset.

Given that Levy, himself an immigrant from Morocco, commanded wide support among the Oriental community, his placement of eighth on the list was credited to the Ashkenazim bias inherent within the party structure. The final round of voting appeared to confirm such prejudice: amid rumours of pacts between the largely Ashkenazim supporters of Shamir, Moshe Arens, and Ariel Sharon, the election for the top 28 positions on the Likud list, during which central committee members placed seven candidates in order of preference in four separate rounds of voting, resulted in Levy achieving only fourth place behind Shamir, Arens, and Sharon.

Believing that his placement did not reflect his popular support among Likud voters, Levy gave one week's notice, effective from 29 March 1992, of his intention to resign from the party. This ultimatum presented Shamir with an acute dilemma. The relative strength of Arens and Sharon indicated strong support for retention of the Occupied Territories throughout the Likud central committee. Indeed, Shamir was concerned that failure to comply with a hardline agenda towards Middle East peace would translate into greater support for Tehiya, Tsomet, and Moledet. However, concern at the possible erosion of Oriental support for Likud forced Shamir into striking a political deal with Levy. In return for withdrawing his impending resignation, Shamir promised that the position of Foreign Minister and deputy Prime

Minister would be offered to Levy in the event of a Likud victory in June. Such political brinkmanship provoked an angry response from Arens and exposed new schisms within the leadership. The deal, cut at the expense of the erstwhile Defence Minister, did little to mitigate the rancour and bitterness that continued to plague the Likud throughout its election campaign.[14]

The acceleration of the settlement programme was, therefore, contingent on the needs of party unity. It was also a direct riposte to Washington after it refused to compromise on conditions set forth over Israeli access to the loan guarantees. Consequently, Sharon stated that construction in the Occupied Territories would continue 'without concern for either the elections or the resumption of the peace talks'.[15] This declaration was echoed by Shamir at election rallies throughout Israel. Speaking before party supporters in Jerusalem, he proudly stated:

> From 1977, all Israeli governments regarded the liberated parts of our homeland as more than collateral for a time when negotiations are held, as an integral part of the country to which the people of Israel have returned. The settlement in these areas has become one of the cornerstones of the government's policy – and not out of political considerations, not only out of security considerations, but for the simple reason that these parts are ours and will remain ours forever.[16]

A clear reaffirmation of the guiding ethos behind the Likud Party notwithstanding, to view the election campaign through an ideological prism was to obscure the development of public opinion away from consolidation of *Eretz Y'Israel*. One poll, conducted by the Dahaf Research Institute for the Tel-Aviv-based ICPME throughout February 1992, showed 63 per cent of Israelis in favour of an Israeli-Palestinian settlement, premised upon land for peace.[17] A more sophisticated picture of the Israeli electorate had been produced in 1990 by the Israeli political scientist Elihu Katz. Rather than a straight division between 'hawks' and 'doves' over the issue of the territories, Katz sketched the emergence of a third body of public opinion, which he termed security hawks, or more euphemistically, 'dawks'. His research showed that 30 per cent of Israelis approved the return of the territories, while 40 per cent supported the concept of *Eretz Y'Israel* wholeheartedly. However, 30 per cent, the security hawks, were willing to compromise over the territories if sufficient security guarantees were forthcoming.[18]

These findings, as Hadar points out, indicated that Israeli public opinion was far more sanguine over the future of the Occupied Territories than was the Likud leadership. Moreover, Katz's research suggested that 35 per cent of Likud supporters viewed themselves as security hawks. Given the dependence upon United States financial and military aid to ensure strategic security, the deterioration in bilateral relations with Washington over loan guarantees was identified by this group as detrimental to Israel's long-term security needs and interests.[19] Clearly, such sentiment was amplified by the impact of Soviet immigration on Israeli society. While a demographic boost to Israel as a nation, the conditions imposed by ideological orthodoxy on the very process of absorption undermined the economic and military security of that selfsame nation. Failure to comprehend this dimension of immigration helped to shift the support of the security hawks towards the political agenda of the centre left. Therefore, as a transnational flow, migration complicated the security arrangements of the Jewish State at the level of interstate co-operation, thus moving societal support away from the Likud coalition government.

Movement was also discernible in the attitudes of Israel's Oriental community towards the Likud agenda. Reflecting on the social and economic costs wrought by mass *aliyah*, many within the community questioned the precedence placed by Likud in consolidating *Eretz Y'Israel* over the more immediate needs of Israeli society. One Oriental protest group, the Movement for a Halt to Immigration, announced in May 1992 its intention to field candidates for the Knesset, declaring that 'Israel is incapable of absorbing the Russian immigrants in the present political circumstances'.[20] Though very much a fringe group – their platform, a direct contravention of the Law of Return, placed them in the role of political pariahs – their position won some sympathy from a community that felt it had borne a disproportionate burden in the absorption of Soviet Jewry.

The Likud campaign singularly failed to address social and economic problems that Soviet Jewish immigration had imposed upon Israeli society. Emphasis was continually placed upon consolidating Israel's legitimate hold on the territories, a process which assumed that the loyalty of immigrants would be forthcoming simply because of their perceived aversion to any organization tainted with an apparently discredited ideology. Such assumptions undermined a cohesive and effective election campaign among Soviet *olim*, a marked contrast with the political capital that the centre-left parties invested in the new immigrants.[21]

Moreover, adherence to the revisionist concept of *Eretz Y'Israel* precluded any concerted attempt to tackle the mounting social and economic dislocation presented by the great wave of Soviet *aliyah*. According to a quarterly report issued by Peace Now in the summer of 1992, April, May and the beginning of June saw work commence on 4,000 new housing units over the Green Line. The allocation of funds to settlement construction had already resulted in the cancellation of eight road projects which were needed to ease the growing traffic congestion in and around Tel-Aviv.[22]

The Politicization of Soviet Jewish Aliyah
The development of political identity among the immigrant community reflected three interconnecting factors: past experience in the Soviet Union; present experience of *mizug galuyot*; and the perception or misperception of party élites in determining the exact impact of these two environments on Soviet Jewish political allegiance. Past experience alone suggested that the political right stood to accrue the maximum benefit from immigration. Such judgements assumed this *aliyah* to be an extension, albeit far larger, of the immigrant wave of the 1970s, which had since shown a predilection for the Likud and parties to the right.

Certainly, one poll conducted among immigrants during the course of 1990, showing a majority in favour of consolidating Israeli rule over the Occupied Territories, intimated a continuity in this political preference.[23] However, such comparisons disguised fundamental differences between the two immigrant waves which helped form disparate political identities. The most notable immigrants of the 1970s had been the refuseniks, people such as Ida Nudel, Yosef Mendelevich, Yuli Edelstein, and Nathan Sharansky, the products of urban, distinctly European environments. Yet among Soviet Ashkenazim Jewry, their attachment to Zionism remained very much the exception rather than the rule. The majority of Jews allowed to emigrate by the Soviet authorities came from the outlying regions of the Soviet Union, notably Georgia, Moldova, and Uzbekistan.

The absorption of this wave gave rise to the phenomenon of 'Instant Patriotism', an intense vituperation of the Arab world that even surpassed the more extreme rhetoric of the far right in Israel. In part a reflection of the persecution that they had endured, it was also a powerful means to establish credibility with, and acceptance by, the Israeli people. It is thus not surprising that a high proportion of the 1970s immigrant wave settled in the West Bank. Indeed, Sharansky's wife, Avital, established close ties with Gush Emunim.[24]

By contrast, the urban origins and the paucity of Zionist identification marked Soviet *aliyah* from 1989 onwards. This did not necessarily negate the prevalence of revisionist views concerning the future of the territories among *olim*. Such sentiment was, according to party workers active among new immigrants, a product of their collective experience of Soviet society. This included an education that had justified the use of force towards an ideological end, most notably in Czechoslovakia and Afghanistan.[25] None the less, immigrants developed a marked tendency to congregate around the urban sprawl of Israel's coastal plain. Not only were employment opportunities deemed to be more readily available, but such areas represented the continuity of an urban existence, easing the process of absorption and integration into Israeli society. Yet the magnitude and density of immigrants soon exposed inherent faults within the absorption process that the Likud government failed to redress. Accordingly, immigrant support for territorial consolidation, however latent, was overshadowed by the more immediate issues of economic and social well-being.[26]

A direct relationship existed between Likud absorption policy and the emergence of an immigrant political identity. This proved largely to be a product of their previous political environment, although a criticism of present absorption policy was also clearly present. Conditioned to believe in an absolute, single truth, immigrants found the political pluralism of Israeli politics uncongenial to their immediate experience. To this extent, immigrant disillusion was derived from the absence of political certainty, a process that could deliver economic and social well-being, rather than a reasoned appreciation of the diffuse nature of Israel's political system.[27]

Organizations designed to serve the interests of Soviet Jewry did already exist in Israel. The most prominent of these was the

Soviet Jewish Zionist Forum, or Forum, headed by Nathan Sharansky. Forum was an important conduit for immigrants to apply pressure on government, particularly over housing and employment. It produced monthly newsletters detailing retraining programmes and job vacancies, while placing a limited legal service at the disposal of the *olim*. Moreover, Forum had been active in highlighting the shortcomings of direct absorption in meeting the needs of old and infirm immigrants.[28]

Given his personal commitment to Zionism, coupled with an obvious concern for the welfare of the Soviet immigrant community, Sharansky appeared the natural choice to lead an immigrant party list for the thirteenth Knesset. Indeed, a poll conducted in October 1990 by Public Opinion Research of Israel suggested that 60 per cent of Soviet *olim* supported the establishment of an independent immigrant party.[29] However, because of his reputation, the former refusenik enjoyed only limited appeal among the new wave of *aliyah*. According to Shai Grishpon, himself a former immigrant and a Mapam party activist, Soviet *olim* viewed Sharansky as an establishment figure rather than somebody with whom they could readily identify.[30]

Indeed, Sharansky personified the clear differences between the immigrants of the 1970s and the present wave of *aliyah*. The closed nature of Soviet society not only disabused most Jews of a political and national identification with Zionism, but also of an appreciation for those who were struggling to assert that very identification in their attempts to emigrate. Therefore, the image of Sharansky as a human rights activist, a profile that dominated Western perceptions of the refuseniks, proved alien to the experience of his erstwhile compatriots. Hence, the status accorded refuseniks in general, and Sharansky in particular, met the disapproval of the majority of *olim*. From their perspective, he remained 'too rich, too Zionist, and too well-connected'. In short, it was not his political opinions that alienated Soviet immigrants – Sharansky espoused views sympathetic to the right of the political spectrum – but his influence and social standing within the host society.[31]

The impact of such sentiment was to negate any effective attempt by Sharansky in forming a political party. Moreover, any effort to harness immigrant discontent required a comprehensive political programme capable of unifying the demands of single-issue pressure groups. These ranged from Community of *Aliyah*

90 (Kehela Aliyah 90), to the Community of Chernobyl (Kehela Chernobyl), the Community of Single Mothers (Kehela Michparot Had Horiot), and the Community of Doctors (Kehela Rofim).[32] The demands of these groups, though representing individual needs, were essentially eclectic in nature, highlighting the preponderance of social issues in determining an immigrant agenda.

The magnitude of Soviet Jewish *aliyah* was reflected in the mass expansion of the Russian-language media throughout Israel. This included the publication of three different daily newspapers and up to 12 weekly newspapers. These ranged in style and content from serious broadsheets through to the more sensationalist tabloids such as *Panorama*. Unlike their Hebrew counterparts, stories detailing the social problems of this *aliyah* were common fare throughout the Russian media. Yet the very ownership of this media undermined concerted support for an immigrant party among the *olim*. *Nasha Strana*, a Russian-language broadsheet established in the 1970s, was controlled by the Histadrut. *Ma'ariv*, appreciating the potential of the Russian-language market, founded *Vremya*, before a dispute over wages and contracts saw its most talented journalists leave en masse for *Vestiye*, a paper established under the auspices of the main circulation rival of *Ma'ariv, Yediot Aharanot*.[33]

These papers had their own vested political interests and harnessed tales of immigrant hardships towards those ends. Immigrant parties were unable to compete with the fiscal power and distribution networks that the major parties could command in the struggle for the votes of their Soviet compatriots. Thus the Labour party was able to place full-scale advertisements in *Vremya*, which castigated the Likud government over the number of Soviet *olim* involved in prostitution. While concern among immigrant parties over this painful social issue proved just as great, financial constraints imposed strict limits on the capital that could be invested in political campaigning through the media. This undermined the appeal of immigrant parties among the *olim*, creating the impression that only the established parties carried the necessary weight to address immigrant concerns.[34]

A clear case in point proved to be the fate of the largest immigrant party to contest the Knesset election, Da, an acronym for Democracy and *Aliyah*. Da was founded in March 1992 under the leadership of Yuli Kosharovsky, himself a former refusenik who had made *aliyah* to Israel in 1983. The Da party platform was a clear reflection of immigrant concerns: deregulation of the economy to promote job creation, the separation of 'church from state', the implementation of a civil rights law, and the drafting of all citizens, irrespective of religious commitment, into the IDF.[35]

Such policies should have attracted sufficient support among immigrants to win at least three Knesset seats, enabling Da to hold the balance of power between the two main political blocs. Certainly, a poll conducted during the course of November 1991 suggested that an established immigrant party would command up to 40 per cent of the immigrant vote.[36] These hopes were dashed following the June election: Da received 12,000 votes only, inadequate to support even the mandate of one Knesset member. While in part due to insufficient time required to organize his campaign effectively, Kosharovsky blamed his electoral defeat on the exiguity of his party's financial support.[37]

The whole issue of ethnic 'Russian' parties had proved controversial with the Israel electorate. Socio-economic issues dominated the Da Party platform, issues that carried a broader appeal across the strata of Israeli society. Indeed, because *aliyah* represented a consensual pillar of Zionism, some leading activists, including Sharansky, felt that the whole issue of absorption should become subject to a collective political programme. Noticeably, however, Da had remained non-committal in articulating a party position on the Occupied Territories. Kosharovsky had called for the issue to be put to a national referendum, but this statement said more about the need to avoid dissonance within his own party than it did about a steadfast commitment to such a course of action.[39]

None the less, when combined with the potential of its ethnic base, Da aroused considerable antipathy among the Israeli electorate. Many felt that, if successful, sufferance of a parochial agenda by the majority party would lead to policy outcomes inconsistent with broad-based national support. Such hostility was already evident towards the religious parties whose concessions, exacted in support for a wider political programme, often conflicted with the wishes of a largely secular society. Yet inadequate funds, the inability to establish an effective party network in just three months, and the failure to mount any effective media campaign disabused Da of any hope that it would become a net beneficiary of the process of coalition politics in Israel.

The failure of Da to become a political force had another, albeit less obvious, dimension. At the party's founding convention, Yuli Kosharovsky declared that:

> Although we are centrists, this doesn't mean that we don't have views concerning security. If we can find solutions for socio-economic problems, and create conditions conducive to a warm reception for massive immigration, then we'll make progress in that direction as well. With substantial population growth security will no doubt improve and we will be in a better position to negotiate the future of the territories.[39]

This statement clearly inferred that strategic security was conditional upon the successful absorption of Soviet Jewish *aliyah*. Therefore, precedence accorded to the socio-economic needs of immigrants would endow Israel with *future* strategic benefits. Rather than assuming that absorption of the *olim* and state security were mutually interdependent in the present as Labour held, Kosharovsky implied a sequential approach had to be taken. If priority were given now to the socio-economic well-being of the immigrants, it would *later* lead to enhancing the security of the state. While social security remained the dominant concern among Soviet *olim*, strategic security, deeply ingrained within the collective conscience of this *aliyah*, remained a potent force in helping to determine voting behaviour. The success of the centre left was to show that the relationship between security and immigrant welfare could be concurrent, rather than one having to follow on from the other.[40]

Labour, Rabin, and Soviet Jewish Immigration
In December 1990, a nationwide opinion poll commissioned by the Histadrut-controlled newspaper, *Davar*, registered support for the Labour Party at 21 per cent, an all-time low. Even with the inclusion of Mapam, Ratz, and Shinui, the centre left could only attract the support of 33 per cent of those interviewed, down seven percentage points on electoral support that the centre left had enjoyed in the 1988 national elections.[41] Moreover, support for Likud appeared strong among Soviet immigrants: in April 1991, it stood at 46 per cent against 21 per cent for Labour. Although this gap had somewhat narrowed by the following November – of those *olim* polled, 36 per cent voiced support for

Likud compared to 26 per cent for Labour – Yitzhak Shamir remained the preferred immigrant choice for Prime Minister, gaining a 68 per cent approval rate. By contrast, Labour leader, Shimon Peres, attracted support from only 21 per cent of Soviet immigrants.[42]

The decline in popular support for the Labour party was the outcome of public dismay with the internecine strife within the party hierarchy. This unease throughout the party, a product of personal and political rivalry between Peres and Yitzhak Rabin, obscured the development of a coherent, structured opposition to the Likud coalition government. As party leader, Peres had presided over four electoral defeats, a record brought into sharp relief by his failure to achieve a Knesset mandate following the collapse of the National Unity Government in March 1990. Moreover, Peres, perhaps unfairly, had earned a widespread reputation for expending political capital on the Palestinian issue, rather than addressing the more urgent social and economic problems wrought by Likud policies.[43]

For his part, Rabin remained suspicious of Peres, not least because of their long-standing rivalry over the party leadership. As a former IDF Chief of Staff, Prime Minister, and Defence Minister, his security credentials were impressive. Indeed, as Defence Minister at the begining of the *intifada,* it was Rabin who introduced the so-called 'Iron Fist' or the use of 'force, power and blows', in an attempt to reassert Israeli control of the West Bank and Gaza Strip. Although such punitive measures met with national and international condemnation, not least from sections of the Israeli media, they enjoyed broad support among Israelis themselves.[44]

The immediate need to crush the Palestinian uprising did not, however, reflect Rabin's view on the overall need for territorial compromise. Although dismissive of any return to Israel's pre-1967 borders and the establishment of a Palestinian state, Rabin conceded the validity of the need to exchange land for peace. On 21 November 1991, in a speech before the Israeli Labour Party convention, Rabin declared his belief that Israel would have to relinquish control of 'many kilometres' if regional peace were to be realized.[45]

While helping to synthesize factional positions over this issue, the leadership of the party remained unresolved. Indeed, it was the belief that it would remain a divisive issue, negating any attempt to run an effective campaign, that persuaded Shamir to dissolve the Knesset and bring forward the national election from November to June 1992. However, elections for both the Labour leadership and party list produced a unified, rejuvenated political force, capable of attracting support beyond its traditional Ashkenazim constituency. On 19 February 1992, in direct elections for the leadership among the party membership, Rabin received 40.5 per cent of the vote, six percentage points ahead of Peres and enough to secure his mandate for the party leadership.[46]

If the election of Rabin was a victory for the security 'hawks' within the party, the selection of the party list produced tangible rewards for the 'doves'. While Peres gained second place on the party list, his Knesset supporters achieved more remarkable success. The election of Avraham Burg, Ora Namir, and Haim Ramon, all self-proclaimed 'doves', to three of the top ten positions on the party list came at the expense of the 'hawks' within the party. Moreover, the election of Burg to the third slot on the party list reflected the widespread sympathy that had accompanied his call for a clear separation of 'church and state' at the 1991 party convention.[47]

In sum, elections for the leadership and Knesset list produced a party with a broad-based appeal. Rabin's reputation on strategic issues blunted criticism from the Likud that any Labour government would have a debilitating effect on Israel's security. Indeed, these very credentials were a positive asset in attracting support from disaffected security 'hawks' in the Likud and, more importantly, capturing the immigrant vote. To this end, Rabin's reputation, harnessed to the relatively young, 'dovish', and secular profile of the party list, produced a political agenda that struck at the very core of immigrant concerns: socio-economic needs and physical security.

This was clearly reflected in the priorities that Rabin had outlined for the party even before his election to the Labour leadership. At the beginning of February, during the course of an interview with the Egyptian daily *Al-Ahram*, Rabin declared his outright opposition to settlement construction in the West Bank and Gaza since it was not in Israel's political interests – a veiled reference to the fractious state of bilateral relations with Washington. Rabin went on to make an explicit causal link between the building of settlements and the deleterious effect that this had upon the absorption of Soviet Jews.[48] Three weeks later,

Rabin elaborated on his position, delineating between what he termed security settlements and political settlements. The former he defined as contingent on the strategic security of the Jewish State and constituted for the most part kibbutzim and moshavim in sparsely populated areas along the length of the Jordan valley. The latter, mostly situated in and around areas of Palestinian urban density, did little to enhance Israeli security, the yardstick by which Rabin judged the utility of all such developments. Continuing along this vein, Rabin declared:

> Furthermore, our main task is fighting unemployment to allow hundreds of Jews to come here from the former USSR. If we seriously want to help the young Israeli generation of those who served in the army – and it is a fact today, every fourth released soldier is unemployed – if we want to construct a healthy society and economy, in parallel with a political process while protecting Israel's security, we have to foresake the current order of priorities according to which money is being wasted on political settlements. This is the main bone of contention between us and the Likud.[49]

This agenda was broad in its appeal, providing a synthesis between the hitherto competing demands of strategic and socioeconomic security. Moreover, not only did it reject the legitimacy of political settlements, but it proposed that talks over interim Palestinian autonomy on the West Bank and Gaza Strip should develop into some framework invested with empirical meaning. Rabin, throughout his election campaign, made clear his intent to reach agreement on Palestinian autonomy within six to nine months of taking office. This was not, at least overtly, viewed as recognition of a nascent Palestinian state. Rather, it was a structure that would alleviate the physical, economic, and moral burden of occupation, while leaving Israel in control of areas deemed vital for security.[50]

Such thinking rejected the *ideological* borders of *Eretz Y'Israel*, but accepted the need of a *security* border for the protection of the State of Israel. The juxtaposition of the two is more than an exercise in political semantics. In this case, the term *ideological* border conferred legitimacy on Israel's claim to all land west of the Jordan river, irrespective of the presence of the Palestinian Arabs. For its part, the term *security* border suggests the extent of Israeli influence, rather than claim, over the same land. It confers ideological legitimacy on the State of Israel but is, to all intents, a defensive buffer for the protection of that state, rather than a territorial claim to the West Bank and Gaza Strip. The territory between the borders of the state, and, excluding Jerusalem, the security boundary of the Jordan river, encompassed the envisioned area of Palestinian autonomy.

These declarations of territorial intent remained subject to conflicting variables, not least the reaction of the Palestinians themselves. None the less, the Labour agenda remained coherent in its view that societal and strategic security were not mutually exclusive. Settlements remained the key obstacle to progress on regional peace, the acquisition of loan guarantees, and their use as a ready panacea for immigrant absorption and wider socio-economic concerns. By linking the investment of financial and political capital in settlement construction to the degradation of the strategic and socio-economic security of the Jewish State, the Labour alignment produced a platform more attuned to the needs of Israelis in general, and the Soviet *olim* in particular. In short, the Labour agenda addressed the needs of both state and societal security.[51]

Therefore, attempts by Likud to discredit the opposition by invoking a comparison with the failed model of Soviet socialism found little favour among the immigrants. Likewise, Labour proved more adept at canvassing for support among Soviet Jews. Its election broadcasts included subtitles in Cyrillic, a technique copied by the Likud only at a relatively late stage of the campaign. Labour focused much attention on the progress of Shimon Peres in his attempts to learn Russian, clearly demonstrating that the interests, culture, and language of this *aliyah* concerned the party élite. Indeed, in newspapers throughout the former Soviet Union, Labour placed political advertisements in an attempt to attract support from prospective emigrants to Israel.[52] Parallels with their former homeland were also used to justify the Labour agenda. The ethnic conflict in Azerbaijan was one graphic example used to illustrate the consequences of the failure to achieve territorial compromise between two competing national identities.[53]

The appeal of the Labour campaign found a receptive audience among the Soviet immigrants. With over three months to go before polling day, soundings among *olim* indicated that 43 per cent favoured the centre-left parties against 27 per cent for the Likud and parties to the right.[54] But the economic and political effects wrought by Soviet Jewish *aliyah* went beyond shaping the perceptions and attitudes of the immigrant community. Increasingly, Oriental voters, the traditional bastion of Likud Party support, questioned the party commitment to the esoteric consolidation of *Eretz Y'Israel* over the more prosaic, but equally pressing, concerns of socio-economic security. Oriental Jewish support for the Likud was far more diffuse than identification with one ideological tenet of Zionism. Support for Israeli rule over the Occupied Territories was, as David Hall-Cathala suggests, a product of social status. It allowed Palestinian Arabs access to the more menial jobs in the Israeli market, positions that had previously been the allocated lot of the Oriental community. Return of the territories, it was widely felt, foreshadowed the return of economic and social servility under a Labour-dominated Ashkenazim establishment.[55]

Soviet Jewish immigration proved crucial in undermining such perceptions and questioned the historical relationship between a large section of Israeli society and the ruling state élite. Apprehension was readily apparent over the intellectual challenge that this *aliyah* presented to the status of some sections of the Oriental Jewish community, but the priority placed upon ideological dogma over the financial needs of society produced widespread disaffection with the Likud throughout the Oriental community. Migration to Israel proper now threatened their social status more than did any threat to relinquish territory and its reservoir of cheap Arab labour. Furthermore, continued construction in the Occupied Territories appeared prejudiced against the status of the Oriental community. It denied access to the loan guarantees needed to alleviate the economic burden imposed by mass *aliyah* on Israelis in general, and the Oriental community in particular. The warm welcome accorded Rabin in Oriental communities, a man previously associated with the Ashkenazim élite, was in stark contrast to the hostile reception that met Shamir as he toured development towns, previously the backbone of Likud Party support.[56]

Maintaining support among the immigrant community throughout the election campaign remained, however, a priority for Labour campaign managers. In appearances before immigrant communities, Rabin laid careful emphasis on the Russian origins of his parents, highlighting the continuity from the pioneering efforts of Zionist settlers from Tsarist Russia to the present wave of Soviet *aliyah*. Indeed the last campaign speech Rabin made before polls opened on 23 June was to Soviet Jews in Tel-Aviv.[57] With a platform that recognized the multifaceted nature of security, Labour appeared set to capture the largest proportion of the immigrant vote.

The Israeli Left and the Soviet Jews

Political expediency, as much as ideological affinity, led to the creation of Meretz (Energy) at the beginning of February 1992, an alignment of Ratz (the Citizens Rights Movement), Shinui, and Mapam Parties. All retained their own autonomous party structures, but the raising of the electoral threshold required to take one Knesset seat from 1 to 1.5 per cent of votes cast led to the presentation of a single list by this tripartite alliance. The political diversity between the parties was mainly confined to differences over the structural base of the Israeli economy: Mapam's adherence to large-scale state intervention, a product of its ideological heritage, contradicted the free market liberalism advocated by Shinui leader Amnon Rubenstein.[58]

This disparity was, however, more than offset by a shared commitment to civil rights, electoral reform, and Palestinian self-determination. Such a platform entailed a clear separation of religion from the state and an end to settlement on all land over the Green Line. This strident secularism was designed to appeal to three main target groups: young Israelis disaffected with the leverage exercised by the religious parties over a civil laity; Israeli Arabs disabused of a strong commitment to the non-Zionist Hadash (Communist) party following the collapse of the Soviet Union; and Soviet Jewish immigrants disillusioned with their experience of *mizug galuyot*.[59]

Despite an agenda designed to appeal to all these target groups, the immigrant vote was accorded high priority. To this end, Ratz and Mapam ran separate campaigns that, while mutually supportive, placed particular emphasis on a certain aspect of the Meretz platform, and appealed to certain age groups. Indeed, Mapam had long been active among the immigrant community, reflecting a belief that many *olim* still remained sympathetic to the basic tenets of socialism. For Mapam, they represented the potential to revive the party's ailing fortunes across the Israeli political landscape. At the time of the formation of Meretz, Mapam had already established firm, if somewhat limited support, among Soviet Jewish communities.[60]

Under the auspices of Hymie Borschstein, Mapam established an Absorption Forum that deliberately set out to connect regional peace with the successful integration of Soviet Jewry. In so doing, Mapam emphasized the failure of the free market to equate with immigrant aspirations. This theme appealed directly to the family structure of *olim* whose work experience in the former Soviet Union had allowed for both husband and wife to pursue distinct careers. The use of seminars and rallies to support this message was the preferred strategy of Mapam, with particular emphasis placed upon convening such events in the north of the country. In this endeavour, Mapam had considerable success in the formation of Mapam Party cadres among the older *olim* who could disseminate party literature throughout the immigrant community. Such cadres, particularly conspicuous in Haifa, were mainly comprised of immigrants already in their sixties and seventies, often former members of the CPSU, who still identified with the strong socialist ethos held then by Mapam.[61]

Mapam established a direct correlation between economic investment needed to meet immigrant concerns and the total cessation of construction activity throughout the Occupied Territories. This led to the promotion of what Mapam Party officials termed its 'National Plan', a nationwide project designed to reinvest funds allocated to settlements under the Likud for the widespread construction of new roads and public utilities inside the Green Line. Futhermore, the plan outlined the need for increased state investment in high-technology industries that could utilize skills already held in abundance by Soviet Jews. However, while undoubtedly the recipient of widespread empathy among Soviet *olim*, much of this plan already formed part of the Labour party manifesto whose mass party structure threatened to overwhelm Mapam/Meretz on this issue alone. Therefore, Meretz concentrated its resources on the promotion of civil rights, an issue that affected so many Soviet immigrants, as the central theme of its election manifesto. Given the rejection of the Burg proposal by the Labour Party leadership, a proposal that had called for the division of religion from state, it was also an area in which Meretz could enjoy a unique political monopoly on the centre left.

While all the constituent parties of Meretz made the causal link between civil rights, secularism, and the nebulous position of many immigrants in Israeli society, it was Ratz, as *the* civil rights movement, which carried the main responsibility for eliciting support among Soviet Jews on the strength of this issue alone. As with Mapam, Ratz had already established ties with the immigrant community that pre-dated the formation of Meretz. These included the employment of new *olim* as counsellors and lawyers whose main task was to outline immigrant rights and social benefits to their erstwhile compatriots. Moreover, the presence of Ratz Knesset Member, Yossi Sarid, on the barricades during the August 1991 Moscow coup was used by the movement to illustrate its commitment towards democratic secular norms, both in Israel and the former Soviet Union.[62]

Under the auspices of Dr Benny Temkin, Ratz launched a campaign that made a connection between civil rights and economic development for immigrants, and full withdrawal from the Occupied Territories. In pamphlets that were disseminated among *olim* at specially convened rallies, Ratz/Meretz highlighted the economic benefits that could accrue to Israelis and immigrants alike if territory for peace was to be imbued with some empirical meaning. The appearence of International Business Machines and Motorola in Israel, following the conclusion of the Camp David agreement, was one example used to stress the level of advanced economic investment Israel could accrue if regional co-existence and stability were forthcoming.[63]

The benefits of such an arrangement were self-evident to an *aliyah* anxious to update and utilize skills acquired in the former Soviet Union. Yet the emphasis placed upon these perceived benefits was, as Temkin readily conceded, also necessary to overcome the territorial claustrophobia which impinged upon the collective pysche of this immigrant wave and, therefore, its fundamental attitude towards land for peace. This emphasis, central to the alignment platform, was intended to reflect a moral dimension that could appeal to the generic immigrant experience of the former USSR. Having endured official discrimination under the Soviet authorities, *olim* were challenged to justify the subjugation of Palestinian Arab rights that continued occupation of the West Bank and Gaza necessarily entailed. Moreover, the very act of occupation was presented to immigrants as alien to the democratic norms that distinguished Israeli political discourse within the Green Line. Such moral argument distinguished the Meretz platform from that of the Labour Party, whose hardline credentials, personified in the figure of Rabin, negated any serious debate over the morality of occupation.[64]

Yet civil rights for *olim* remained the area in which Ratz/Meretz held greatest sway over the immigrant community. Its strident secularism dovetailed with the immediate profile of this *aliyah*, a confluence that sought to undermine the constraining influence that religious structures – parties and laws that were endorsed by the state élite – enjoyed over a largely secular society. The change of values wrought by Gorbachev within the Soviet Union meant that many *olim* were already receptive to the ideas of civil rights and democracy. In this regard, Ratz/Meretz presented the question of mixed marriages, where a partner or child was not Halachically Jewish, thereby precluding full Israeli citizenship and concomitant social welfare benefits, as a potent example of the basic denial of these civil rights.[65]

This was important for Soviet immigrants because it represented a clear rejection by Meretz of the political monopoly enjoyed by the religious parties in defining the social base and ethnological structure of the Jewish State. Meretz made the clear distinction between the rights of people to engage in religious practice, and the extent to which such practices should be allowed to inhibit the secular nature of Israeli society. Such sentiment challenged the existing priorities of the Shamir government that continued to place the portfolios of Education and Interior under the aegis of religious ministers. Accordingly, Ratz/Meretz made electoral reform and the introduction of a written constitution enshrining citizens rights in accordance with secular, rather than Halachic law, central tenets of their election campaign.[66]

These policies enjoyed widespread sympathy, in particular, among young first-time voters, disenchanted with the political distortion that allowed a minority to influence the free expression of secular norms. It was a platform premised on a clear separation of religion from state, and, accordingly, one that espoused the introduction of civil marriage and divorce as a civic right for all Israelis. While pervasive in their secular appeal, such policies were particularly attractive to the many immigrants who had encountered discrimination under the Likud coalition government. In seeking to apply a uniform, secular criterion in determining the character of *aliyah*, and presenting this as an issue of civil rights, Meretz was to elicit strong support from the Soviet immigrants in the forthcoming national election.[67]

On the vexed issue of territorial compromise, both the Meretz alignment and Labour Party were supported by the work of the Tel-Aviv based International Centre for Peace in the Middle East, the ICPME. Although committed to the pursuit of regional peace, regardless of 'nationality, ideology, religion, or political affiliations', its approach towards an Arab-Israeli discourse placed it as a societal actor firmly within the remit of the centre left. Through educational programmes, including seminars, lectures by prominent political figures, and the training of peace educators, the ICPME aimed to break down the stereotypical view of Arabs that appeared particularly prevalent among young Israelis. In so doing, it was hoped that the erosion of core democratic values, attributed by the ICPME to Israel's continued rule over the territories, could be reversed.[68]

The ICPME were quick to respond to the political potential that Soviet Jewish *aliyah* represented. In accordance with its self-proclaimed agenda, the Centre, in the summer of 1991, authorized the establishment of a 'Public Education Project' specifically designed for new Soviet *olim*. This had three main components: a course for Young Community Leadership (YCL); publications in Russian that addressed the central crux of the Arab–Israeli conflict; the establishment of public seminars, workshops; and local meetings that focused on the socio-economic needs of the immigrant community at large.[69]

The main objective of the YCL course was to establish a network of 'local, grassroots activists' who could disseminate the aims and ideals of the ICPME throughout their particular communities. Initially, the YCL attracted 160 Soviet Jews, all trained academics whose period of residence in Israel ranged from six months to three years. Under the auspices of staff members drawn from the Centre, a series of district meetings, combined with a series of bi-weekly, nationwide workshops over a nine-month period, were used to instil the ethos behind the ICPME down to these prospective moderators. The publication of Russian-language material, designed to provide the YCL and the wider immigrant community with a more diverse view of Israeli society, was complemented by a high profile campaign in the Russian language media. In full-page advertisements, the ICPME endorsed its support for the Madrid Peace Conference, and reminded the Likud coalition government that the principle of territory for peace enjoyed the backing of at least half of the Jewish State.[70]

The programme was a severe test of the Centre's resources. In particular, the shortage of ICPME staff proficient in the Russian language remained acute. This reflected the enmity in which the centre left had been held by the previous wave of Soviet *aliyah*. As the ICPME readily conceded, the political position of these former immigrants, many of them ex-dissidents, remained vehemently right-wing and opposed to any form of territorial compromise. Moreover, it soon became apparent that the course faced a credibility problem if it failed to present and explain the right-wing agenda. As the products of a sophisticated system of disinformation, participants remained suspicious of any political programme that ignored the presentation of opposing positions.[71]

The language barrier was surmounted in two, complementary ways. All participants were required to have a basic grasp of Hebrew, implying that the immigrant should have studied at an *ulpan* for at least four months. The majority of lectures were, therefore, delivered in simplified Hebrew, sufficient to impart the complexities of the Israeli political system to the YCL students. Where lectures were necessarily complex, consecutive translation was provided by the handful of ICPME staff familiar with the Russian language. The issue of credibility was addressed by making the programme relevant to the everyday lives of the wider immigrant community. Not only were the YCL students presented with opposing views from politicians on the political right, but they were also instructed in the best means to approach the complexities of Israel's overburdened bureaucratic system. The practical benefits of the course allowed the ICPME to legitimize its more abstract goals, enabling its mandate to enjoy wider support among the immigrant community.[72]

Of the original 160 participants, 100 eventually completed the course. On returning to their respective communities many became active on municipal education committees, organized immigrant workshops on peace and co-existence, became active among immigrant students at Ben Gurion University in Beersheba, and involved in community work with the Bedouin Arabs of the Negev region. In a more populist move, ICPME, in conjunction with Peace Now activists, organized the day-long 'Seminar on Wheels' in December 1991. Over 1,800 immigrants were taken by bus over the Green Line where, at appropriate locations, lecturers and interpreters highlighted the visible disparities between government investment in settlement construction and fiscal expenditure within Israel proper.[73]

With this network of committed activists established before the collapse of the Likud coalition government, the ICPME was able to provide invaluable support for the centre left in their election campaigns among the Soviet *olim*. This included supplementary literature designed to cultivate a critical appreciation of the economic, moral, and human costs entailed in Israel's settlement in the Occupied Territories. In one such pamphlet, the ICPME invoked the spectre of Afghanistan, Vietnam, and Lebanon to illustrate the magnitude of human suffering that military occupation over an alien people necessarily entailed. This was an emotive appeal to immigrants whose children would, in future years, bear the burden of military service in the West Bank and Gaza Strip if territorial compromise were not forthcoming. While hard to measure the overall impact of ICPME projects on the immigrant community, their work none the less helped to cultivate an awareness of the centre left among Soviet *olim*.[74]

The Election Results

On the eve of the national elections, the annual report of the State Comptroller was published, revealing the extent of Israel's problem in attempting to absorb the Soviet Jews. The greatest criticism was reserved for the Minister for Housing, Ariel Sharon, whose staff were accused of misappropriation of public funds for personal benefit, and awarding construction contracts on the basis of political affiliation rather than open competition. Moreover, the purchase of mobile homes deemed necessary to solve the housing crisis, was, according to the report, more expensive than investment in public housing construction. With the release of the report, Israel's Attorney General, Yosef Harish, opened a criminal investigation into the allegations it contained, most notably the links between the ministry and private building contractors. As one commentator observed, 'the report served as the last straw that broke the ruling party's back'.[75]

On 23 June 1992, Yitzhak Rabin was duly elected as Prime Minister of Israel, with nearly 60 per cent of the immigrant vote going to the Labour Party or Meretz alignment. Collectively, the immigrant vote translated into six to eight seats for the new Labour coalition government, giving Rabin a two-seat majority in the Knesset even without support from any party in the religious camp. In forming his new cabinet, Rabin was careful to place Meretz members Shulamit Aloni and Yair Tsaban in the Education and Absorption portfolios respectively. This was a deliberate move to reverse three years of religious influence over the absorption process, thus fufilling election pledges made to Soviet Jews to secularize absorption structures.[76]

In total, the Labour Party won 44 seats, representing 34.66 per cent of votes cast while Meretz won 12 seats, some 9.58 per cent of votes cast. By contrast, Likud was reduced to 32 Knesset seats, polling 24.89 per cent of votes cast. Among Soviet *olim*, Likud attracted only 18 per cent of the immigrant vote, just seven percentage points ahead of votes cast for the Meretz alignment. In the development towns, formerly the bastions of Likud party support, Shamir was abandoned by large numbers of Oriental voters who preferred to abstain, rather than cast their votes for alternative parties. If Soviet Jews had punished Likud for its policies by favouring the centre left, the Oriental community spurned Shamir for failing to address the socio-economic problems that accompanied this *aliyah* and affected most Israelis.[77]

The defeat of his party elicited an unusual degree of candour from the outgoing premier. In an interview with the Israeli evening paper *Ma'ariv*, Shamir declared:

> I would have conducted the autonomy negotiations for ten years, and in the meantime we would have reached half a million souls in Judea and Samaria. I didn't believe there was a majority in favour of *Eretz Y'Israel*, but it could have been attained over time... Without such a basis there would have been nothing to stop the establishment of a Palestinian state.[78]

That Shamir failed to realize this long-term strategy was the result of the dynamics unleashed by Soviet Jewish *aliyah*. The domestic challenges presented by mass migration required the support of international actors, most notably the United States. The dissonance in policy positions between Shamir and the Bush administration undermined the credibility of the Likud coalition government throughout Israel. Economic well-being was subsumed by an ethos that placed the sanctity of the land over the common health of society. The failure of the Likud leadership was to appreciate fully the seismic transformations that had taken place in the arena of international politics. The very magnitude of Jewish emigration called into question the threat perceptions that had dominated international politics since 1945. No longer could Israel's settlement in the Occupied Territories take place in a vacuum, excused and silently condoned by Washington because of its perceived role as a regional strategic asset. Therefore, while Soviet Jewish *aliyah* strengthened the demographic base of the Jewish State, it undermined the power of the Likud coalition government, and negated any attempt by Shamir to fuse ideological orthodoxy with the security, both social and strategic, of the Jewish people.

In this process, Soviet immigration was *the* catalyst for change in Israel's political discourse. Not only were immigrant votes decisive in the victory of the centre left, but the scale of *aliyah* affected all Israelis, highlighting the costs imposed by Likud's agenda on the populace at large. In voting for a new state élite in the centre left, Israelis made the cognitive connection between the welfare of the state and substantive progress towards Palestinian territorial autonomy. On 13 July 1992, the Israeli Knesset approved the formation of a Labour coalition government under the leadership of Yitzhak Rabin. Based on agreement between Labour, Meretz, and Shas, and able to count on the support of five more Knesset seats held by the non-Zionist Hadash and Arab Democratic parties, the government was the most dovish in Israel's history.[79]

In presenting his new cabinet before the Labour Party central committee, Rabin outlined his government's main national priorities: the establishment of autonomy – self rule – for the Palestinians in the Occupied Territories; the reallocation of funds from political settlements to socio-economic programmes within the Green Line; the rehabilitation of bilateral relations with the United States, leading to the acquisition of $10 billion in loan guarantees.[80] The causal relationship between these priorities required that progress on the issue of settlements be made before Israel could gain access to the loan guarantees and their concomitant socio-economic benefits. Accordingly, on 16 July 1992, Israel's new Housing Minister, Binyamin Ben Eliezer, announced a settlement freeze and the cancellation of contracts for 3,000 housing units in the Occupied Territories. In so doing, the minister declared that, 'We want to end the process of one Israel for 3,900,000 Jews and another Israel of 100,000 Jews. We want to start to provide answers to the basic problems of Israeli society in unemployment, housing for young couples and *aliyah*.'[81]

Moreover, the massive programme in road construction throughout the West Bank was severely curtailed. This was significant because according to the Labour MK, Ephraim Sneh, road construction had formed part of a Likud plan for the gradual cantonization of 'Judea and Samaria'.[82] Such actions helped Washington adopt a benign approach to the issue of the loan guarantees. On 11 August 1992, during the course of a summit meeting at Kennebunkport, Maine, President Bush informed Rabin that he would submit to Congress the legislation required to allow Israeli access to the guarantees. Two months later, on 5 October, Congress duly approved the allocation of the $10 billion, to be issued over a five-year period. The loans were agreed on condition that they pertained to immigrant absorption and resettlement in areas which 'were subject to the administration of the Government of Israel before June 5 1967'.[83]

Yet simultaneously, Rabin was looking to invest the Madrid peace process with greater practical meaning. His personal commitment to oversee an agreement on Palestinian autonomy within six to nine months may have appeared somewhat optimistic, but Rabin was clearly preparing Israelis to accept psychologically changes in the existential borders of the Jewish State. This not only included concessions to Palestinian Arabs, but also to Syria over the issue of the Golan Heights. When the government said that Israel would withdraw not *from* the Golan but *on* the Golan, it conveyed the message that while still committed to the military security of the state, it would none the less be willing to make some territorial compromise. This position encompassed the principle of land for peace as the basis for negotiation with Israel's Arab interlocutors.[84]

That Rabin was able to countenance the idea of such territorial concessions was the direct result of the impact that Soviet Jewish *aliyah* had on Israeli society, and its interactive effect on Israel's relationship with other nation-states. It brought to an end 15 years of Likud adherence to the ideological sanctity of *Eretz Y'Israel*, and allowed a more substantive position to be taken regarding the principle of territory for peace. Not only did this lead to severe curtailment of construction activity in the Occupied Territories, but eventually it paved the way towards mutual recognition between Israel and the PLO. Israel has never been able to define its borders. Nevertheless, the election of the Rabin government marked a watershed in Israeli politics, representing as it did an outright rejection of a Jewish State whose borders were based upon mystical, historic, and Biblical associations. Towards that end, the mass *aliyah* of Soviet Jewry played the defining role.

Conclusion

Attempting to use Soviet Jewish immigration to achieve an ideological end proved an expensive gamble for the Likud. It remained immune to a new Middle East agenda, dismissed arguments over demographics, and ignored the very real needs of its own Jewish population. Shamir's disastrous handling of the absorption process, his narrow interpretation of security needs, and a belief that this *aliyah* would reproduce the ideological allegiance of previous immigrant waves served only to alienate the new Soviet *olim* from the very concept of Zionism that he sought to promote.

The ability to harness this discontent proved to be decisive for the centre left and the election of Rabin. While predominantly a vote over socio-economic, cultural, and security issues, the Soviet Jews, in conjunction with many Israelis, provoked a *mahapach* in Israel's territorial agenda with its Arab neighbours. As the former Defence Minister, Moshe Arens, readily conceded in the aftermath of Likud's electoral defeat, 'A part of the public does not see the slogan *Eretz Y'Israel* as an adequate response to the complexities of problems associated with the Palestinians in the territories.'[85]

Until the Declaration of Principles, signed between the PLO and Israel on 13 September 1993, the mandate achieved by the Labour coalition government led to what can be termed a negative definition of the Jewish State – that is, a rejection of the borders inherent within the concept of *Eretz Y'Israel*. It rejected the notion of religious and historical absolutes regarding revisionist claims to the territories and moved the issue from Israel's perspective back to the utility of the territories on security grounds alone. In short, the government of Yitzhak Shamir paid the political price for making the needs of societal security subservient to the consolidation of an ideological goal. Consolidation of this goal became subject to increasing pressure by actors, both state and non-state, in both domestic and international politics. The interaction between these two, and most notably, the impact that Washington's actions had upon Israel's domestic milieu, exposed structural limitations in the ability of the Jewish State to cope with the demands of mass *aliyah*. This at least prompted progress over the issue of territorial compromise because of the multidimensional view that now governed the issue of security in the new Labour coalition government. As Rabin himself remarked:

We should back away from illusions and seek compromises in order to reach peace or, at least, make practical moves to promote it. We should drop the illusions of the religion of *Eretz Y'Israel* and remember that we must take care of the Israeli people, society, culture, and economy, that a nation's strength is not measured by the territories it holds but by its faith and its ability to cultivate it social, economic and security systems.[86]

NOTES

1. 'Tehiya Announces Decision to Quit Government', *BBC-SWB*, ME/1280 i(b), 17 Jan. 1992; Ian Black, 'Far Right Provokes Israeli Election', *The Guardian*, 20 Jan. 1992.
2. Ian Black, 'Shamir Says Settlements Will Continue', *The Guardian*, 21 Jan. 1992.
3. Leon T. Hadar, 'The 1992 Electoral Earthquake and the Fall of the "Second Israeli Republic"', *Middle East Journal*, Vol.46, No.4 (Autumn 1992), p.602.
4. David B. Capitanchik, 'A Guide to the Israeli General Election 1992', *Institute of Jewish Affairs Research Report*, No.3 (1992), p.14; Edith Coron, op.cit., p.121.
5. Reich *et al.*, op. cit., p.50.
6. Hadar, op. cit., p.595.
7. Reich *et al.*, op. cit., p.50.
8. Herb Keinon, 'Strategies to Woo Immigrant Voters', *The Jerusalem Post International*, 4 Jan. 1992.
9. Avishai Margalit, op. cit., p.23.
10. Ian Black, 'Claiming a Free Lunch in the House of Greater Israel', *The Guardian*, 14 Feb. 1992.
11. Ian Black, 'Blackmailing for a Little Milk and Honey', *The Guardian*, 7 Feb. 1992. Data for the October 1990 poll was taken from Reich *et al.*, op. cit., p.52.
12. Interview with Svetlana Raviv, Absorption Director for the Holon Histadrut Workers' Council, Holon, 27 June 1992.
13. 'Shamir and Sharon Comment on Occupied Territories Settlement', *BBC-SWB*, ME/1313 A/1, 25 Feb. 1992; 'Top Economic Figures Call for Compromise with USA on Loan Guarantees', *BBC-SWB*, ME/1313 A/1, 25 Feb. 1992.
14. Ian Black, 'Squabbling Tribes of Israel', *The Guardian*, 1 April 1992; Capitanchik, op. cit., pp.19–21.
15. 'Minister Says Construction Drive Will go on Regardless of Elections and Talks', *BBC-SWB*, ME/1357 A/9, 16 April 1992.
16. 'Israel: Shamir says West Bank and Gaza to Remain Israeli "Forever and Ever"', *BBC-SWB*, ME/1362 A/6, 23 April 1992.
17. This opinion poll, conducted by the Dahaf Research Institute on behalf of the ICPME, found that 85 per cent of those polled favoured advancement of the peace process. A further 43 per cent were for a comprehensive peace settlement including security guarantees for a return of most of the Occupied Territories. Only 18 per cent supported full annexation of the Occupied Territories. For the full text see *ICPME Newsletter* (English, Arabic, Hebrew), No.2 (March 1992).
18. Hadar, op. cit., p.610.
19. Ibid., p.610.
20. 'Movement for a Halt to Immigration Will Run for Knesset', *BBC-SWB*, ME/1378

A/5, 12 May 1992.
21. Ian Black, 'Israel's Big Battalions Vie for Immigrants' First Votes', *The Guardian*, 10 June 1992.
22. 'Peace Now's Report on Building of Settlements in the Occupied Territories Disputed', *BBC-SWB*, ME/1411 A/7, 19 June 1992; Ian Black, 'Israel Explores the Scars Left by Falling Scuds', *The Guardian*, 18 Jan. 1992.
23. Margalit, op.cit., p.52.
24. Interview with Shai Grishpon, Immigrant liaison official for Mapam, Mapam Party headquarters, Tel-Aviv, 23 June 1992.
25. Ibid.
26. Prior to 1989, around 90 per cent of the Israeli population lived in urban areas. This was largely due to the suburbanization of Israel's two largest cities, Haifa and Tel-Aviv. See Alan Kirschenbaum, Migration and Urbanization: Patterns of Population Redistribution and Urban Growth', in Goldscheider (ed.), op. cit., pp.65–88.
27. Reich *et al.*, op.cit., p.52.
28. Naomi Shepherd, *The Russians in Israel: The Ordeal of Freedom* (London: Simon and Schuster, 1993), p.62; Coron, op. cit., p.71; Roberta Cohen, op. cit., p.73.
29. Reich *et al.*, op.cit., p.52.
30. Interview with Shai Grishpon.
31. Sarah Helm, 'A Lonely Prisoner of Zion', *The Independent*, 7 October 1992. The refuseniks of the 1970s were widely regarded as national rights, rather than human rights activists. Their belief in their divine right to live in *Eretz Y'Israel* convinced many that this right alone superseded the human, civic, and national rights of the Palestinians. See also Herb Keinon, 'The politics of disgruntlement', *The Jerusalem Post International*, 4 Jan. 1992.
32. Interview with Lesya Shtane-Smirnoff, immigrant campaign worker for Ratz/Meretz, Tel-Aviv, 23 June 1992.
33. Shepherd, op. cit., pp.208-9. Other newspapers included *Novosti* and *Nyezavisimaya Gazeta*.
34. *The Guardian*, 7 Feb. 1992.
35. Herb Keinon, '"Objects of Paternalism" Say Yes to their own Party', *The Jerusalem Post International*, 18 April 1992.
36. Herb Keinon, 'Extra Soup Kitchens Needed for Immigrants', *The Jerusalem Post Internaional*, 21 Dec. 1991.
37. Shepherd, op. cit., pp.208–9.
38. *The Jerusalem Post International*, 18 April 1992.
39. Ibid.
40. Although Da remained the largest immigrant party, its impact was probably dented further by the profusion of immigrant parties that were established on an ad hoc basis in the run-up to the June 1992 election. For example, Robert Golan, a former activist with Sharansky's Forum, founded Tali – the Movement for the Renewal of Israel. However, its platform was no different from that of Da. See Herb Keinon, 'New Immigrant Party', *The Jerusalem Post International*, 11 April 1992.
41. Sarah Honig, 'Poll Shows Labour at an All Time Low', *The Jerusalem Post International*, 29 Dec. 1990.
42. Yosef Yaakov, 'Soviets Assure Israel *Aliyah* will be Allowed to Continue', *The Jerusalem Post International*, 19 July 1991; Herb Keinon, 'Land of Opportunity is Russia Not Israel Say Some *Aliyah* Activists', *The Jerusalem Post International* 23 Nov. 1991.
43. Between 1984 and 1986, as Prime Minister in a Government of National Unity, Peres was primarily responsible for curbing Israel's hyper-inflation, and the withdrawal of the IDF from most of Lebanon where in two years it had lost over 600 dead.
44. Geoffrey Aronson, *Israel, Palestinians, and the Intifada: Creating Facts on the West Bank* (London: Kegan Paul/Institute for Palestine Studies, 1987), p.328; Phil Marshall, *Intifada* (London: Bookmarks, 1989), pp.13–14.

45. Ian Black, 'Israel's Divided Opposition Reaches Policy Compromise', *The Guardian*, 22 Nov. 1991.
46. Sarah Honig, 'After Rabin, Shamir Victories, Infighting starts in Likud and Labour', *The Jerusalem Post International*, 29 Feb. 1992.
47. Sarah Honig, 'Labour Chooses Young, Dovish Leadership', *The Jerusalem Post International*, 11 April 1992; Ian Black, 'Israel's Opposition Fields Young Doves', *The Guardian*, 3 April 1992.
48. Interview with Yitzhak Rabin, *Al-Ahram*, 3 Feb. 1992, cited in 'Yitzhak Rabin Says Talks with Palestinians are Main Priority', BBC-SWB, ME/1298 A/6, 7 Feb. 1992.
49. 'Israel: Labour Party Leader Rabin Comments on US Loan Guarantees, Settlements', BBC-SWB, ME/1312 A/12-13, 24 Feb. 1992.
50. 'Israel: Yitzhak Rabin Promises Agreement on "Autonomy Within Six to Nine Months"', BBC-SWB, ME/1319 A/15, 3 March 1992.
51. 'Israel: Rabin Promises Agreement with Palestinians, Stop Funding of Settlements', BBC-SWB, ME/1353 A/3, 11 April 1992.
52. Capitanchik, op. cit., p.16.
53. *The Jerusalem Post International*, 4 Jan. 1992.
54. *Hadashot*, 20 March 1992.
55. Hall-Cathala, op. cit., pp.94-7.
56. Hadar, op. cit., p.613. According to press reports cited by Hadar in *Ha'aretz*, Shamir was accorded a particularly hostile welcome in the development town of Beersheba.
57. *The Guardian*, 10 June 1992; Richard Beeston, 'Likud Brace for Return to Unity Coalition', *The Times*, 23 June 1992.
58. *Financial Times*, 5 February 1992. In the outgoing Knesset, Ratz held 5 seats, Mapam 3 seats, and Shinui 2 seats.
59. Ian Black, 'Israel's Meretz Party Sees Friend and Foe in Labour', *The Guardian*, 12 June 1992.
60. Reich *et al.*, op. cit, p.50.
61. Interview with Hymie Borschstein, Chairman of the Mapam Absorption Forum, Mapam Party headquarters, Tel-Aviv, 16 Nov. 1992.
62. Interview with Lesya Shtane-Smirnoff, Ratz/Meretz, Tel-Aviv, 18 Nov. 1992.
63. Ibid. See also the Meretz pamphlet, *Osnovnye Polozheniya Platformi: Meretz* (Basic Political Platform: Meretz), produced by the Meretz alliance in the run-up to the June 1992 election. In relatively simple terms, this outlined the Meretz agenda, emphasizing its policies towards territorial compromise, the economy and society, civil rights, *aliyah* and absorption, citizens rights, religion and the state, the position of women in Israeli society, and its approach towards equal rights for Israeli Arabs.
64. The economic benefits to be accrued from territorial compromise had already formed part of the Ratz political agenda to capture immigrant support before the foundation of Meretz. See *The Jerusalem Post International*, 4 Jan. 1992. The moral objections to Israeli rule over the territories were outlined in *Osnovnyo Poloseniya Platformi: Meretz*, 1992.
65. See the entries 'Grazhdanskiye Prava' (Citizens Rights) and 'Religiya i Gosudarstvo' (Religion and State) in *Osnovnye Polozheniya Platformi: Meretz*.
66. Interview with Lesya Shtane-Smirnoff, Tel-Aviv, 18 Nov. 1992.
67. This populist message included a pledge by Meretz to legislate for fundamental reform to the Law of Return. A bill was subsequently presented to the Knesset by Meretz/Ratz MK Dedi Zucker.
68. For a detailed discussion of the origins of the ICPME, see Hall-Cathala, op. cit., pp.139-40.
69. 'Public Education Project for New Russian Immigrants: Interim Report', ICPME, Tel-Aviv, Nov. 1991.
70. These Russian language publications included, 'Obshchyestvo, Ekonomika i Bezopasnost: Kakoi Myezhdu' (Society, Economy, and Security: What's between), and,

'Religiozye Nasiliye v Izrallye' (Religious Coercion in Israel).
71. 'Public Education Project for New Russian Immigrants: Interim Report', ICPME, Tel-Aviv, Nov. 1991.
72. Ibid.
73. ICPME *Newsletter* (English and Hebrew), No.1 (Jan. 1992). With an increase in numbers the programme was revised and relaunched in April 1993. Among those who addressed the *olim* at the Green Beach Hotel, Netanya, during their bi-weekly conventions, was Israeli Deputy Foreign Minister, Yossi Beilin, a key player in negotiations that led to the Declaration of Principles. See 'Thinking and Doing Something About Peace, Democracy and Co-existence', ICPME *Newsletter*, No. 2 (June 1993). Beilin addressed the immigrants at Netanya on 3 July 1993.
74. The image of Afghanistan, Vietnam and Lebanon haunting Israeli society was presented by Yigal Amitai and Yuliya Wolfovich, *Territorii!? Tsyennost'eli Oboza* (Territory!? Benefit or Burden) (Tel-Aviv: ICPME, 1992), p.6. See also the Hebrew language pamphlet, 'Facts and Figures about the Social Gap in Israel', ICPME (May 1992). This highlighted the nationwide disparities in government policies that favoured investment in the territories.
75. Bill Hutman and Asher Wallfish, 'Comptroller Blasts Sharon and Misrule by His Aides', *The Jerusalem Post International*, 9 May 1992; Hadar, op. cit., p.597.
76. Ian Black, 'Soviet Influx Tips the Balance', *The Guardian*, 25 June 1992.
77. David B. Capitanchik, 'The Stalemate is Broken: The 1992 Israeli General Election', *The Institute of Jewish Affairs Research Report*, No.4 (1992), pp.4–7.
78. *Ma'ariv*, 26 June 1992.
79. Hadar, op. cit, pp.615–16.
80 'Rabin Addresses Labour Party Central Committee: Presents Labour Ministers', *BBC-SWB*, ME/1432 A/2, 14 July 1992.
81. 'Housing Minister on Settlement Freeze: Denies Declaring War on Settlers', *BBC-SWB*, ME/1435 A/1, 17 July 1992.
82. 'Minister on Cuts in "Politically Motivated" Construction Programmes', *BBC-SWB*, ME/1441 A/10, 24 July 1992.
83. For the full text of the terms governing Israeli access to the loan guarantees, see *The Journal of Palestine Studies*, Vol.XXII, No.2 (Winter 1992), pp.158–61. As part of the package Israel was required to reform its industrial base, implement privatization and embark on trade liberalization. Israel was also required to 'substantially increase' its purchase of goods and services from the United States.
84. Ian Black, 'Rabin Admits Need to Concede on Golan', *The Guardian*, 10 Sept. 1992.
85. Aren's remarks were quoted by *The Guardian*, 27 June 1992.
86. 'Rabin Says a Nation's Strength Not Measured by the Territory it Holds', *BBC-SWB*, ME/1477 A/4, 4 Sept. 1992.

8 Conclusion

Writing in the wake of the June 1992 election, Leon T. Hadar posed the question of why so many experts had failed to foresee the defeat of the political right in Israel. He concluded that the answer lay in the traditional framework that had been consistently applied to explain Israeli political behaviour.

> This paradigm did not explain in an effective way the relationship between the Israeli political system and foreign policy outcomes, on the one hand, and the pressure from the Middle Eastern and international environment, including ties with Washington, on the other hand. It was based very much on the notion that Israel and the international system operate without reference to one another, as though each were in its own watertight compartment. According to this view, Israelis debate their domestic and foreign policies among themselves with little input from the outside world, reach a consensus about what constitutes their national interests, ignore the views of foreign powers, and then make their choices through the ballot box.[1]

The impact of Soviet Jewish migration to Israel between 1989 and 1992 highlights the paucity of this framework. Indeed, this book has sought to demonstrate how migration as a transnational flow created a clear linkage between Israel's domestic political environment and the conduct of foreign policy by the Likud coalition government.

This is not to suggest, however, that the problems associated with absorbing Jews from the former Soviet Union have been solved by the present Israeli government, or that the centre left continues to enjoy widespread support among the *olim*. They have voted only once in a national election and have yet to build a core allegiance to any particular political or ideological agenda, something that 25 years in opposition allowed the Likud Party to achieve with the Oriental community.² As Israel's single largest ethnic community, Soviet Jews hold considerable sway in deciding the future political direction of Israel. Failure by the Rabin government to provide adequate levels of strategic, as well as social and economic, security for Israelis and *olim* alike could well undermine popular support for the present Labour coalition government and its regional agenda.

Indeed, the local government elections throughout Israel on 2 November 1993 brought into sharp relief the power that immigrants could wield. The results demonstrated a clear swing to the right, with Likud-sponsored mayors making inroads into previously safe, Labour-controlled municipalities. The most notable of these was Jerusalem, where the veteran Labour incumbent, Teddy Kollek, was ousted by the Likud candidate, Ehud Olmert. It was estimated that Olmert received over 80 per cent of Soviet immigrant votes cast.³

Moreover, in belated recognition of the political power accruing to the immigrant vote, the Likud Central Office began to explore ways in which immigrants could be recruited into the party structure. Under the auspices of Likud MK and member of the *Aliyah* and Absorption Committee, Efraim Gur, the party began to explore the possibility of establishing an immigrant forum as a means to anchor support for the Likud among the wider immigrant community. In a memorandum to party members, Gur remarked that the establishment of such a forum was important because 'as the largest Jewish community in Israel, the Soviet Jewish vote will fundamentally affect future election results. Therefore the Likud needs to formulate a strategy that will deal effectively with immigrant absorption from the former Soviet Union'.⁴

This was as much an acknowledgement of the contradictions that had afflicted absorption policy under the government of Yitzhak Shamir, as the need to create party political structures attuned to immigrant needs. In short, failure to attend to the burden of societal security associated with mass *aliyah* compromised the regional agenda of the last Likud coalition government. Not only did this result in the election of a new government, but one whose leadership clearly identified the establishment of a benign external environment with the well-being of Israeli society at large.

Conclusion

Speaking before a seminar of new immigrants from the former Soviet Union on 3 July 1993, Israel's Deputy Foreign Minister, Yossi Beilin, elaborated upon this theme. Noting that Israel had the potential to develop a sophisticated industrial base capable of competing with the best in the world, he reminded his audience that such potential would never be realized if Israel continued to spend 20 per cent of its gross domestic product per annum on defence. In reference to those who believed that Israel remained an island impervious to world opinion, Beilin remarked that the Labour Party regarded the Jewish State as a member of the world community and would implement foreign policy accordingly. This not only included Israel's relationship with the major state actors, but included the position of Israel within the regional milieu of the Middle East and the prospects of peace with the Arabs. While clearly stating that this would not be achieved in a day, Beilin declared that: 'It [peace] can be achieved however within a reasonable period and we are not talking here in tens of years. We are talking about a couple of months to a year or two years at the very maximum.'[5] Two months later, on 13 September 1993, the interim agreement on Palestinian self-rule in Jericho and the Gaza Strip was signed in Washington between Israel and the PLO.

By regarding migration as a transnational flow, this book has attempted to gauge the impact that Soviet Jewish *aliyah* has had upon Israel between 1989 and 1992. It has been the contention of this thesis that mass Soviet Jewish immigration has had a profound effect upon Israel with implications for future stability in the Middle East. In so doing, Israeli conceptions of security were broadened beyond the parameters of strategic concerns, allowing debates concerning societal security to become complementary with, rather than subordinate to, debates on the physical well-being of Israel as a nation-state. The dynamics behind the re-evaluation could not have been appraised or fully understood by the application of a simple state centric approach. This would have taken insufficient account of Soviet migration as a transnational flow, and the manifold social pressures that this produced upon the government of Yitzhak Shamir. Accordingly the framework outlined in Chapter 1 allowed for an analysis of the four main themes:

1. The impact of Soviet Jewish migration on Israel's relationship with both state and non-state actors. The issue of Soviet

Jewry remained a function of superpower politics, the scope and pace of emigration remaining subject to the fluctuating fortunes of the relationship between Washington and Moscow. As shown in Chapters 2, 4, and 6, Soviet Jewish migration complicated the relationship not only between the superpowers, but between the superpowers and regional states, as well as among the regional states themselves. These effects included not only the discord between Tel-Aviv and Washington over the loan guarantees, but also subsequent Arab responses to mass *aliyah*. While the Arabs were unable to formulate a cohesive strategy, their representations to Washington exacerbated Israel's absorption difficulties. These difficulties in turn were compounded by an acute shortage of Palestinian construction workers.

2. The impact of Soviet Jewish migration on security. Undeniably, the arrival of so many immigrants strengthened the central tenet of Zionism, 'the ingathering of the exiles', but the utility of immigrants in achieving an ideological end exposed divisions inherent within the conceptual basis of Zionism as outlined in Chapter 3. Indeed, the pursuit of an ideological goal, Jewish sovereignty over those areas deemed to constitute *Eretz Y'Israel*, adversely affected Israel's ability to implement a strategy designed to mobilize from the international environment the resources required for immigrant absorption. Moreover, as Chapter 4 argued, the structure of Israel's economy precluded the adoption of any effective form of accommodational or restructural mobilization strategy in an effort to obtain the required resources from Israeli society.

Although the Likud coalition government gained access to loan guarantees worth $400 million, it was insufficient to raise the necessary revenue required for effective immigrant absorption. However, compromise over an ideological goal proved anathema to the Likud and its right-wing allies. It is perhaps ironic that the reluctance by Likud to restructure the Israeli economy lay in the perceived impact that this would have on their most loyal constituents. Yet ultimately, pursuit of a regional agenda, dictated by ideological orthodoxy, provoked an international response whose domestic impact undermined the position of the Likud among bastions of previous right-wing support.

3. The impact of Soviet Jewish *aliyah* on societal security. The volume and intensity of this *aliyah* aroused questions concerning societal security among both the Soviet *olim* and Israelis alike. The

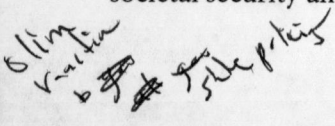

costs of absorption affected the social, economic, and cultural well-being of large sections of Israeli society, a process amplified by the failure of the Likud coalition government to implement an adequate mobilization strategy as was previously demonstrated. This produced widespread antipathy towards immigrant needs from the recipient society, particularly among some sections of Israel's Oriental community. As discussed in Chapter 5, such a milieu degraded the effectiveness of *mizug galuyot*, resulting in widespread introversion among the *olim*. This problem was especially acute among those immigrants with professional qualifications whose existence in caravan parks and some development towns allowed little opportunity for skills obtained in the Soviet Union to be used.

The power exercised by the religious authorities over a largely secular, non-Zionist immigrant wave, only provoked further disenchantment among the *olim* with the agenda of the state élite, dependent as this was on religious party support in government and the Knesset. With the failure of the *aliyah* cabinet to co-ordinate an effective construction programme inside the Green Line, the result of nepotism and inefficiency as much as ideological preference, Soviet immigrants and increasing numbers of Israelis began to question the practical implications involved in pursuing the agenda set by Shamir's government.

4. The impact of Soviet Jewish *aliyah* on regional order. The election result of June 1992 was tangible evidence of the effect that Soviet Jewish migration as a transnational flow had upon the domestic equilibrium of Israeli society. Not only were the votes of the *olim* crucial to the success of the centre left, but the net effect of migration on society disabused many Israelis of continued support for an agenda that subordinated internal needs to an ideological goal. The outcome of the election had a direct bearing on the ascendancy of the centre left whose own agenda proved more amenable to territorial compromise. This has had clear repercussions upon regional order, resulting in Israel's adoption of a more tangible approach to the pursuit of Middle East peace as outlined in Chapter 7. Indeed, while migration reinforced the central tenet of Zionism, its impact upon the wider Zionist debate demonstrated that Israel's borders remained both permeable and malleable to the impact of mass *aliyah* as a transnational flow.

In conclusion, no Israeli government could have accurately forecast the mass influx of Jews from the former Soviet Union, let alone foreseen the social and economic costs involved. Yet the policies pursued by the Likud coalition government resulted in widespread discontent among Israelis and immigrants alike. Failure to implement radical steps to cope with absorption was ultimately the product of an interpretation of Zionism that placed the land above the people, a process that ignored the growing need of societal security throughout Israel. In short, the Shamir government became too obsessed with the need to consolidate Israeli rule over the Occupied Territories, a process that prejudiced the establishment of an effective infrastructure required to create new homes and meaningful employment.

Diversion of resources from the territories to ease the social dislocation resulting from Soviet *aliyah* would not have been enough by itself, but it would have secured much needed support from Washington. The failure of the Likud leadership, however, to appreciate the changing international and regional environment, particularly in the aftermath of the Gulf War, demonstrated the continuing influence of *Eretz Y'Israel* as the ideological prism through which the Likud continued to perceive the Middle East. Accordingly, Soviet Jews provided a means, albeit through a large shift in the population of established citizens, by which Israeli rule over the territories could be consolidated. The practicalities of ruling over nearly two million Palestinian Arabs, as well as 700,000 Israeli Arabs within the Green Line, proved of little consequence to the political right. While the creation of new settlements, particularly the 'Stars Programme' was a deliberate attempt to usurp any Palestinian claim to statehood, developments in the Middle East, particularly in the aftermath of the Gulf conflict, allowed insufficient time for the Likud to attract sufficient numbers of Israelis to the Occupied Territories.

As such, attempts by the Likud to use Soviet Jewish *aliyah* as a means to an ideological end proved to be an expensive gamble. In pursuit of its regional agenda, the government of Yitzhak Shamir felt itself impervious to international pressure, dismissed arguments over demographics, and ignored the very real societal needs of its population. The resulting backlash proved calamitous for the Likud, but fundamental in conflating Israeli conceptions of strategic and societal security in accordance with a new set of regional and domestic priorities.

It would be foolhardy to predict specific outcomes in the volatile arena of Middle East politics. But if some regional

Conclusion

accommodation is eventually to be reached between Israel, the Palestinians, and the wider Arab world, the effects wrought by Soviet Jewish *aliyah* between 1989 and 1992, could at least in part be responsible for the laying of new foundations for hope throughout the region.

NOTES

1. Leon T. Hadar, op. cit., p.605.
2. Interview with Shai Grishpon, Mapam party headquarters, Tel-Aviv, 23 June 1993.
3. Nathan Sharansky, 'No Integration Without Representation', *The Jerusalem Report*, Vol.IV, No.15 (2 Dec. 1993), p.35.
4. Text of proposal by Likud MK Efraim Gur, The Likud Central Office, Knesset, Jerusalem, 17 Nov. 1993.
5. Speech by Israeli Deputy Foreign Minister and Labour MK Yossi Beilin to Soviet *olim*, Netanya, 3 July 1993.

Appendix

JEWISH EMIGRATION FROM THE USSR: 1968–90

1968–70	4,235	1980	21,471
1971	13,022	1981	9,447
1972	31,681	1982	2,688
1973	34,733	1983	1,314
1974	20,628	1984	896
1975	13,221	1985	1,140
1976	14,261	1986	914
1977	16,736	1987	8,155
1978	28,864	1988	18,965
1979	51,320	1989	71,217
		1990	186,815

JEWISH EMIGRATION FROM THE USSR: 1968–90

	1989	1990	1991	1992
Jan		4,836	13,360	6,285
Feb		6,628	7,164	4,286
Mar		7,077	13,336	5,071
Apr		11,062	16,286	4,668
May		10,293	16,048	3,552
June	657	11,259	21,372	3,943
July	801	15,739	10,325	5,066
Aug	938	17,617	8,943	5,122
Sept	1,231	18,725	9,877	6,793
Oct	1,516	20,324	9,845	6,901
Nov	1,936	25,186	8,090	6,579
Dec	3,558	35,295	145,005	65,079

Figures for Soviet Jewish Emigration from the Soviet Union supplied by Soviet Jewry Research Bureau, National Conference on Soviet Jewish *Aliyah* and by the Communications Department, Joint Israel Appeal, London.
*Denotes total Soviet Jewish *aliyah* between January and June 1989.

Select Bibliography

A. PRIMARY SOURCES

1. *Persons Interviewed*

Posts indicated were held by interviewees at the time of interview.

Tamara Amitai, Haifa, 22 November 1992. Author of children's books and peace activist.

Yigal Amitai, Haifa, 22 November 1992. Freelance journalist with *Ha'aretz* and co-ordinator of the immigrant seminar programme for the International Centre for Peace in the Middle East.

Dr Yossi Beilin, Netanya, 3 July 1993. Israel's Deputy Foreign Minister and a Labour Member of the Knesset.

Hymie Borschstein, Tel-Aviv, 16 November 1992. Chairman, Mapam Party Absorption Forum for new immigrants.

Avraham Burg, Knesset, Jerusalem, 23 November 1992. Labour Member of the Knesset and Chairman of the Select Committee on Education.

Edith Coron, Jerusalem, 1 July 1993. Middle East correspondent for *Liberation*.

Shai Grishpon, Tel-Aviv, 23 June 1993. Mapam Party worker with special responsibility for immigrant absorption.

Professor Avi Harrell, Tel-Aviv, 24 November 1992. Physician at the Ichilov hospital in Tel-Aviv and a member of the Presidium of the Council for Soviet Russian Jewry.

Marina Heifetz, Tel-Aviv, 24 June 1993. Recent immigrant and lawyer with Ratz.

Leonid Kilbert, Netanya, 3 July 1993. Independent film maker and journalist. Previously a physicist and former refusenik in the Soviet Union.

Svetlana Raviv, Holon, 27 June 1993. Director of immigrant absorption for the Histadrut Trade Union Federation.

Lesya Shtane-Smirnoff, Tel-Aviv, 18 November 1992 and 23 June 1993. Campaign co-ordinator for Meretz and Ratz Party worker for immigrant absorption.

Other information was obtained in conversations with numerous immigrants from the former Soviet Union, particularly in Haifa and the immigrant caravan park at Neve Carmel.

2. *Official Party and Government Publications*

International Centre for Peace in the Middle East, *Aniya Irha Kolmim: Vudot Vemisparim al hapar Hahebrati beIsrael*, May 1992.

_____.*44-aya Godovshchina Provozglashyeniya Nyezavisimosti Izraelya*, 9 April 1992.

_____.*Territorii!? Tsyennost ili Oboza*, May 1992.

Ministry of Immigrant Absorption, Department of *Aliyah* and Absorption of the Jewish Agency, *Aliyah: Karmaey Spravochnik*, 1992.

_____.*Kudsniki, Artisti, Pistyeli*, January 1992.

_____.*Naochniye Rabotniki*, 1992.

_____.*Pryamaya Absorbstziya: Tablitza, Denesnoy, Pomoshchi*, 1 April 1993.

_____.*Vasha Professiya v Izraelya: Spetzialisti v Oblasti EBM*, 1992.

Ratz/Meretz, *Osnovnye Polozheniya Platformi: Meretz i Demokratiya Izraelya*, May 1992.

3. *Documents and Papers.*

Robert O. Freedman, 'Soviet Jewish Immigrants and Israel's Election', paper presented as part of a US State Department briefing for the future American Ambassador to Israel, Mr Harrop. Washington, D.C, 30 July 1991.

Select Bibliography

Efraim Gur MK and member of *Aliyah* and Absorption Committee, 'Proposal for the Recruitment of *Olim* to the Likud Party and the Establishment of an Immigrant Forum', Likud Central Office, Knesset, Jerusalem, 17 November 1993.

International Centre for Peace in the Middle East, 'Public Education Project for New Russian Immigrants: Interim Report', Tel-Aviv, November 1991.

B. SECONDARY SOURCES

1. Books

Arian, Asher, *Politics in Israel* (Chatham, NJ: Chatham House Publishers, 1989).

Aronson, Geoffrey, *Israel, Palestinians and the Intifada: Creating Facts on the West Bank* (London: Kegan Paul/Institute for Palestine Studies, 1987).

Avishai, Bernard, *The Tragedy of Zionism: Revolution and Democracy in the Land of Israel* (New York: Farrar, Straus, Giroux, 1985).

Bennigsen, Alexandre, Paul Henze, George Tanham, and S. Enders Wimbush, *Soviet Strategy and Islam* (New York: St Martins Press, 1989).

Beschloss, Michael R. and Strobe Talbott, *At the Highest Levels: The Inside Story of the End of the Cold War* (London: Warner Books, 1994).

Blatt, M., Uri Davis, Paul Kleinbaum (eds), *Dissent and Ideology in Israel: Resistance to the Draft 1948-1973* (London: Ithaca Press, 1975).

Borovik, Artyom, *The Hidden War* (London: Faber and Faber, 1990).

Bowker, Mike and Phil Williams, *Superpower Detente: A Reappraisal* (London: Royal Institute of International Affairs/Sage, 1988).

Brecher, Michael, *Decisions in Israel's Foreign Policy* (Oxford: Oxford University Press, 1974).

_____, *The Foreign Policy System of Israel: Setting, Images, Process* (Oxford: Oxford University Press, 1972).

Brenner, Lenni, *The Iron Wall: Zionist Revisionism from Jabotinsky to Shamir* (London: Zed Press, 1984).

Breslauer, George W. (ed.), *Soviet Strategy in the Middle East* (London: Unwin Hyman, 1990).

Cobban, Helena, *The Palestinian Liberation Organization: People, Power, and Politics* (Cambridge: Cambridge University Press, 1990).

Coron, Edith. *Le Dernier Exode: Les Juifs Sovietiques en Israel: Recontre et Desillusion* (Paris: Francois Bourins, 1993).

Crockatt, Richard. and Steve Smith (eds), *Cold War: Past and Present* (London: Allen and Unwin, 1987).

Fletcher, William, *Religion and Soviet Foreign Policy, 1945-70* (London: Royal Institute for International Affairs/Oxford University Press, 1973).

Freedman, Robert O. (ed.), *The Intifada: Its Impact upon Israel, the Arab World and the Superpowers* (Miami: Florida International University Press, 1991).

_____(ed.), *Soviet Jewry in the Decisive Decade* (Durham, NC: Duke University Press, 1984).

_____, *Soviet Policy Towards Israel under Gorbachev* (New York: Centre for Strategic Studies, Washington, D.C/Praeger, 1991).

Garthoff, Raymond L, *Détente and Confrontation: American-Soviet Relations from Nixon to Reagan* (Washington, D.C: Brookings Institution, 1985).

Gazit, Shlomo and Zeev Eytan (eds), *The Middle East Military Balance, 1990-91* (Tel-Aviv: Jaffee Center for Strategic Studies, 1992).

Gilbert, Martin, *The Jews of Hope* (London: Macmillan Press, 1984).

Golan, Galia, *Moscow and the Middle East: New Thinking in Regional Conflict* (London: Pinter/Royal Institute for International Affairs, 1992).

_____, *Soviet Policies in the Middle East: From World War II to Gorbachev* (Cambridge: Cambridge University Press, 1990).

Goldscheider, Calvin (ed.), *Population and Social Change in Israel* (Boulder, CO: Westview Press, 1992).

Select Bibliography

Green, Stephen, *Living By the Sword: America and Israel in the Middle East, 1968–87* (London: Faber and Faber, 1987).

Hall-Cathala, David, *The Peace Movement in Israel, 1967–87* (New York: St Martins Press, 1990).

Hirst, David, *The Gun and the Olive Branch: The Roots of Violence in the Middle East* (London: Faber and Faber, 1984).

Hosking, Geoffrey, *A History of the Soviet Union* (London: Fontana, 1985).

Jansen, Michael, *Dissonance in Zion* (London: Zed Press, 1987).

Jennett, Christine and Randal G. Stewart (eds), *Politics of the Future: The Role of Social Movements* (Melbourne: Macmillan Press, 1989).

Keller, Adam, *Terrible Days: Social Divisions and Political Paradoxes in Israel* (Amstelveen, Holland: Cypres, 1987).

Keohane, Robert O and Joseph S. Nye (eds),. *Transnational Relations and World Politics* (Cambridge, MA: Harvard University Press, 1972).

Klinghoffer, Arthur with Judith Apter, *Israel and the Soviet Union: Alienation or Reconciliation?* (Boulder, CO: Westview Press, 1985).

Kochan, Lionel (ed.), *The Jews in Soviet Russia since 1917* (London: Oxford University Press/Institute of Jewish Affairs, 1978).

Kritz, Mary M., Charles B. Keely and Silvano M. Tomasi (eds), *Global Trends in Migration: Theory and Research on International Population Movements* (New York: Center for Migration Studies, New York, 1983).

Kyle, Keith and Joel Peters (eds), *Whither Israel? The Domestic Challenges* (London: RIIA/I.B.Tauris, 1993).

Lane, David, *The End of Inequality? Class, Status, and Power under State Socialism* (London: Allen and Unwin, 1982).

Laquer, Walter and Barry Rubin (eds), *The Israel-Arab Reader* (Harmondsworth: Penguin, 1984).

Levin, Nora, *The Jews in the Soviet Union since 1917: Paradox of Survival* (London: I.B. Tauris, 1990).

Light, Margot, *The Soviet Theory of International Relations* (Brighton: Harvester Press, 1988).

Luckas, Yehuda (ed.), *The Israeli-Palestinian Conflict: A Documentary Record, 1967–70* (Cambridge: Cambridge University Press/ International Centre for Peace in the Middle East, 1992).

Lynch, Allan, *The Soviet Study of International Relations* (Cambridge: Cambridge University Press, 1989).

Marshall, Phil, *Intifada: Zionism, Imperialism, and Palestinian Resistance* (London: Bookmarks, 1989).

Melman, Yossi and Dan Raviv, *Behind the Uprising: Israelis, Jordanians, and Palestinians* (Westport, Connecticut: Greenwood Press, 1989).

Migdal, Joel S. *Strong Societies and Weak States: State-Society Relations and State Capabilities in the Third World* (Princeton, New Jersey: Princeton University Press, 1988).

Morgenthau, Hans J., *Politics Among Nations* (New York: McGraw-Hill, 1993).

Moskovich, Wolf, *Rising to the Challenge: Israel and the Absorption of Soviet Jews* (London: Institute for Jewish Affairs, 1990).

O'Brien, Conor Cruise, *The Seige: The Saga of Israel and Zionism* (London: Weidenfeld and Nicholson, 1986).

Ovendale, Ritchie, *The Longman Companion to the Middle East since 1914* (Harlow: Longman, 1992).

_____, *The Origins of the Arab-Israeli Wars* (Harlow: Longman, 1992).

Peri, Yoram, *Between Battles and Ballots: Israeli Military in Politics* (Cambridge: Cambridge University Press, 1985).

Pinkus, Benjamin, *The Jews of the Soviet Union: The History of a National Minority* (Cambridge: Cambridge University Press, 1989).

Piscatori, James P. (ed.), *Islamic Fundamentalisms and the Gulf Crisis* (Chicago: American Academy of Arts and Sciences, 1991).

Quandt, William B., *Peace Process: American Diplomacy and the Arab-Israeli Conflict since 1967* (Washington, DC: Brookings Institution/University of California Press, 1993).

Reich, Bernard and Gershon R. Kieval, *Israel: Land of Tradition and Conflict* (Boulder, CO: Westview Press, 1993).

_____ (eds), *Israeli Politics in the 1990s: Key Domestic and Foreign Policy Factors* (Westport, Connecticut: Greenwood Press, 1991).

Rodinson, Maxime, *Israel and the Arabs* (Harmondsworth: Penguin, 1985).

Rothman, Jay, *From Confrontation to Co-operation: Resolving Ethnic and Regional Conflict* (London: Sage, 1992).

Salitan, Laurie P., *Politics and Nationality in Contemporary Soviet–Jewish Emigration, 1968–89* (London: St Antonys/Macmillan Press, 1992).

Sawyer, Thomas E., *The Jewish Minority in the Soviet Union* (Boulder, CO: Westview Press, 1979).

Schiff, Zeev and Ehud Ya'ari, *Israel's Lebanon War* (London: Unwin, 1984).

Sheffer, Gabriel (ed.), *Modern Diasporas in International Relations* (London: Croom Helm, 1986).

Shepherd, Naomi, *The Russians in Israel: The Ordeal of Freedom* (London: Simon and Schuster, 1993).

Shindler, Colin, *Ploughshares into Swords? Israelis and Jews in the Shadow of the Intifada* (London: I.B. Tauris, 1991).

Silberstein, Laurence J. (ed.), *Jewish Fundamentalism in Comparative Perspective: Religion, Ideology and the Crisis of Modernity* (New York: New York University Press, 1993).

Swirski, Shlomo, *Israel: The Oriental Majority* (London: Zed Press, 1989).

Waever, Ole, Barry Buzan, Morten Kelstrup, and Pierre Lemaitre, *Identity, Migration and the New Security Agenda in Europe* (London: Pinter Publishers, 1993).

Waltz, Kenneth, *Theory of International Politics* (New York: McGraw-Hill, 1979).

Weingrod, Alex (ed.), *Studies in Israeli Ethnicity: After the Ingathering* (New York: Gordon and Breach, 1985).

Wolffsohn, Michael, *Israel: Polity, Society and Economy, 1982-1986* (New Jersey: Humanities Press International, 1987).

Yaniv, Avner (ed.), *National Security and Democracy in Israel* (London: Lynne Rienner Publishers, 1993).

Zaslavsky, Victor. and Robert J. Brym *Soviet Jewish Emigration and Soviet Nationality Policy* (London: Macmillan Press, 1983).

2. Monographs

Capitanchik, David. 'A Guide to the Israeli General Election, 1992', *Research Report No.3* (London: Institute of Jewish Affairs, 1992).

_____. 'The Stalemate is Broken: The 1992 Israeli General Election', *Research Report No.4* (London: Institute of Jewish Affairs, 1992).

Feldman, Shai and Heda Rechnitz-Kijner, 'Deception, Consensus, and War: Israel in Lebanon', *Jaffee Center for Strategic Studies Paper No.27* (Tel-Aviv: Tel-Aviv University/Jerusalem Post, 1984).

Lawrence, Timothy, 'The Soviet Nationalities Question: Disintegration in the 1980s and 1990s', *Manchester Papers in Politics* (Manchester: Department of Government, University of Manchester, 1991).

Loescher, Gil 'Refugee Movements and International Security', *Adelphi Paper No.268* (London: International Institute of Strategic Studies, 1992).

More, James W., *'Aliyah* and the Demographic Balance in Israel and the Occupied Territories', *The Norman Paterson School of International Affairs Occasional Papers series No.1* (Ottowa: Carleton University, 1992).

Nosenko. Vladimir I., 'The Transformation of the Soviet Stand on the Palestinian Problem', *Dayan Center Occasional Papers No. 109*. (Tel-Aviv: Dayan Center for the Middle Eastern and African Studies, Tel-Aviv University, 1991).

Teitelbaum, Joshua, 'The Arabs and the New Wave of Jewish Immigration to Israel: Back to Old Ideology?', *Data and Analysis* (Tel-Aviv: Dayan Center for Middle Eastern and African Studies, Tel-Aviv University, 1990).

3. Journal and Book Articles

Ahmed, Mohammed Sid, 'Consequences of Perestroika', *Middle East Report*, Vol.20, Nos. 3/4 (May–August 1990), pp.58–9.

Al-Haj, Majid, 'Soviet Immigration as Viewed by Jews and Arabs: Divided Attitudes in a Divided Country' in Calvin Goldscheider (ed), *Population and Social Change in Israel* (Boulder, CO: Westview Press, 1992), pp.89–108.

Al-Qattan, Leenah, 'Soviet Jews and Israel: Immigration and Settlement: A Selected Bibliography', *Journal of Palestine Studies*, Vol. XXII, No. 2 (Winter 1993), pp.125–41.

Aronson, Geoffrey, 'Full Steam Ahead in the West Bank', *Journal of Palestine Studies*, Vol. XXI, No. 1 (Autumn 1991), pp.115–19.

_____ 'Soviet Jewish Emigration, the United States and the Occupied Territories', *Journal of Palestine Studies*, Vol. XIX, No. 4 (Summer 1990), pp.30–45.

Baram, Haim, 'Immigration in Perspective', *Middle East International*, No. 368 (2 February 1990), pp.4–5.

Barnett, Michael, 'High Politics is Low Politics: The Domestic and Systemic Sources of Israeli Security Policy, 1967-1977', *World Politics*, Vol. XLII, No. 4 (1990), pp. 529-62.

Baskin, Gershon (ed.), 'Water: Conflict or Cooperation', *Israel/Palestine Center for Research and Information*, Vol. 2, No. 2 (March 1993), pp.1–11.

Beit-Hallahmi, Benjamin, 'A "Miracle" Made in Washington and Moscow', *Middle East Report*, Vol. 20, Nos. 3/4 (May–Aug 1990), pp.46–7.

Ben-Meir, Alon, 'Israelis and Palestinians: Harsh Demographic Reality and Peace', *Middle East Policy*, Vol. 2, No. 2 (1993), pp.74–86.

Blankfort, Jerry, 'Bush Locks Horns with Shami', *Middle East Report*, Vol. 21, No. 6 (November-December 1991), pp.38–9.

Bull, Hedley, 'The State's Positive Role in World Affairs', *Daedulus*, Vol. 108, No. 4 (Fall 1979), pp.111–23.

Buzan, Barry, 'Societal Security, State Security, and Internationalization', In Ole Waever et al., *Identity, Migration and the New Security Agenda in Europe* (London: Pinter Publishers, 1993), pp.41–58.

Cohen, Benjamin, 'An Insecure Future for Israel's Immigrants', *Middle East International*, No. 404 (12 July 1991), pp.17-18.

Cohen-Almagor, Raphael, 'The *Intifada*: Causes, Consequences, and Future Trends', *Small Wars and Insurgencies*, Vol. 2, No. 1 (April 1991), pp.12-40.

Cohen, Roberta, 'Israel's Problematic Absorption of Soviet Jews', *Innovation*, Vol. 4, Nos. 3/4 (1991), pp.65-87.

Cohen, Stuart A., 'Changing Emphases in Israel's Military Commitments, 1981-91: Causes and Consequences', *Journal of Strategic Studies*, Vol. 15, No. 3 (September 1992), pp.330-50.

'Course for Young Community Leadership for Russian Immigrants', *International Centre for Peace in the Middle East News Letter*, No. 1 (January 1992), p.3.

Demchenko, Pavel, 'Between Hammer and Anvil', *Asia and Africa Today*, No. 6 (September-October 1991), pp.4-9.

Doron, Gideon and Gad Barzilai, 'The Middle East Power Balance: Israel's Attempts to Understand Changes in Soviet-Arab Relations', *International Journal of Intelligence and Counter-intelligence*, Vol. 5, No. 1 (1993), pp.35-47.

Dowty, Alan, 'Emigration and Expulsion in the Third World', *Third World Quarterly*, Vol. 8, No. 1 (January 1986), pp.151-76.

Eisenberg, Laura Zittrain, 'Passive Belligerency: Israel and the 1991 Gulf War', *Journal of Strategic Studies*, Vol. 15, No. 3 (September 1992), pp.304-29.

'Either Territories or Immigrants', *International Center for Peace in the Middle East News Letter*, No.1 (January 1992), pp.2-3.

Friedgut, Theodore, 'The Welcome Home: Absorption of Soviet Jews in Israel', In Robert O. Freedman (ed.), *Soviet Jewry in the Decisive Decade* (Durham, NC: Duke University Press, 1984), pp.68-78.

Gilison, Jerome M., 'Soviet Jewish Emigration, 1971-80: An Overview', In Robert O. Freedman (ed.), *Soviet Jewry in the Decisive Decade* (Durham, North Carolina: Duke University Press, 1984), pp.3-16.

Gitelman, Zvi, 'Moscow and the Soviet Jews: A Parting of the Ways', *Problems of Communism*, Vol. XXIX. (Jan.-Feb. 1980), pp.18-34.

Select Bibliography

_____. 'Soviet Jewish Immigrants to the United States: Profile, Problems, Prospects', In Robert O. Freedman (ed.), *Soviet Jewry in the Decisive Decade* (Durham, NC: Duke University Press, 1984), pp.89–98.

Goodman, Hirsh, 'Why Israel went into Battle', *The Jerusalem Report*, Vol. IV, No. 7 (12 Aug. 1993), pp.10–11.

Goodman, Jerry, 'The Jews in the Soviet Union: Emigration and Its Difficulties', In Robert O. Freedman (ed.), *Soviet Jewry in the Decisive Decade* (Durham, NC: Duke University Press, 1984, pp.17–28).

Gruen, George E., 'The Impact of the *Intifada* on American Jews', In Robert O. Freedman (ed.), *The Intifada: Its Impact upon Israel, the Arab World, and the Superpowers* (Miami: Florida International University Press, 1991, pp.220–66).

Hadar, Leon T., 'High Noon in Washington: The Shootout over the Loan Guarantees', *Journal of Palestine Studies*, Vol. XXI, No. 2 (Winter 1992), pp.72–87.

_____. 'The 1992 Electoral Earthquake and the Fall of the "Second Israeli Republic"', *Middle East Journal*, Vol. 46, No. 4 (Autumn 1992), pp.594–616.

Halevi, Yossi-Klein and Tom Sawiki, 'Its Better Here Than There', *The Jerusalem Report*, Vol. IV, No. 13 (4 Nov. 1993), pp.18–22.

Hilterman, Joost R., 'Settling for War: Soviet Immigration and Israel's Settlement Policy in East Jerusalem', *Journal of Palestine Studies*, Vol. XX, No. 2 (Winter 1991), pp.71–85.

Horowitz, Dan, 'The Israeli Concept of National Security', In Avner Yaniv (ed.), *National Security and Democracy in Israel* (London: Lynne Rienner Publishers, 1993), pp.11–53.

Inbar, Efraim, 'Attitudes Towards War in the Israeli Political Elite'. *Middle East Journal*, Vol. 44. No. 3 (Summer 1990), pp.431–45.

Irwin, Zachary, 'The USSR and Israel', *Problems of Communism*, Vol. XXXVI (Jan.-Feb. 1987), pp.36–45.

Karsh, Efraim and Inari Rautsi, 'Why Saddam Hussein Invaded Kuwait', *Survival*, Vol. XXXIII, No. 1 (Jan.-Feb. 1991), pp.18–30.

Kidron, Peretz, 'Euphoria and Alarm', *Middle East International*, No. 401 (31 May 1991), p.4.

_____, 'Knives Make Repression Harsher', *Middle East International*, No. 397 (5 April 1991), pp.8–9.

_____, 'The Sword at Israel's Throat', *Middle East International*, No. 404 (13 Sept. 1991), pp.4–6.

King, John, 'Job Problems Face Israel's Soviet Immigrants', *Middle East International*, No. 374 (27 April 1990), pp.19–20.

Kolker, Fabian, 'A New Soviet Jewry Plan', In Robert O. Freedman (ed.), *Soviet Jewry in the Decisive Decade* (Durham, NC: Duke University Press, 1984), pp.79–88.

Korey, William, 'Soviet Decision-Making and the Problems of Jewish Emigration Policy', *Survey*, Vol. 22, No. 1 (Winter 1976), pp.112–31.

Lahav, Pnina, 'The Press and National Security', In Avner Yaniv (ed.), *National Security and Democracy in Israel* (London: Lynne Rienner Publishers, 1993), pp.173–95.

Legrain, Jean François, 'A Defining Moment: Palestinian Islamic Fundamentalism', In James P. Piscatori (ed.), *Islamic Fundamentalisms and the Gulf Crisis* (Chicago: American Academy of Arts and Sciences, 1991), pp.70–87.

Marcus, Jonathan, 'Israel's General Election: Realignment or Upheaval?', *International Affairs*, Vol. 68, No. 4 (1992), pp.693–705.

Margalit, Avishai, 'The Great White Hope', *New York Review of Books*, Vol. XXXVIII, No. 12 (27 June 1991), pp.19–25.

'Messengers of Peace, Democracy, and Co-existence: ICPME Trains Future National and Communal Leaders', *International Centre for Peace in the Middle East News Letter*, No. 1 (April 1993), pp.9–10.

Neff, Donald, 'Bob Dole Squares up to Israel', *Middle East International*, No. 374 (27 April 1990), pp.3–5.

Newman, David and Tamar Hermann, 'A Comparative Study of Gush Emunim and Peace Now', *Middle Eastern Studies*, Vol. 28, No. 3 (July 1992), pp.509–30.

Norton, Augustus Richard, 'The Future of Civil Society in the Middle East', *Middle East Journal*, Vol. 47, No. 2 (Spring 1993), pp.205–16.

'On the Emigration of Soviet Jews', *Israel and Palestine Political Report*, (May 1990), pp.4–8.

Pallis, Elfi, 'Israel's $10 Billion Loan Guarantee: Is it Needed?' *Middle East International*, No. 410 (11 Oct. 1991), pp.18–19.

_____. 'The Likud Party: A Primer', *Journal of Palestine Studies*, Vol. XXI, No. 2 (Winter 1992), pp.41–60.

Peretz, Don, 'The Impact of the Gulf War on Israeli and Palestinian Political Attitudes', *Journal of Palestine Studies*, Vol. XXI, No. 1 (Autumn 1991), pp.17–35.

_____. 'The *Intifada* and Middle East Peace', *Survival*, Vol. XXXII, No. 5 (Sept.-Oct. 1990), pp.387–401.

Peterson, M. J., 'Transnational Activity, International Society, and World Politics', *Millennium*, Vol. 21, No. 3 (Winter 1992), pp.371–88.

Piscatori, James P., 'Islamic Fundamentalism in the Wake of the Six Day War: Religious Self-Assertion in Political Conflict, in Laurence J. Silberstein (ed.), *Jewish Fundamentalism in Comparative Perspective: Religion, Ideology, and the Crisis of Modernity* (New York: New York University Press, 1993), pp.79–93.

Ramzani, R.K., 'Iran's Foreign Policy: Both North and South', *Middle East Journal*, Vol. 46, No. 3 (1992), pp.392–412.

Reich, Bernard, Noah Dropkin and Meyrav Wurmser, 'The Impact of the Soviet Jewish Vote on the Israeli Knesset Election', *Middle East Insight*, Vol. VIII, No. 4 (March–April 1992), pp.48–55.

_____. 'Soviet Jewish Immigration and the 1992 Israeli Knesset Elections', *Middle East Journal*, Vol. 47, No. 3 (1993), pp.465–78.

Rekhess, Elie, 'The Arab Nationalist Challenge to the Israeli Communist Party, 1970–85', *Studies in Comparative Communism*, Vol. XXII, No. 4 (Winter 1989), pp.337–50.

Rubenstein, Colin. 'Zionism: The National Liberation Movement of the Jewish People'. In Christine Jennett and Randall G. Stewart (eds), *Politics of the Future: The Role of Social Movements* (Melbourne: Macmillan Press, 1989), pp.262–90.

'Russian Immigrants: Thinking and Doing Something About Peace, Democracy, and Co-existence', *International Center for Peace in the Middle East News Letter*, No. 2 (June 1993), pp.9–10.

Sabella, Bernard, 'Russian Jewish Immigration and the Future of the Israeli-Palestinian Conflict', *Middle East Report*, Vol. 23, No. 3 (May–June 1993), pp.36–40.

'Salute to *Aliyah*: Ingathering '91', *Tel-Aviv University News*, (Fall 1991).

Sawiki, Tom, 'A Wedding Banned', *The Jerusalem Report*, Vol. IV, No. 21 (24 Feb. 1994), pp.14–15.

Sergeyev, S., 'Reactionary Theories of Political Zionism', *Zionism: Enemy of Peace and Social Progress*, Issue 2 (Moscow 1983), pp.5–38.

Sheffer, Gabriel, 'Political Aspects of Jewish Fundraising for Israel', in Gabriel Sheffer (ed.), *Modern Diasporas in International Politics* (London: Croom Helm, 1986), pp.259–93.

Smooha, Sammy, 'Part of the Problem or Part of the Solution: National Security and the Arab Minority', in Avner Yaniv (ed.), *National Security and Democracy in Israel* (London: Lynne Rienner Publishers, 1993), pp.105–27.

'Soviet Anti-Zionist Committee Press Conference', *Zionism: Enemy of Peace and Social Progess*, Issue 4 (Moscow 1985), pp.5–25.

Sprinzak, Ehud, 'Politics, Institutions and Culture of Gush Emunim', in Laurence J. Siberstein (ed.), *Jewish Fundamentalism in Comparative Perspective: Religion, Ideology, and the Crisis of Modernity* (New York: New York University Press, 1993), pp.117–47.

Spulbeck, Suzanne, 'Integration and Identity: The Immigration of Jews from the former USSR to Germany', *Analysis: Institute of Jewish Affairs*, No. 3 (March 1993), pp.1–6.

'Survey of Israel: At Ease in Zion', *The Economist*, Vol. 330, No. 7847 (22-28 Jan. 1994), pp.1–22.

Swann, Robert, 'A Change of Dutch Heart', *Middle East International*, No. 414 (6 Dec. 1991), p.14.

Szulc, Tad., 'The Great Soviet Exodus', *National Geographic*, Vol. 181, No. 2 (Feb. 1992), pp.40–65.

Waever, Ole 'Societal Security: The Concept', In Ole Waever *et al.*, *Identity, Migration, and the New Security Agenda in Europe* (London: Pinter Publishers, 1993), pp.18–40.

Wallender, Celeste, 'Third World Conflict in Soviet Military Thought: Does New Thinking Grow Prematurely Grey?', *World Politics*, Vol. XLII No. 1 (1989), pp.31–63.

Weinbaum, Marvin J., 'The Israel Factor in Arab Consciousness and Domestic Politics', *Middle East Policy*, Vol. II, No. 1 (1993), pp.87–102.

Willis, Aaron, 'Redefining Religious Zionism: Shas' Ethno-Politics', *Israel Studies Bulletin*, Vol. 8, No. 2 (Fall 1992), pp.3–8.

Zolberg, Aristide R., 'International Migrations in Political Perspective', in Mary M. Kritz *et al.*, *Global Trends in Migration: Theory and Research on International Population Movements* (New York: Center for Migration Studies, New York, 1983), pp.3–27.

Zuyenko, Oleg, 'A "Russian" Party', *Asia and Africa Today*, No. 6 (Nov.–Dec. 1991), p.29.

4. Unpublished Papers

Freedman, Robert O., 'Jewish Emigration as a Factor in Soviet Foreign Policy Toward the United States and Israel in the Gorbachev Era', unpublished Paper, 1992.

Weiner, Myron, 'The Political Aspects of International Migration', paper presented to the International Studies Association, London, 30 March 1989.

5. Newspapers

France:
Le Monde.

Israel: In English.
The Jerusalem Post.
The Jerusalem Post International.
Israel: In Hebrew.
Al Hamishmar.
Davar.
Ha'aretz.
Hadashot.

Ma'ariv.
Yediot Aharanot.

Israel: In Russian.
Nasha Strana.
Novosti.
Novosti Nedli.
Nyozaveezemaya Gazeta.
Panorama.
Vremya.

Soviet Union:
Izvestia.
Pravda.

United Kingdom:
BBC *Summary of World Broadcasts for the Middle East.*
The Daily Telegraph.
Financial Times.
The Guardian.
The Independent.
The Independent on Sunday.
The Sunday Times Magazine.
The Times.

United States of America:
International Herald Tribune
New York Times.
Washington Post.

7. *Television and Radio Broadcasts*

Corbin, Jane, *Panorama*, BBC 1, 22 June 1992.

Reynolds, Paul, *International Assignment*, BBC Radio Four, 5 June 1987.

Simon, Stewart, *Analysis*, BBC Radio Four, 27 Jan. 1994.

_____ *File on Four*, BBC Radio Four, 22 Oct. 1991.

Vine, Jeremy, *Today*, BBC Radio Four, 8 May 1992.

Index

Abna al-Balad (Sons of the Land), 171–2
Abram, Morris, 44
Abu Sharif, Yahya, 169
Afghanistan, Soviet invasion of, 26; 204
Agudat Y'Israel, 133
al-Asad, President Hafiz, 8, 36; speech to Syrian Revolution Youth Federation, 154; 161
Aley Zahav, settlement of, 110
Aliyah, comparative scale of, 1; definition of, 9; difficulties in assessing scale of, 75; decline in the level of, 131,142
Aliyah Cabinet, 77, 79, 85, 98; budget for immigrant absorption, 84; failure to co-ordinate absorption strategy, 81
Aliyah 90 (All Israeli Federation of Public and Professional Organizations of *Olim*), 127
Algeria, 159
Allison, Graham, 5
Allon, Yigal (Allon Plan), 58
al-Maguid, Esmat Abd, 169
al-Qaddafi, Mu'ammar, and reaction to Soviet Jewish migration, 156, 159
Aloni, Shulamit, 204
al-Qassim, Marwan, 158
Amash, Az al-Din, 173
American–Israel Public Affairs Committee (AIPAC), 88, 91, 92, 109, 136
Amidar Construction Company, 99-100
Amitai, Tamara, 146
Amitai, Yigal, 131
Amnesty International, 4
Amutah Housing Co-operative, 99-100
Andropov, Yuri, 22
Angola, 20
Anti-Semitism (*see also* Pamyat), 22, 26, 35, 39, 121
Anti-Zionist Committee (AKSO), *see* Soviet Union
Arab League, 162, 165
Arafat, Yasser, views of Soviet Jewish migration, 157, 162, 164, 168

Arara, village of, 173
Arens, Moshe, 110, 167, 184-5, 208
Arian, Asher, 132
Ariel, Israeli settlement of, 66, 103-5
Armenian earthquake, 47
Ashdod, 63
Ashkenazi Jews, dominance of in Israel, 32, 62; Oriental Jewish view of, 145; view of Soviet Jews, 146
Audizhan (Uzbekistan), 121
Avney Hafetz, settlement of, 105
Azerbaijan, 196

Baghdad, 1990 Arab conference in, 154, 162-5
Baker, James (*see also* United States), 88; loan guarantees and the issue of fungibility, 89–90; 92, 110, 161–62, 166
Barenboim, Daniel, 43
Barnett, Michael, domestic and international levels of resource mobilization, 2, 5–7, 12, 87
Bedouin Arabs, 67, 130, 202
Beersheba, Soviet Jewish settlement in, 145–6
Beilin, Yossi, 215
Begin, Binyamin, and the Revisionist concept of Zionism, 58
Begin, Menachem, 62
Belonogov, Aleksandr, 42, 161
Ben-Aharon, Yossi, 160
Ben Eliezer, Binyamin, 206
Ben Gurion, David, and 'Jewishness', 10; 61-2, 63, 136
Ben-Porat, Miriam, 79, 101
Benvenisti, Meron, 103
Ben-Yemini, Dror, 173
Betar, settlement of, 179
Bolshoi Ballet, 47
Borschstein, Hymie, 199
Bovin, Aleksandr, 42
Brecher, Michael, 10–11

Brezhnev, Leonid, 19, 37
Brit Shalom, 60
Bronfmann, Edgar, 45
Bruno, Michael, 82
Brutents, Karen, 44
Buber, Martin, 60
Buchbut, Shlomo, 110
Burg, Avraham, 139, 194, 199
Bush, George (*see also* United States of America), 46, 77, 92-3, 107-8, 161, 162, 165, 166, 207

Camp David Agreement, 28, 41
Canada, 27
Carmiel, area of, 101
caravan parks (*see also* Neve Carmel), settlement of Soviet Jews in, 119, 138
Carter, President Jimmy, 20, 21
Chernobyl, 122
civil society, concept of, 3, 5
Cohen, Melvin, 98
Cohen, Ran, 103
Committee for the Present Danger, 20

DA (Democracy and *Aliyah*), 181, 190-2
Damascus, 36
Darousha, Abd el-Wahab, 175
Davar, 192
Declaration of Principles, 208, 215
Democratic Front for Peace and Equality, 173, 175
Democratic Front for the Liberation of Palestine, 58
Deri, Rabbi Aryeh, 132-3, 134, 135, 136, 138
Der Judenstaat, 61
Derkovsky, Oleg, 42
Detente, *see* United States of America
de Tocqueville, Alexis, 4
Dinitz, Simcha, 78-80, 165
Dole, Senator Robert, 88
Dragunskii, David I., 36
dropout syndrome (*see also* Noshrim), 27-8
Druze, reaction to Soviet Jewish migration, 130, 155-6, 174
Dzasokhov, Aleksandr, 41

Eban, Abba, 68
Edelstein, Yuli, 187
Eliashu, Efrat, 67
Egypt, 158
Elon, Amos, 132
Eitan, Lieutenant General Rafael, 70
Ethiopia, 20
Ethiopian *olim*, and relationship with Soviet Jews, 147-8

European Community, 159

Fahd, King of Saudi Arabia, 158
Faris, Hussein, 172
Fourth Geneva Convention, 103
France, and the *pieds noirs*, 9
Freedman, Robert O., 45
Frenkel, Ya'acov, 95

Gafni, Arnon, 86
Galilee, settlement of immigrants in, 63, 67, 68, 98, 130
Gaza, *see* Occupied Territories
Germany, the migration of Soviet Jews to, 142
Gilison, Jerome, 23
Gilo, settlement of, 163
Gitelman, Zvi, 33
Glassman, Alec, 182
Golan Heights, 43, 107, and Israeli withdrawal from, 207
Gorbachev, Mikhail, December 1988 speech before the United Nations, 16, 48; and New Political Thinking, 40-1; 154, 160; and the Soviet Jews, 38, 39
Gordon, Uri, 78, 80-1, 126
Goronetsky, Lev, 142
Greenpeace, 4
Grishpon, Shai, 189
Gulf Crisis 1990-1, 101,166, 168, 218
Gur, Efraim, 2143
Gush Emunim, 4, 60, 68, 93, 188

HaAm Ahad (Asher Ginsberg), 60
Ha'aretz, 106, 131, 171
Hadar Ha'Carmel, *see* Haifa
Hadar, Leon T., 181, 186, 213
Hadash, see Democratic Front for Peace and Equality
Haifa, 64; Israeli Arab protest in, 171; numbers of Soviet Jews living in, 64, 100, 105, 124, 146
Haggada, 137
Hague Convention, 103
Halacha, 132, 135, 138-9, 149, 201
Hall-Cathala, David, 197
Hamas, and view of Soviet Jewish immigration, 164
Ha'patish, 173
Harawi, President Elias, 8
Harel, Israel, 93
Harish, Yosef, 204
Harell, Professor Avi, 125
Hassan, King of Morocco, 160
Hawatmeh, Nayif, 58
Hebrew Immigrant Aid Society (HIAS), 34, 50

Index

Heifetz, Marina, 138-9
Helsinki Final Act of the Conference of Security and Co-operation in Europe, 37, 39, 46, 157–8
Herut Party, 62
Horowitz, Dan, 69
Herzl, Theodore, 61
Herzog, President Chaim, 126
Histadrut trade union movement, 61, 82, 85-6, 94, 127-8
Hussein, King of Jordan, at the Baghdad summit 164; threat of military action against Israel over Soviet Jewish *aliyah*, 158
Hussein, President Saddam, 90, 159, 162–4
Husseini, Feisal, 168, 173

Ighbarieh, Raja, 171
Ihud group, 60
Institute of World Economy and International Relations (IMEMO), 42
International Business Machines (IBM), 200
International Centre for Peace in the Middle East (ICPME), 136, 174, 185; and work among Soviet *olim*, 202–4
International Covenant on Civil and Political Rights (ICPR), 36
Intifada, 46, 65, 71, 80, 155, 164, 173, 193
Iraq, invasion of Kuwait, 46, 71, 89, 159, 165; missile attacks upon Israel, 71, 91, 167; war with Iran, 159
Ireland, 159
Israel (*see also* Occupied Territories), concept of *Eretz Y'Israel*, 12, 58; financial debt to Washington, 166; migration from, 59; National Unity Government, 65, 66, 81, 83, 89, 192; origins as a state, 61–2; restrictions on economic reform in, 82, 84–5, 216; settlement in Occupied Territories, 58, 64–5, 69, 76, 107, 163; unemployment in, 125
Israeli Arabs, 99, 111, 130, 218; reaction to Soviet Jewish *aliyah*, 155, 170–4; support for Islamic politics, 170; unemployment among, 170
Israel Defence Forces (IDF), impact of *aliyah* on budget, 86; origins of, 61; opinion on the Occupied Territories, 69–72
Israel Land Authority (ILA), 97, 100

Jabotinsky, Vladimir, 62
Jackson-Vanik Amendment, 19, 21, 45–6

Jaffee Centre for Strategic Studies, 70
Japan, 96
Jasr el-Zarka, village of, 173
Jerusalem, construction in 78, 90; settlement of Soviet Jews in, 67, 89–90, 105–7, 163; Temple Mount shooting, 90
Jewish Agency, 34, 66, 134, 138; and covering absorption costs, 83; housing plans in the Occupied Territories, 104; and 'Operation Exodus', 78; *shlichim* in, 121–2, 128, 147;
Jordan, Hashemite Kingdom of, 8, 58, 62, 158, 164
Jordan Times, 168
Judea and Samaria, *see* Occupied Territories

Kahane Commission, 3
Katz, Elihu, 185–6
Kessar, Yisrael, 86
kibbutzim, 61, 65, 129-30, 137, 145
Kiryat Gat, 63
Kiryat Malachi, 143
Kiryat Shemonah, 145
Kiryat Yam, 100
Kleiner, Michael, 135
Klibi, Chedli, 158
Kohl, Chancellor Helmut, 9
kolkhozy, 130
Kollek, Teddy, 66, 214
Kook, Rabbi Yitzhak HaCohen, 59
Kook, Rabbi Zvi HaCohen, 60
Kosharovsky, Yuli, 190–2
Kosygin, Alexei, 22

Labour Alignment (*see also* Peres and Rabin), 61, 72, 139; elections to the party list, 194; national election of, 204–5; support among Soviet Jews, 192–3
Lahat, Shlomo, 68
Law of Return, definition of, 9, 49, 119, 134-5, 138, 142, 186
Lebanon, 8, 35, 36, 65, 96, 204
Leibowitz, Yeshayu, 61
Leningrad Trial, 18
Levy, David, 90, 103, 167, 184–5
Libya, 41
Likud (*see also* Shamir), 62–3, 65; formation of coalition government, 72, 133; elections for the party list, 184; relationship with Soviet Jews, 181–6; views on the Occupied Territories and Soviet Jews, 68, 93
Lissak, Professor Moshe, 131
Lithuania, 161

loan guarantees, 87–8, 91, 144, 167, 173, 179, 207, 216

Ma'alot, 110
Ma'ariv, 205
Madrid Peace Conference, 93, 95, 108, 202
Ma'aleh Adunim, Israeli settlement of, 102, 106, 162
Magnes, Dr Judah, 60
Mansour, Attallah, 172
Mapai party, 61, 63
Mapam, 61, 181, 189, 192, 198–9
Meir, Golda, 25, 29-30, 83
Meese, Edwin, 49
Mena, David, 124
Mendelevich, Yosef, 187
Meretz (Energy), 174, 181; formation of 198; political platform of, 198-201; 204, 205, 206
Migration, *see* transnationalism
Millennium, 1
Ministry of Immigrant Absorption (*see also aliyah* cabinet, Rabbi Yitzhak Peretz), 31, 75, 78, 79, 80, 81, 83, 132, 136, 141
Ministry of the Interior (*see also* Rabbi Aryah Deri), 141
Mirsky, Georgy, 42
Mitzna, Major-General Amram, 70
Mizug galuyot, concept of, 31; impact of upon Soviet Jews, 118, 127, 131, 134, 143, 149, 187, 198, 217
Mo'dai, Yitzhak, 77, 85–6, 91; problems with *aliyah* cabinet, 95, 107–8; request for loan guarantees, 167
Morocco, 159
Moledet party, 109, 179, 182, 184
Moscow, *see* Soviet Union
moshavim, 65
Motorola, 200
Mubarak, President Hosni, 158, 162, 164

Nachman, Ron, 66, 107
Namir, Ora, 194
National Conference on Soviet Jewry, 46
National Religious Party (NRP), 132
Ne'eman, Yuval, 109, 179
Negev, settlement of immigrants in, 63, 67, 68, 98, 130
Neve Carmel, caravan park of, 147-8
Nitze, Paul, 20
Northern Ireland, 8
Norton, Augustus Richard, 4
Noshrim, 17, 28, 33, 40, 48, 50; and the Dutch Embassy, 48; in the Netherlands, 142

Nudel, Ida, 37, 187

Occupied Territories, as part of Israel, 57, 58; 64, 65, 67, 68, 76, 89, 95, 102-4, 155–6, 173, 182, 205–6
Olmert, Ehud, 105, 214
Ofarim, settlement of, 109
Oren, Haim, 110
Oriental Jews, 10, 29-30, 32; absorption of, 63–4; impact of Soviet Jewish *aliyah* upon, 85, 119, 143-4, 145, 146, 147; links with Israeli Arabs, 172–3; rejection of Likud, 186, 197; social status of, 29–31
Otdel Vizy i Registratsii (OVIR), 23, 25–6, 38
Oz, Amos, 123

Palestinians (*see also intifada*), 3, 8, 9, 46, 65, 66, 67, 101, 182, 200, 218 Israeli government plans to reduce dependence upon, 85, 168; view of Soviet Jewish *aliyah*, 155, 157, 158, 159, 168–71, 207–8
Palestinian Liberation Organization (*see also* Arafat), 46, 65, 66, 68, 157, 158, 159, 160, 168, 180, 207
Palgi, Arieh, 159
Pamyat, 42, 121
Panterim Shehorim (Black Panthers), 30–1
Peace Now, 4, 186
Peled, Matityahu, 71
Peres, Shimon, 44, 81, 82, 89, 193, 196
Peretz, Rabbi Yitzhak, 85, 101, 119, 132–3, 134, 135, 136, 137, 145
Peterson, M.J, 1-2, 5
Perle, Richard, 20
Plotzker, Sever, 94
Polyakov, Vladimir, 41
Porush, Menachem, 102
Primakov, Yevgeny, 42

Qaddumi, Faruq, 158
Qatzrin, 101
Quayle, Vice-President Dan, 163, 167

Rabin, Prime Minister Yitzhak, 32; definition of security border, 195–6; selection as Labour leader, 193–4; election as Prime Minister, 204, 206, 207–9; and Palestinians, 193, 194, 195, 196, 206; and Soviet Jews 194–8
Rager, Yitzhak, 145
Rakah (Israeli Communist Party), 171
Ramon, Haim, 194
Ratz, 138, 181, 192, 198, 200
Ratzner, Lieutenant-Colonel Michael, 69

Index

Reagan, President Ronald, 20, 34, 44, 49, 79
Revava, settlement of, 106
Reykjavik, summit at, 44
Refuseniks, *see* Soviet Jews
Rishon Le Zion, 169
Rubenstein, Amnon, 198
Rubin, Amos, 75

Sadat, President Anwar, 19, 27
Sarid, Yossi, 200
Saudi Arabia, 158-9, 167
Sawyer, Thomas, 22
Schultz, Secretary of State George, 36
Shamir, Yitzhak, 1, 44, 48, 58, 94-6, 179, 183-4, 214; Arab pressure upon 160, 169; collapse of coalition, 109, 179; electoral defeat of, 204-5, 208, 214; formation of coalition government, 66, 75, 133; Greater Israel speech, 57, 89, 156, 165, 185; press censorship and Soviet Jews, 80; settlement of immigrants, 73, 75-6, 89, 96-7; Soviet Jewish support for, 193; views on United States, 92, 180
Sharansky, Anatoly (Nathan), 37, 136, 187, 189
Sharansky, Avital, 188
Sharon, Ariel, 3; allegations of corruption against, 99, 184, 204 as Minister for Agriculture, 70; as Minister for Housing and Construction, 77, 79, 90, 95-9, 103, Stars programme, 104-8, 218
Shas (Sephardi Tora Guardians Party), 132-3
Shevardnadze, Eduard, 46, 162
Shinui, 181, 192, 198
Shomron, Lieutenant-General Dan, 71
Shoval, Zalman, 92-3
Sid-Ahmed, Mohamed, 157
Slepak, Vladimir, 37
Sneh, Brigadier-General Ephraim, 104, 207
societal actors, definition of, 2
societal security, concept of, 9; impact of Soviet Jewish *aliyah* upon, 216, 217-8
Soshani, Uri, 99
Sofer, Ovadia, 43
South Africa, 67
Soviet Jews, and absorption basket, 83-4; absorption of in the 1970s, 31-3; attachment to Zionism, 27, 122; diploma tax upon, 24; educational profile of, 119, 124; effect of Gorbachev's reforms upon, 39-40, 120-1, 122; ethnic composition of, 23-5, 33-4; expected numbers of Soviet Jews in 1990, 75-6; Jews from Georgia, 23 31, 32, 120, 124, 127; from Russia and Ukraine 24, 25, 33, 122; gender and Soviet Jewry, 123-4; housing crisis, 101, 118, 128-30; immigration to Israel in the 1970s, 28-35; immigration to the United States in the 1970s, 33-4; impact upon 1993 Israeli municipal elections, 214; numbers settled in the Occupied Territories, 105-6, 162; politicization of, 180, 187-92; prostitution among, 128, 189; refuseniks, 16, 37-8, 39, 187, 189; religious influence upon, 134-5, 137, 138-40; Russian language media, 190; terror attacks upon, 169; under and unemployment among, 125, 127, 129 131; views on the Occupied Territories, 183, 188
Soviet Jewish Zionist Forum, 136, 189
Soviet Union (*see also* Gorbachev), Anti-Zionist Committee in, 35, 42; *glasnost* and *perestroika*, 38, 39, 41, 51; Letter of 39, 17; Moscow coup of 1991, 200; migration policy in the 1970s, 16-17; migration regime in the 1970s and 1980s, 23-6, 35-8; relationship with the Arab world, 27, 35, 41, 46, 160; relationship with the United States, 19-22, 34, 36, 45, 160, 161, 216; view of Zionism, 26, 41-3
stars programme, *see* Sharon
state elite, concept of, 2-3, 12
Stevenson Amendment, 20, 45
Strategic Arms Limitation Talks (SALT), 19, 20, 21, 28, 45
Suslov, Mikhail, 22
Svissa, Yemin, 173
Syria, 36, 41, 68, 159, 162, 207

Tarasov, Gennady, 160
Tehiya party, 109, 179, 182, 184
Temkin, Dr Benny, 200
Tel-Aviv, 64; capacity to absorb immigrants, 67; numbers settled in, 105, 124
Tonnies, Ferdinand and the concept of *Gemeinschaft*, 3
Toubi, Toufiq, 171
Transnationalism, as a concept, 1-2; migration as a transnational flow and activity, 1, 7-9, 11, 12-13, 106, 212-17
Trans-Siberian railway disaster, 47
Tsaban, Yair, 204
Tsomet party, 182, 184
Tulkarm, 106

Umm al-Fahem, town of, 170
United Jewish appeal (UJA), 79
United Kibbutz Movement (UKM), *see* kibbutzim
United Nations Resolutions 92, 242, 338, 425
United States of America (*see also* loan guarantees, Soviet Union), aid to Israel, 88, 165–6; and American Jewry 21, 45, 49-50, 135; Central Intelligence Agency report on Soviet Jews, 162; condemnation by Arab states, 159, 160, 165–6; conditions set for loan guarantees, 92, 144; immigration quotas, 48-50, 155; US State Department, 75, 105; view of *detente*, 19, 21; view of Israeli settlement policy, 87, 89, 107, 175, 205
Universal Declaration on Human Rights, 28
Upper Nazareth, 101, 111, 131

Vienna, 27
Vietnam, 20, 204
Vilnai, Major-General Matan, 70

Vorontsov, Yuli, 43

Waever, Ole, 3-4
Washington, *see* United States of America
Washington Summit, 161
Weiner, Myron, 7
West Bank and Gaza Strip, *see* Occupied Territories
West Bank Data Base Project (WBDBP), 102, 103, 166
Western Sahara, Moroccan settlement of, 8
Women in Black, 4

Yakovlev, Aleksandr, 42
Yordim, see Noshrim

Zalah, Sheikh Riyad, 172
Ze'evi, Rehavam, 109, 179
Zionism, 58; origins and development of, 59–62
Zionist Federation, 142
Zivs, Samuil L., 36, 37
Zolberg, Aristide R., 7
Zucker, Dedi, 104, 108